THE

MUSHROOM

FEAST

BOOKS BY JANE GRIGSON:

The Art of Charcuterie

Good Things

Food with the Famous

Fish Cookery

The Mushroom Feast

English Food

Jane Grigson's Fruit Book

Jane Grigson's Vegetable Book

The Enjoyment of Food

THE MUSHROOM FEAST

JANE GRIGSON

The Lyons Press

Reprinted by arrangement with Alfred A. Knopf, Inc.

Library of Congress Cataloging-in-Publication Data
Grigson, Jane.
    The mushroom feast / Jane Grigson.
        p.   cm.
    Originally published: New York: Knopf, 1975.
    Includes index.
    ISBN 1-55821-194-2
    1. Cookery (Mushrooms)   I. Title
    [TX804.G77 1992]
    641.6'58—dc20
                                        92-13373
                                        CIP
Printed in the United States of America

Illustrations by Yvonne Skargon

10 9 8 7 6 5 4 3 2 1

For Geoffrey,

remembering Maurice

Acknowledgements

The author wishes to thank Mrs. D. Rogers for her translation of Pasternak's "Going Mushrooming"; Miss Kathleen Topham, of the Mushroom Growers' Association in London; and Mr. K. G. Pointing, Divisional Director of Darlington Mushrooms in Bradford-on-Avon.

FOREWORD

*"But when all's said and written,
there is nothing better than field mushrooms
that you have gathered yourself,
on toast, for breakfast."*

Jane Grigson's epilogue to a mushroom feast that embraces an entire globe of fungi, from the cèpe de Bordeaux to the wood ears of China, is deceptively simple and yet completely evocative of Grigson's world, whether she addresses fruits, vegetables, charcuterie, or as here mushrooms. As an eater, cook, writer, wife, and mother, Grigson is rooted in the earth of England and of France, whether digging up turnips in her garden in Wiltshire or searching for the first girolles in the woods of the Bas-Vendômois. Wherever she is, she speaks in the active voice and in first-person plural, extending the "we" of her husband and daughter to include friends and acquaintances and finally a global and invisible community of fellow mushroom gatherers, toast makers, breakfast eaters. She makes every reader a part of this extended family, with whom she can't wait to share information, recipes, lore, anecdotes, history, poetry, and pleasure in the good things of this world.

Because she is so firmly rooted in the countryside, in the fields around Broad Town and the woods around the village of Trôo, she can descry through the smog of urban industrialization a more ancient and enduring European landscape that connects England to the Continent, past to present, and cooks to writers in illuminating that common landscape. She moves at ease through space and time, in one breath quoting a Pasternak poem on mushrooming, in another citing a seventeenth-century recipe from La Varenne for scrambled eggs and mushrooms, in a third reciting a mushroom haiku from a nineteenth-century Japanese poet. In the fertile compost of her imagination and memory, all kinds of mushrooms—historical, poetical, botanical—sprout and spread.

But she is no gassy internationalist. What persuades us to join in her mushroom quest is her direct and immediate relation to the object in hand, how it looks, feels, smells, and how to deal with it in a practical hands-on way. Her description of Chinese wood ears, for example, is arresting: "The crumpled blackish muddle of dried wood ears resembles the charred remains of a log before it finally disintegrates to ash." But what compels us is her anticipatory question, "How can such an unpromising substance come to be worth eating?" Without attempting to turn wood ears into silk purses, she advises us to chew a small piece once it has been soaked and swollen into a cloud-like shape. "It is almost entirely texture, with the faintest air of mushroom flavour that one seems to smell rather than taste."

Practical advice includes, of course, cost. Noting the affinity of fish and mushrooms in hundreds of classical dishes, such as Escoffier's sole à la bonne femme, she advises thrifty British cooks to look for substitutes for sole. "Always keep a look-out for John Dory. Its large lugubrious head, and the black 'fingerprints' of Saint Peter, one on either side, where he picked the fish up, make it easy to recognize," and most important, "the price is ridiculously low for such an exquisite fish." To a good housewife, cost is never irrelevant, and what delights her in a brandade de morue truffée is its "irreverent combination of the cheapest, most despised fish of all (despised at least by some cookery writers and many English people), salt cod, with the most expensive of all fungi, truffles."

Her section on truffles voices her same commonsense, anti-snobbish attitude toward a commodity valued too often for cost alone. After quoting Colette, Raymond Oliver, Apicius, Pliny, and Ada Boni, she offers an irresistibly simple recipe for oeufs en cocotte aux truffes, advising the penurious to use a tiny tin of truffles or truffle peelings. "Naturally all the other ingredients must be of first-class quality—genuinely fresh farm eggs, the best unsalted butter from Normandy, freshly ground black pepper, and if possible cream with a slight tang from a farm producer rather than one of the large factory-dairies." As for truffles as an aphrodisiac, a no-nonsense British skeptic can't resist twitting the amorous French. "Certainly I would expect the provider of truffles to gain his point more rapidly—all other things being equal—than the provider of panhaggerty or shepherd's pie. Or of haggis and bashed neeps, however abundant the whisky. More than that cannot be claimed, I think, for any food."

She supports her claims for mushroom pleasures with the most minutely detailed, eclectic, witty, and wayward testimony, which leads us far from wood and field. Sometimes it's a single punch line, as in this description of the wood mushroom rubber brush, or pig's trotter: "Under its pinkish-yellow cap, there are not gills or tubes, but spines reminding one of a rubber toothbrush." Sometimes it's a political critique revealing centuries of British-French rivalry, as when she introduces an English hare soup with its French title, potage de levraut à l'anglaise, and notes that the English in the eighteenth century were famous for their abundance of meat and game. "Foreign travellers exclaimed, with a tone of priggish shock, that the British working classes ate *meat*, and not just occasionally but often. The unspoken conclusion was that it would all come to no good. But in fact we escaped the excesses of revolution. Can we ascribe this to meat-eating by the lower orders in the eighteenth century?" The question, again, is pragmatic.

But beyond practical information on the best edible mushrooms, how they grow, how to preserve them by drying or pickling or freezing, how to sauce them or stuff them or add them to soups, meat, poultry, game, or how to put them in a pie or make a sandwich of them—beyond all this, it's the small exact domestic detail of the gardener, the cook, the woman in a house in the countryside that sticks in the mind. For escargots à la poulette, which mixes snails in a mushroom sauce, she remarks that the dark-speckled garden snail and the brown and white vineyard snail are found both in the countryside of England and of France. "Often when I put the milk bottles out on a wet night, I see a good number of garden snails moving majestically up the doorsteps and over the porch, or humping along the gravel."

Who would not want to join the procession of snails up the doorsteps and over the porch, and on into the kitchen where the mistress of the hearth would show us, after swishing the snails several times in salt water to clean them, how then to remove them from their shells with a needle "which has been stuck eye-end into a kernel of corn"? So practical. So simple. Like eating field mushrooms that you have gathered yourself, on toast, for breakfast.

—Betty Fussell, 1998

INTRODUCTION

The idea of writing this book came to us in the woods of the commune of Trôo, a village of the Bas-Vendômois, where for the last twelve years we have made a second home in the human dovecot of its sheltering cliff. Our first guide to that secret countryside, the key to our explorations, and our great friend, was a local vineyard-owner called Maurice. With a gentle humour at our French and our ignorance—"Pauvres paysans," he would say—he initiated us into the two main occupations of the neighbourhood, wine-making and mushroom-hunting. On the second subject at least, we were not so ignorant as he thought, but our French hampered explanations. We kept quiet and learnt about wild mushrooms from quite a different point of view.

To him (and to his neighbours) mushroom-hunting was part of the waste-nothing philosophy he had inherited from his farming peasant ancestors, a philosophy which is dying out as time becomes a more precious commodity than wild sorbs or service berries or Spanish chestnuts or the small hard round pears of outlying fruit trees. In the case of wild mushrooms, though, time is not reckoned to be more precious than the flavour of girolles, ceps, morels and field mushrooms. These mushrooms have long been appreciated by chefs of the high cooking tradition in France: there is no question of allowing them to go to waste as we do so unregardingly.

So in that part of France, and I am sure in many others as well, and in Poland, Italy, Czechoslovakia and so on, there exists a large invisible community of mushroom-hunters. The concentration of eyes downwards, the careful tread of boots, require peace. Sunday is the occasion. Woods which have been silent most of the week, come alive. The crackling of dry twigs announces our presence to all the others whom we cannot see, a more frequent shushing up of dead leaves, then the triumphant shout of our daughter, who has found the first girolles of the day. Maurice's dog squawks as we all close in swiftly on the fruitful corner, with encouraging noises for the sharp-eyed novice. Then we all spread out again, and a busy silence returns. One is isolated, all sense of time goes in the velvet warmth of the young trees. Suddenly some more girolles appear, or the moist brown head of a cep, and without meaning to, I shout aloud.

My voice
Becomes the wind;
Mushroom-hunting.

"Becomes the wind," because nobody takes any notice; I am too old to need encouraging, I am merely doing what we are all there to do. That haiku is perfect. It was thought or spoken—one could not in the first instance say "written"—by the Japanese poet Shiki, in the nineteenth century. He must have worked it out a little ruefully, as he walked on with his eyes moving forward and back across the ground. After a few expeditions one's eyes are trained to work in detached efficiency: one has time for reflection.

My own thoughts go to the mushroom-hunting parties of Tolstoy's *Anna Karenina.* In the false, airless suspense of forests, where reality is quite driven out by stillness, feelings become magnified, silences deeper but misleading. When we go into the bank on market day, the following Wednesday, we find out just how misleading. As we take our place at the counter, with farmers and farmers' wives in black, the young clerk smiles at us.

"Did you have much luck on Sunday?"

"Luck? Sunday?"

"Yes, Sunday. We heard you in the woods at Les Hayes. We heard Sophie shouting *girolles.*"

Everyone listens. Everyone smiles. We love Montoire and its gentle friendliness of life. After the wide uninhabited farmlands of Wiltshire, one forgets that the French countryside is still full of ears as well as eyes. The silence of that wood was an illusion. Our English accents had first betrayed us; the easier French of our small daughter calling to Maurice in her high, clear voice had completed the giveaway. Tolstoy could have written a scene from that Sunday afternoon, adding love disappointed, the coincidence of discovery. Or he might have been content, as we were, with family peace and mushrooms.

Days in the wood end early. Even the thin, leafless hazel copse subdues a flaring sunset. We are glad to come out into the less sombre light of the road, glad to see the car against the skyline beyond the brambles by a roadside chapel. We pile the baskets into the back, stopping to look at their strong, graceful curves. We recall for the hundredth time with Maurice how he made them during the winters, with cane from osiers at the edge of his vineyard. Every time these thoughts, repeated and savoured in a ritual dialogue, go with the mushrooms lying in the sturdy baskets; now that Maurice is dead, we repeat the dialogue but go home without him.

We light the lamp quickly, and pour out a drink. One of us separates out the picking, the *cueillette*. Someone else gets down the mushroom book. I go into the large old fireplace which is now my kitchen, light the candles because it is nearly dark, quickly assemble butter, oil, garlic, onions, cream—the things we are going to need for the mushroom feast.

Every mushroom is checked, stalk and all, before the blemishes are cut away and the earth removed. This is the essential discipline. After twenty years of mushroom-picking, ten of them in Trôo, we look them over as carefully as if it were the first time. If we were novices, and had had no Maurice and no books, we would take our baskets in to the local chemist for him to see. He expects to do this, and during the autumn season will arrange a display in his window, with models of lurid colouration, plans, charts, and printed instructions, plus a few ferns and stuffed pheasants for atmosphere. It is good to have personal help, as well as a book of identification. I say this with feeling, because of the recent adventures of a young couple in Guernsey which were reported in one of the national Sunday papers in England.

One morning early, they found some delicious-looking mushrooms on the lawn. They had popped up overnight. This had never happened before, so they checked them with a mushroom reference book, and identified them as being perfectly safe.

They each had six for breakfast. As mother-in-law was cooking them, the girl said jokingly, "If anything happens to us, you'll look after the baby, won't you?" They sat down at table, and enjoyed their mushrooms enormously. They tasted as delicious as they looked. Life went on, the young woman fed her baby, and all was well—for twelve hours.

Then the pains began, diarrhoea, and vomiting which came too late (as it always does with the kind of mushroom they had eaten) to prevent the poison being absorbed. The doctor arrived, spotted what was wrong, being a mushroom-fancier himself, and checked his diagnosis against the new crop of identical mushrooms which had helpfully sprung up on the lawn. He flew his patients immediately to London, with the news that they had eaten the Death Cap, *Amanita phalloides*. They were not likely to live. No one does. The symptoms come too late for remedies. The wife fell into a coma. The hospital doctors rang a colleague at the Hospital Beaujon in Paris, where they may see as many as a hundred cases of similar poisoning a year. At last someone had the idea of passing her blood through an artificial liver. After four times on the machine, she began to recover. Remarkably, her husband survived with ordinary medical care, and the baby, who might have been poisoned through her mother's milk, showed no discomfort at all.

I tell you this story not to put you off, but to show that reference books are not a talisman (and the illustrations in *this* book are decorative—not for identification purposes). Even the best reference books must be used with understanding. In a way, it is most important of all to recognize the very few *fatal* mushrooms (other kinds can upset your stomach, or taste bitter—hardly any will kill you). When you come across them, snap them over with your foot or stick, then crush them, so that no one else will be tempted to take them home. Avoid touching them with your hands or gloves.

On the other hand, don't be like the woman in this village who met my husband halfway up the hill on his way back from a most successful mushroom expedition. He had found an unexpected patch of morels. She did not know him, but with Christian valour walked up to him, knocked the basket out of his hands, and jumped about all over the beautiful mushrooms, which had been giving him such delight. "Don't want to see you in the churchyard tomorrow," she said with gruff friendliness, and strode off into the darkness in true heroic fashion, not waiting to be thanked. He stood gazing after her, speechless, unable to move as he contemplated the wreck of the spectacular dinner he had planned.

In the United States, mushroom fever is growing—a consequence of learning more about the environment. It's the reward after the hard slog of persuading the greedy and acquisitive to respect the earth, which has put up with their unlovely ways. Ever since the composer John Cage started the New York Mycology Society, similar societies have been started all over the country, particularly in university towns, or in places with a large population from the mushroom-minded countries of Europe. If you join the local chapter's outings, the problem of identification is dealt with automatically and efficiently. Older, more knowledgeable members and experts— usually of European origin, with a long family tradition of mushroom-hunting—see that the less experienced make no mistakes.

Another point, do not think that forests or fields are the only places to look. You can have surprises. A letter in the *Times* described something quite extraordinary. As a boy during the First World War, this letter writer had been at school in Worcestershire, in the Midlands of England. It was an old grammar school, but only one part of the original building remained—this was an eight-sided bell tower of 1552. The ground floor part was used by the boys as a bicycle shed. It was paved with stone slabs about four feet square, and, as it turned out, four inches thick.

One day, one of the pupils tripped over the edge of a paving stone which had lifted, and fell into a muddle of pedals and handlebars. At the sight of his son's scarred face, the father made a fuss with the school authorities, and the slab was prised up with crowbars so that it could be relaid. Underneath the stone was a mass of mushrooms, which had apparently lain dormant since the sixteenth century until about 1918, when "they had combined to lift several hundredweight of solid stone. The school janitor assured us that they made very good eating with his breakfast bacon."

This is the point—good eating. The best of the wild mushrooms —ceps, girolles, morels, field mushrooms—have the highest place in grand cookery, particularly in France but in other countries of mainland Europe as well. They have become part of the classic dishes of this tradition—and by classic I mean the very best of their kind, which because of their quality remain untouched through generations of changing taste. The flavour of such mushrooms rises above the main ingredients, like a fine descant which turns a familiar carol into something new, something more enjoyable than one had ever thought possible. In this matter, the semi-cultivated truffle is the greatest of all. Even when tinned, it breathes flavour through a fairly solid dish of pork or chicken or cured sausage. My own favourites are ceps, because of their texture, and the powerful earthy delicacy which marries so well with simple things like potatoes, as well as with chicken and veal dishes of first-class cookery. Morels are in the same bracket, but we rarely find enough of them.

Do not despise, as one can do so thoughtlessly, the neat white button of the commercial mushrooms, the *champignons de Paris*. They deserve the name, for they really are the Paris mushroom. Although people have been gathering wild ones from the earliest food-gathering days, it was not until the seventeenth century that their mysterious growth was enough understood to provide a basis for cultivation. First, of course, one had to find the right variety. Forest mushrooms are tricky (though the Chinese and Japanese were to cultivate them, in imitation of Europe, in the eighteenth century). Field mushrooms mature too quickly.

The first time mushrooms were referred to as a crop, in any language, was in 1600, by Olivier de Serres, the great agriculturist, in his *Théâtre d'Agriculture des Champs*. He appears, though, to be talking about occasional, haphazard cultivation, a kind of cos-setting of natural growth. The true domestication dates from about 1678. The botanist Marchant gave a demonstration to the Académie des Sciences in Paris, to show that "the white filaments, which develop in the soil under mushrooms, will, if transplanted into a suitable medium, give rise to more mushrooms"—a discovery that the market gardeners of Paris were quick to profit from. They would certainly have noticed the crops of edible mushrooms which appeared in the autumn, on the hotbeds of manure on which they had been growing summer melons. They may even* have employed Marchant to investigate the life-cycle of the mushroom—this would account for the speed with which they put his results to good use. Travellers were commenting on their presence in the Paris markets by the end of the century. By 1708 they were recognized as one of the decadent attractions of Paris:

* *Edward Hyams,* Plants in the Service of Man *(London: Dent, 1971).*

Muse! sing the man that did to Paris go,
That he might taste their soups and mushrooms know!
Oh! how would Homer praise their dancing dogs,
Their stinking cheese and fricasee of frogs.

The seventeenth century saw the great advance in French cookery. Under the influence of Italy, the hearty Rabelaisian style of earlier times was refined into Europe's greatest cookery. The first modern cookery book, *Le Cuisinier françois,* by La Varenne, came out in 1651 and ran into many editions. Here, finally, the medieval style was discarded. The old recipes for mixtures of sweet and savoury, for dried fruit with fish and meat hashed up together, the kind of thing that still lingers on in England in Christmas mincemeat, are firmly put into the corner. One finds a number of delicious omelettes and egg dishes that make one long to rush into the kitchen and prepare supper. It shows a great enlightenment about food, to parallel the general enlightenment of the period. Delicate flavours, clever contrasts of texture, variation, all come to the foreground. In this new style, mushrooms obviously have an important part. This was signalled by La Varenne's invention of *duxelles,* a store-cupboard seasoning, made by frying chopped mushrooms in butter with chopped onion and garlic, until all the juices evaporate, and the mixture can be put into covered storage jars—or nowadays into the deep freeze. This method of preserving mushrooms could be valuable in America, where cultivated mushrooms vary in supply and price.

Of course, Paris had the best circumstances for mushroom cultivation. Huge quarry caves surrounded the city, and as they were worked out, the stonemasons handed them over to the gardeners. A method was rapidly evolved, an extension of the melon hotbed principle, by which long hummocks of soil and horse manure, as wide as twice the reach of a man's arm, were set like railway lines along the floor of the cave. Until a few years ago one could still see this system in many caves in France, where family enterprises had not yet been bought up by the huge firms. As one went into the cave—women only allowed in after careful enquiries as to whether or not they had "the curse," which in Biblical fashion, was still supposed to blight the crop—the door was carefully closed. The soft air, the steady calm of underground life, closed one in as one abandoned the real world for an Orpheus journey into the depths of the cliff. Suddenly the proprietor's torch would light up the endless lines, spreading from one's feet, dotted all over with the white soft skulls of mushrooms.

Nowadays the large firms still make use of the caves (as they also do in parts of America, and in one place in England). In a village near us at Trôo, appropriately called Les Roches, there are twenty-five kilometres of them warrening the cliff. The plain on top is dotted with chimney-like ventilation shafts, which push up puffs of steamy-looking air (actually dust) over the vines and maize. Down below, at the entrance, there is a bustle of modern machinery and order. Trays stacked with a specially prepared and sterilized growing mixture (one could not call it soil), already sown with mushroom spawn, are trundled into the caves and stacked one on top of the other for their two to three months' stay in their pre-ferred milieu. Looking down the great branches of caves, each with its own name, like a street, you can see that they are carved with accordion pleats which lie towards the entrance, so that you can never quite lose the way. Some are piled with tier upon tier of great oak trays. Other trays are stacked on fork lifts waiting to be removed for emptying and resowing. Far away there is a bobbing of lights and a low hum of chatter. It's like a fairy story, as if the small folk were coming to entice you into their kingdom for seven years. These are in reality the mushroom pickers, with torches on their heads. The foreman in charge knows the plan of the caves by heart. His father and grandfather and great-grandfather, and great, great . . . were stonemasons in these caves. There has never been a time when he did not know them. Now he rejoices that his son will be able to follow him and inherit his knowledge.

The great moment for cultivation was in the twenties, when American scientists published in full and generous detail their per-fected methods. The discovery of how to produce sterilized mush-room spawn had been made, as one would expect, in Paris, at the Pasteur Institute in the 1890s. The French were prepared to supply the spawn, but not to disclose the method of production. This meant that mushrooms were likely to remain the food of rich people, the perquisite of haute cuisine. The Americans broke this monopoly, and their open-minded attitude has now come to prevail in the mushroom industry throughout the world.

The cultivated mushroom is *Agaricus bisporus,* of the same genus as the field mushroom, but another species; it has a better "shelf-life," but less flavour, though it is fair to remember that the small buttons we buy are immature specimens. Freshness and a delightful texture are their strong suit (they make a most delicious salad, when sliced and eaten raw with a good dressing). For long-cooked dishes, garlic and onion are almost always essential, and it is wise to choose the large ones if you can.

Incidentally, the word "mushroom," which we use to cover all manner of fungi, derives from the French *mousseron,* the field mushroom. And the French word goes back to the late Latin *mussiriones,* first recorded in the sixth century.

Agaricus bisporus is not the only mushroom cultivated on a large scale. There is the truffle, the black truffle of France, and the white truffle of Piedmont. More accessible to most of us, in spite of the long journey, is the dried shiitake of Japanese and Chinese cookery. The third biggest business in world terms—one cannot include truffles in the concept of big business—is the growing of the padi-straw mushroom in south-east Asia and Madagascar but, although dried, it is not commonly found in America or western Europe.

Here, then, is the record of one family's pursuit of mushrooms, both wild and cultivated, over the last twenty years. It has given us much pleasure and many enjoyable meals. It has brought us friends, and the increased knowledge of countrysides we would not otherwise have known so intimately or with such love. It has taken us to strange and beautiful places which were there all the time, sometimes right beneath our feet, and never far away. I hope this book will help others to share the same delights.

Jane Grigson

Broad Town and Trôo, 1974

THE BEST
EDIBLE
MUSHROOMS

Below I list the cultivated and wild mushrooms best used in cooking either by themselves or as flavouring ingredients.

Poisonous mushrooms are few; but if you are going to collect them from woods and fields and lawns and roadsides, the culinary mushrooms need to be learnt. Recognition is the safeguard. So use a reliable guide with coloured plates. For the money, the most useful and most easily acquired is *Collins Guide to Mushrooms and Toadstools,* by Morten Lange and F. B. Hora (1963) and for the United States *The Mushroom Hunter's Field Guide* by Alexander H. Smith (University of Michigan Press, 1963) is highly recommended. Some of the very best mushroom illustrations are to be found in the four volumes of the *Nouvel Atlas des Champignons* by Henri Romagnesi, published by Bordas in 1967 under the auspices of the Société Mycologique de France, and for America the richly illustrated *Mushrooms of North America* by Orson K. Miller, Jr. (Dutton, 1972).

Many more kinds than I have listed are edible, and a few of them are delicious. I have omitted kinds at all difficult to identify, and also one or two which our mushroom books follow each other in praising too highly. One of these is the Saint George's mushroom (*Tricholoma gambosum*) of the early summer. People often dislike its mealy scent and taste, though it does, I admit, look exceptionally pure, clean and appetising. Others are the coarse and sturdy blewit or blue-leg (*Tricholoma saevum*) of late autumn meadows, not as pleasant-flavoured as the slighter wood-blewit (*Tricholoma nudum*), which I include below, though it is sometimes on sale in shops and on market stalls in the Midland counties; and the rather overenthusiastically named *Lactarius deliciosus* of conifer woods, an orange mushroom which weeps orange tears.

General preparation of mushrooms
With the exception of morels and of course the dried mushrooms of all kinds, expose mushrooms to water as little as possible. A quick rinse under the tap, or a careful wipe with a clean damp cloth, should be enough. Cut off any blemished parts and the earthy base of the stalks. Do not peel mushrooms.

On the whole, wild mushrooms exude more liquid when exposed to heat than cultivated ones (though this often depends on the season and place where they have been growing). You can start off with the intention of frying them in a little butter, and find that the frying pan is soon overflowing and the mushrooms considerably reduced in size. If this happens, drain off the liquid and use it for soup or a sauce, and start again in a clean pan with a fresh lump of butter. If there is only a moderate amount of liquid, you can get rid of it by raising the heat—but be careful not to overcook the mushrooms. This is a danger with girolles, which always remain slightly chewy, and can be overcooked to toughness.

It follows that you need to allow more wild mushrooms when you are substituting them for cultivated mushrooms in a recipe, though sometimes quantity is compensated for by the extra flavour. Remember, too, that dried mushrooms often have a most concentrated richness, so that what seems at first sight an extravagant purchase turns out in the end to be quite reasonable. I can recommend drying your own mushrooms at home. It's a simple business, as you will see on page 31. The results cannot fail to be successful so long as you always dry perfect, unblemished ones.

On page 66 you will find Jason Hill's basic recipe for all fungi.

All the fungi in the following list, except the truffles and the four species from the Far East, grow in Britain and North America. The illustrations are not for the purpose of identification.

THE CULTIVATED MUSHROOM (*Agaricus bisporus*)

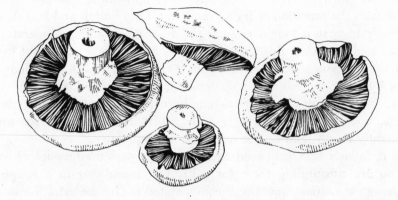

These are the mushrooms we buy fresh and immature from the greengrocer, and with which most of the recipes in this book are concerned. They come in three grades, according to size: the smallest are known as buttons; the medium-sized as cups; and the largest, most strongly flavoured are known as open or flat mushrooms. Very often the sizes are mixed together, which is not ideal for the cook. *Agaricus bisporus* is sometimes to be found wild, not in grass, but along roads, even in towns, pushing up between paving stones.

COOKING: Fry, grill or broil, bake. Use in soups, sauces, stuffings, stews. Delicious uncooked in salads, particularly with shellfish.

FIELD MUSHROOM, MEADOW MUSHROOM
(*Agaricus campestris*)

The mushroom, none better, of old meadows and downland. Probably the kind which the Franks of northern France called by a name from which we have 'mushroom,' by way of French. In the sixth century a Greek doctor wrote out some Latin notes on food for Theodoric, King of the Ostrogoths. "Fungi of all kinds," he told the king, "are heavy and hard to digest. The better kinds are mushrooms (*mussiriones*) and truffles."

C O O K I N G : As for cultivated mushrooms, and, when available, always to be preferred on account of their exquisite flavour; in particular in the following recipes:

Eliza Acton's mushrooms au beurre
Mushroom pie
Champignons à la crème
Field mushroom stew from Holland
Champignons farcis
Champignons à la bordelaise
Aubergines (eggplant) with mushrooms
Deep-frozen fish with mushrooms
Smoked haddock kulebiaka
English game pie
Côtes de chevreuil Saint-Hubert

HORSE MUSHROOM (*Agaricus arvensis*)

A mushroom of pastures, like the field mushroom. The two kinds often grow together. Don't be put off—some people are—by the smell (aniseed), the yellow tint in the cap, and the grey rather than pink colour of the gills. The horse mushroom is hardly less good to eat than the field mushroom.

COOKING: See field mushroom and cultivated mushroom.

MOREL, MERKEL, SPONGE MUSHROOM
(*Morchella esculenta* and *Morchella vulgaris*)

Dried or canned, from France, the ingredient of many notable dishes. The commoner, or less uncommon, of the two is M. *esculenta*. They push up in the spring and are abundant in some years, easily recognizable by their brownish, pitted sponge-like caps.

C O O K I N G : Morels are usually split down the centre, or sliced, so that all sandy grit and earth can be washed from the intricate convolutions. Put a handful of salt into the washing water, in case there are any ants or other creatures lurking in the crevices. Can be fried, but are best cooked *à la crème,* or with poultry.

Curnonsky's morilles du Jura à la crème
A flan of mushrooms or morels à la crème
Croûtes aux morilles à la normande
Omelette à la provençale
Fish meunière aux morilles
Ragoût de laitances aux morilles
Fillet of beef with morels
Ris de veau (d'agneau) à la crème
Poulet aux morilles

CEP, CÈPE (*Boletus edulis*)

Known as *porcini*—piglets—in Italy.

The true *cèpe de Bordeaux* is *Boletus edulis* (*cèpe* from a Gascon word *cep*, a trunk, because of the fat stem; *boletus* from the Greek word *bolos*, a lump: they come up like lumps in the woodlands). Other kinds of *Boletus* are common and delicious, such as *Boletus luteus* with a slimy yellow-brown cap and *B. granulatus* with a slimy reddish-yellow cap. Both have yellow tubes beneath the cap and grow under conifers, especially pines. A few kinds taste bitter, too peppery, or just dull; but all the *Boleti* are easily distinguished by having crowded tubes instead of gills below the cap. These tubes need not be removed before cooking ceps, so long as they are in good condition. If they look wet and spongy and a little unappetising, it is easy to peel them off, leaving a whitish cap, which cooks to the most delicious, firm, but succulent texture.

The dried ceps of the delicatessens keep their flavour very well, especially the *porcini* imported from Italy.

COOKING: Fry (olive oil is usually, though not always, preferred to butter), grill or broil, bake. Use in soups, sauces, stuffings, stews. Good as cold hors d'oeuvre, when blanched and pickled in an aromatic marinade. Excellent for home drying. With girolles and morels, ceps are the favourite mushrooms of fine cookery. Ceps can replace cultivated mushrooms in almost every recipe with advantage.

Crème de bolets
Mushroom sauce with pasta
Ceps and olive stuffing
Cèpes à la bordelaise
Cèpes sur le gril
Risotto ai funghi
Escoffier's cèpes à la crème
Mushroom loaves
Herrenpilze mit paprika
Cèpes à la génoise
Cèpes au chester
Funghi ripieni
Funghi porcini al tegame
Cèpes farcies
Cèpes Brimaud
Ceps with potatoes
Cep recipes from Apicius
Fish meunière aux cèpes
Truite au pastis
Truite aux cèpes
Paupiettes forestières
Brains baked with mushrooms and cheese
Rognons de veau (d'agneau) panés aux cèpes, sauce Colbert
Poultry and game birds stewed with ceps
Poulet à la dauphinoise
Poularde à la crème, aux cèpes de Revard
Salsa di fegatini
Confit d'oie à la basquaise
Côtes de chevreuil Saint-Hubert

TRUFFLES (*Tuber melanosporum, Tuber magnatum*)

The classic species, the Périgord (black) truffle (*Tuber melanosporum*), and the white truffle (*T. magnatum*) of Piedmontese cookery, are both obtainable in cans. But canning reduces them almost to a rumour of their extraordinary scent and flavour. John Ramsbottom has a splendid chapter on truffles in his *Mushrooms and Toadstools* (1953), with much about the cook's truffle which is found in England, *Tuber aestivum,* and how and where to look for it. The naturalist Sir Tancred Robinson, who first described this English truffle in 1693, nicely called truffles a "delicious and luxurious piece of Dainty"—which they are when fresh.

COOKING: Clean fresh Périgord truffles with a small brush to loosen the earth from their skins. Best simmered in dry white wine (champagne is not necessary) and eaten on their own. Slices of raw truffle are added to stuffings, foie gras and pâté, or slipped under a chicken or turkey skin to perfume the flesh beneath whilst showing sombrely through the skin in unmistakable show.

The Piedmont truffle should be cleaned in the same way, but it is not usually cooked, as exposure to heat spoils the flavour. The most one should do is to warm it through in a little butter. The best way to eat it is in thin shavings on pasta, or with a cheese *fonduta,* or with eggs.

If placed in a covered bowl with some fresh eggs, either the Piedmont or the Périgord truffle will scent them deliciously.

SHIITAKE (*Lentinus edodes*)

Dried, from Japan, where it is cultivated on logs of oak and other trees, one of them the shii—so shiitake, "shii mushroom." The Chinese, perhaps the first to cultivate this mushroom, made great use of it.

COOKING: Needs to be soaked in water for about half an hour to soften the cap (the stalks are discarded). Can then be fried, baked with a stuffing, steamed, or substituted for cultivated mushrooms in western dishes, though the flavour is quite different. Much used as a flavouring for steamed fish, red-cooked meat, soups and so on.

Chawan-mushi
Norimaki-zushi
Tempura
Sukiyaki Dobin mushi
Tung kua t'ung (winter melon soup)
Chinese steamed fish
Red-cooked pork shoulder
Stir-fried chicken with mushrooms
Chicken stuffed with dried mushrooms and chestnuts
Stir-fried Chinese cabbage with mushrooms and bamboo shoots
Aubergines (eggplant) à la chinoise
Sautéed mushrooms
Braised satin chicken

GIROLLE, CHANTERELLE, CHANTRELLE, EGG MUSHROOM (*Cantharellus cibarius*)

The girolle or chanterelle of French cooking. Dried, in food shops, or canned, but common in deciduous woods, where it shows up yellow as apricots against green moss. It smells of apricot, too. The beauty of the colour is matched by the beauty of its form, a curving trumpet, with delicate ribs running from the stalk through to the under edge of the cap like fine vaulting.

COOKING: Fry in butter with chopped onion or shallot, garlic and parsley (but see general instructions, pages 2–3). Delicious in sauces, and with eggs. An incomparable flavour.

Girolles on buttered toast
Girolles à la crème
Girolles à la forestière
Champignons au madère
Girolles with eggs
Paupiettes forestières
Fillet of beef with girolles
Ris de veau (d'agneau) à la crème
Poulet, pintadeau ou dindonneau aux girolles

MATSUTAKE (*Tricholoma matsutake*)

Dried, from Japan, where it grows under pine trees—the matsu, or pine, mushroom. Also canned. It is related to our overpraised Saint George's mushroom (*Tricholoma gambosum*), already mentioned, and to our wood-blewit (*Tricholoma nudum*), which can be used instead of matsutake for the recipes listed below.

COOKING: Dried matsutake will need soaking. See the recipes listed below.

Mushrooms grilled with mirin
Dobin mushi
Matsutake gohan

WOOD EAR (*Auricularia polytricha*)

Dried, from China, where it is both collected and cultivated. A gelatinous species growing on trees, like the European and North American Jew's ear (*Auricularia auricula*), which is so common on branches and trunks of elder. Jew's ear (properly the ear of Judas, who by legend hanged himself from an elder) can be used in the same dishes, but it has less flavour.

COOKING: Soak for half an hour, starting with tepid water. Rinse several times, separating the clusters with your fingers, so that the sandy earth and grit and seeds can fall to the bottom of the bowl.

Pig's liver with wood ears
Braised satin chicken
Pickled cabbage steamed with pork
Yuan Mei's bêche-de-mer gourmet

PADI-STRAW MUSHROOM (*Volvariella volvacea*)

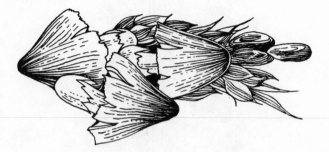

Dried, and sometimes to be had in Chinese stores. Another mushroom grown from early times by the Chinese (on beds of rice straw).

COOKING: Soak 15 minutes in warm water. Used with steamed chicken dishes from southern China.

Steamed chicken with padi-straw (grass) mushrooms

PARASOL MUSHROOM, UMBRELLA MUSHROOM
(*Lepiota procera*)

One of the most delicious mushrooms to eat. Stems uphold a scaly parasol with a boss in the middle. They stand up tall and obvious and surprising on grassy hillsides and banks, on sandy sea margins or on cliff tops by the sea. But it is no good picking them if they are dry or leathery.

COOKING: Can be used in most mushroom recipes, like field or cultivated mushrooms. Delicious when fried and served for breakfast with bacon and eggs; or as a vegetable with a cream sauce. A particularly good mushroom for stuffing—fill them with any good mixture (see stuffing recipes), or in English style with sage and onion stuffing, then place them *open side down* on a greased baking dish. Spear a square of fatty bacon or pork fat on top of each parasol, with a cocktail stick. (When sage and onion stuffing is used, serve them with apple sauce and roast potatoes: this makes a good main course for lunchtime.) Parasol mushrooms are also suitable for drying.

Morilles farcies, en cocotte

FAIRY-RING MUSHROOM, SCOTCH BONNET
(*Marasmius oreades*)

For soups and flavouring. Very common and very good, sometimes found in huge rings of darkened grass. The French *bouton de guêtre,* "gaiter-button." The cap rises to a boss.

COOKING: The small size of this mushroom makes it most suitable for soups and sauces, or in stews. Wash as little as possible. A particularly good mushroom for drying.

Recipes for soups and sauces, in particular *Sauce au beurre aux amandes, ou aux pistaches*

WOOD-BLEWIT, NAKED TRICHOLOMA
(*Tricholoma nudum*)

To be found under deciduous trees or conifers, and in a convenient way appearing now and then on lawn cuttings when they have rotted down. Has violet cap, gills, flesh and stem.

COOKING: Wood-blewits, when fried in butter or baked in the oven, have a fresh flavour that is not unlike new potatoes. Use as a substitute for Japanese matsutake.

Gratin de pommes de terre aux champignons
Gratin de pommes de terre aux cèpes
Pommes de terre aux cèpes
Potatoes with mushroom sauce in the Russian style

OYSTER MUSHROOM (*Pleurotus ostreatus*)

Found, in itself the reverse of decay, in colonies on dying, dead or rotten trunks of beech, ash, and so on. Smoothly suggestive of an oyster in shape and in the blue-grey of its cap. Sold in markets in France.

COOKING: Grill or broil, fry, bake in a cream sauce or with a good stuffing mixture as a gratin.

Champignons au madère

GREEN RUSSULA (*Russula virescens*)

Found in beech woods especially, with a green cap (instead of the startling red or yellow cap of many kinds of *Russula*), and firm white flesh scented like young hazel nuts, and a white leg.

COOKING: Grill or broil, fry, bake and serve with a cream sauce, or snail butter, or fill with a stuffing and bake. It has a fresh flavour, a little like new potatoes from the garden, and can be used for potato and mushroom gratins with great success.

GRISETTE *(Amanita vaginata)*

This delicate grey-capped mushroom, common under beech trees, is the *coucoumel* of French mushroom fanciers, who regard it as one of the best of wild fungi.

COOKING: Fry, grill or broil, bake, etc.; can be used in most mushroom recipes.

RUBBER BRUSH, PIG'S TROTTER
(*Hydnum repandum*)

Deciduous woods. Under its pinkish-yellow cap, there are not gills or tubes, but spines reminding one of a rubber toothbrush.

COOKING: A good mushroom for most recipes, but in particular for a fricassee—fry them in butter, stir in flour and seasoning with spices and chopped parsley, then moisten with meat, chicken, or game stock, and bind the sauce finally with cream and egg yolks.

Champignons au madère
Hannah Glasse's white fricassey of mushrooms

HORN OF PLENTY (*Craterellus cornucopioides*)

Little blackish brown soft funnels common among the rotting autumn leafage under beech trees. Called by the French *trompettes-des-morts*, and funereal in colour certainly.

COOKING: The flavour is disappointing, but the mushroom is used in pâtés and pork cookery by French housewives to give an illusion of truffles. An easily dried mushroom, which can usefully be reduced to mushroom powder.

Longe de porc à la vendômoise

PRESERVED MUSHROOMS, SAUCES, STUFFINGS, AND SOUPS

Mushroom sauces, soups and stuffings are entirely a part of our modern cookery. The Romans ate and enjoyed truffles and a variety of mushrooms, while wondering anxiously if they were poisoning themselves (the antidotes they thought up were many and useless), but it wasn't until the seventeenth century that mushrooms began to be regarded as an essential part of cookery. France led the way. By 1600 a primitive and spasmodic cultivation was being carried on: by the end of the century, the gardeners who supplied Paris with vegetables were able to produce a regular supply of mushrooms as well—to the amazement of travellers. This aroused all the English attitudes of chauvinism in matters of food. Mushrooms were for a time a symbol of Parisian decadence, and made an appearance in a spendid line of verse which goes: "Mangoes, potargo, champignons, caveare."

The earliest kitchen memorial to the newly cultivated mushroom is the seasoning known as duxelles. Onions or shallots are cooked gently in butter, then finely chopped mushrooms are added, and the whole thing is stirred over a moderate heat until all the moisture has evaporated and the mixture is dry enough to be safely stored. By reheating with some wine or sauce, duxelles can be reconstituted and used as a stuffing for vegetables (including mushrooms). The interesting thing is the early recognition that the flavour of forced mushrooms is insipid without the assistance of the onion family. Duxelles is an adjunct of a large, busy kitchen (though a quantity can be made and stored in a refrigerator or deep-freeze): in our small circumstances to-day, at home, we start afresh each time, following the style of modern recipe books, by cooking a chopped onion or shallot gently in butter, before adding the mushrooms. It is a good idea to include a chopped clove of garlic with the onion, because it assists the light flavour of cultivated mushrooms even more than its relations.

The person credited with the invention of duxelles is La Varenne. He started as a scullery boy in the kitchens of Charles II's great-aunt, sister to Henri IV, and rose to the grand office of *écuyer de cuisine* to Louis Chalon du Bled, Marquis d'Uxelles. La Varenne wrote what is in style and arrangement the first modern cookery book, *Le Cuisinier françois ou l'école des ragoûts,* which first came out in 1651, and ran to several editions in the next seventy-five years. Many of his recipes are perfectly easy to follow, and there are some in this book. There is little of the quaintnesses—as they seem to us—of mediaeval cookery, those combinations of overwhelming sweetness with meat, the use of many spices all together in one dish, that linger on in cookery books until the middle of the eighteenth century and even later. The book was dedicated to the Marquis d'Uxelles—so, presumably, was his useful onion and mushroom mixture.

Preserved mushrooms

Duxelles

A few spoonfuls can be used to cut out the early stages of those many recipes which begin with onion and mushrooms sweated slowly together in butter. In normal family circumstances, it is probably more convenient to follow the recipe each time, rather than to prepare duxelles for the store cupboard. But should you be lucky enough to have a glut of field mushrooms in your neighbourhood, or a well-organized deep-freeze, you will find this a useful recipe to know.

For mushrooms which have a fair amount of juice and a tendency to flood the frying pan, wring out the chopped mushrooms in a clean cloth to get rid of as much moisture as possible before cooking.

½ *pound mushrooms, or stalks and trimmings only*
4 *tablespoons butter*
2 *tablespoons oil*
1 *shallot or small onion, minced*
salt, pepper, nutmeg
1 *teaspoon minced parsley*

Chop mushrooms finely. Melt butter and oil, and cook shallot or onion gently without browning it. As it begins to soften, add the mushrooms and go on cooking over a good heat until the mixture is dry but not browned (or burnt). Stir the whole time. Season and add the parsley. When cooled, put into a clean jar, cover and store in the refrigerator; or pack in plastic for the deep-freeze.

TO USE DUXELLES: Mix into the filling for pies and pasties or turnovers, or into a chicken pie. Use as a seasoning for stews, in particular stews of white meat. Duxelles also makes a fine base for a fish which is to be baked whole in the oven; add a little white wine or fish stock to moisten it. Mix with enough béchamel, velouté or espagnole sauce to make a coherent mixture for stuffing vegetables—cucumbers, tomatoes, large mushroom caps. For a quick mushroom sauce, add a spoonful or two to some béchamel or *sauce à la crème*: the same principle can be used to make soup. For recipes of the *en croûte* variety, mix the duxelles with a little wine and spread it over the meat.

Deep-freezing

As cultivated mushrooms are available all the year round at more or less the same price, there is little point in freezing them in any quantity. Field and woodland mushrooms are another matter, though even with them the method has only limited usefulness, as mushrooms should not be kept in the freezer for longer than a month. If you do have a glut of these wild mushrooms, freeze some by all means, but dry the rest as a long-term investment (see directions following).

The main thing to remember is that mushrooms, like any other food for preservation, must be of top quality.

Wash them quickly but thoroughly; 1½ teaspoons lemon juice to each pint of water helps white-fleshed mushrooms to keep their colour. Dry them well. Tiny mushrooms can now be frozen without further preparation. Larger ones should be sliced, or quartered, and lightly fried in butter. Drain and cool them, then pack and freeze in the usual way, allowing ½ inch headroom in the container.

The small mushrooms can be used uncooked in salads—thaw them first. No need to thaw any of them when they are being used in a recipe; they can go straight into the pot or pan as they are.

Drying

In warmer countries one can get away with methods which are decidedly rough and ready. We've often gathered *trompettes-des-morts* or ceps on a swilling day of rain, and just spread them out on newspapers on a camp bed. They've dried in their own time, without going mouldy. But that is in the dry air of the Bas-Vendômois. On sunny days we've left them in the verandah day and night, and the results have also been perfect. I suppose this is why we have lost the habit of drying food in England—one has to be more pedantic here about the method.

However, with an oil-fired stove, drying mushrooms is simple. Trim off any blemished parts—though you should be careful to choose good specimens in the first place—and spread them out on newspaper on the rack above the stove. In a few days they will be dry, almost brittle and much reduced in size. When you are sure of them, pack them into brown paper bags. Polythene or plastic may also be used, but you must be extra sure that all moisture has evaporated; otherwise the mushrooms will go mouldy in the bag.

Another method is to thread alternate mushrooms and pieces of card or stiff paper on string like a necklace. Hang it over a radiator or night storage heater or in the sun (but take it in at night). It can also go into the oven—door open so that any moisture can evaporate quickly—when the cooking for the main meal of the day has finished. Never put them into a temperature higher than 140°F, or they will cook and not dry. A combination of all these methods can be used—the point is to dry the mushrooms as quickly as possible.

To reconstitute the mushrooms, soak them for up to 24 hours, starting with tepid water, the same soaking treatment required for bought dried mushrooms, whether they come from Yugoslavia,

France, Italy, China or Japan. Drain and dry them, and use in sauces, stuffings, stews and vegetable dishes in the usual way. The most successful mushroom for this kind of treatment is undoubtedly the cep. It retains a most remarkable amount of flavour, and completely transforms any dish to which it is added. With smaller quantities of the delicate mushrooms—girolles, field mushrooms and so on—freezing is perhaps the best answer for any you cannot use straightaway, though as they can be kept for only a month, a large surplus will need to be dried if they are not to be wasted. The other alternative would be mushroom ketchup (see recipe in this book).

Mushroom powder

Mushroom powder can be prepared quite simply by crushing ceps or field mushrooms or parasols which have been dried in the usual way (see page 31). This is a more spicey recipe from *Pottery*, a pamphlet which was published anonymously (in fact it was by Cyril Connolly's father) by the London Wine and Food Society in 1946.

5 *quarts mushrooms, sliced*
2 *onions, sliced*
10 *cloves*
1 *ounce powdered mace*
2 *teaspoons white pepper*

Put everything into a large shallow pan, and put at first over a low fire so that the mushroom juices run. Then raise the heat so that the juices can evaporate, but stir everything continuously so that the mushrooms and onions do not burn. Spread out on baking trays and dry in a slow oven—at about 200°F. When perfectly dry, crush to a powder and store in an air-tight container. When using this flavouring, add it to soups and sauces just before serving.

Mushroom ketchup

Mrs Beeton's recipe for mushroom ketchup includes no vinegar, but suggests the addition of a few drops of brandy to improve its keeping qualities. Modern recipes are less prolonged, and rely on vinegar. Not being keen on the brutish flavour of malt vinegar in English preserves, I suggest you use wine vinegar. Mushroom ketchup is a good standby for flavouring many dishes. Field mushrooms or cultivated mushrooms can be used, obviously. In *Food for Free*, Richard Mabey recommends shaggy caps (ink caps as they are often called in England, and shaggy manes in America) on account of the prodigious amount of liquid they will exude. For ceps or girolles, this kind of recipe would be a waste.

3 pounds mushrooms
6 tablespoons salt
⅔ cup wine vinegar
2 teaspoons chopped onion
1 teaspoon peppercorns
1 teaspoon allspice
2 blades mace
½ teaspoon whole cloves
½-inch piece cinnamon

Chop the mushrooms, spread them out in a large bowl, and sprinkle the salt over them. Leave, covered, for two days, stirring and squashing them occasionally. Put with the remaining ingredients into a large pan and simmer for about 2 hours. Leave the lid off, and the liquor will concentrate to a good strong flavour. Pour through a cloth into hot sterilized bottles and seal immediately. If you are using thin-necked sauce bottles, strain the liquor into a clean pan, bring back to the boil and pour into the bottles through a muslin-lined funnel.

Sauces

Sauce suprême

The classical *sauce suprême* of professional kitchens is the height
of luxury on account of its delicate richness and smoothness. It is
based on a carefully made velouté sauce, which is always to hand,
like the other basic sauces. In our kitchens at home, we have to
start from scratch as a rule, so here is a simplified recipe. In
France it is served with poultry, and fine fish, and best of all at
Christmastime, when the truffle season is at its height, with *poularde en demi-deuil*. This 'chicken in half-mourning' is really a
fine boiling fowl with slices of truffle slipped under the skin before
cooking starts, so that the black discs show through in a decorative design, while the meat underneath absorbs the exquisite flavour.

2 ounces (4 tablespoons) butter
2½ tablespoons flour
1¼ cups chicken stock
2 ounces mushrooms, or stalks and peelings, chopped
1⅓ cups heavy cream
2 egg yolks
salt, pepper

Melt the butter and stir in the flour. Heat the stock, then add
it and mix until smooth. Add the mushrooms and leave to simmer
steadily for a minimum of 10 minutes. Stir the cream in gradually,
tasting all the time. Stop when the sauce tastes right to you—the
point is that the longer the sauce has simmered and, therefore, been
reduced, the more cream you will need for the sake of consistency,
and better flavour. Beat up the egg yolks, add a little sauce, and
stir this mixture into the pan. Thicken without boiling over a moderate heat. Correct the seasoning, and, if you like, strain the sauce.

Sauce poulette

A delicate but piquant sauce, based on *sauce suprême*, which goes admirably with poultry, sweetbreads, sheep's trotters, tripe, mussels and firm white fish, as well as all kinds of vegetables. Usually the main item is cooked in an appropriate stock, and then reheated in the finished sauce: the cooking stock is used for the sauce. The final dish has the look of a ragout, and is called *moules*—or whatever else it may be—*à la poulette*. The sauce can, naturally, be served on its own in a separate sauceboat—in this case, one should omit the button mushrooms, or else serve them as a garnish to the main item of the dish.

Ingredients for sauce suprême (*preceding recipe*)
PLUS:
1–3 extra egg yolks
½ pound small button mushrooms
2 ounces (4 tablespoons) butter
juice of a lemon
parsley, chopped

Make the *sauce suprême* as directed, adding the extra yolks to the yolks in the recipe. Meanwhile cook the button mushrooms in the butter. Add them, with lemon juice to taste, and some parsley, to the finished sauce.

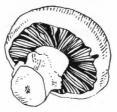

Sauce normande

A fine sauce for fish and egg dishes, which are garnished with mussels or oysters and with mushrooms. The cooking juices of the garnish are an essential part of the flavouring of the sauce. First make a fish stock, by simmering together for 30 minutes:

2 *pounds fish bones and trimmings*
1 *sliced onion*
1 *sliced carrot*
1 *clove*
bouquet garni
2½ *cups cider (or dry white wine)*
1¼ *cups water*

Strain and reduce to 15 ounces, or 2 cups. Season to taste, and use in making the *sauce suprême* on page 34. Add an extra yolk to the thickening.

Have ready:

about ⅓ cup mussel or oyster cooking liquor
about ⅓ cup mushroom cooking liquor
3 *ounces (6 tablespoons) unsalted or lightly salted butter*
2–4 *tablespoons white wine vinegar*
salt, pepper (optional)

Add fish and mushroom liquors to the sauce, reheating it over a bain-marie (double boiler) or very low burner so that it does not boil. Cut the butter into 8 pieces, then, off the heat, whisk pieces into the sauce. Add the vinegar to taste, and more seasoning if required.

Mushroom sauce

If you already happen to have some velouté or béchamel sauce left from another dish, it can easily be turned into mushroom sauce by adding mushrooms cooked in butter, plus some cream if you like. The following recipe, though, is more permeated with the flavour of mushrooms—and this is enhanced with the use of onion and garlic. By increasing the quantity of liquids, this sauce can be turned into mushroom soup. Put it in the blender, or put through a vegetable mill, and add a final seasoning of nutmeg, before reheating.

2 *ounces (4 tablespoons) butter*
6–8 *ounces mushrooms, sliced*

2 *tablespoons chopped onion*
1 *small clove garlic, chopped*
2½ *tablespoons flour*
1¼ *cups chicken stock*
1¼ *cups milk,*
    or ⅔ *cup each milk and light cream,*
    or ⅔ *cup each light and heavy cream*
salt, cayenne pepper
extra knob of butter

Melt the butter and cook the mushrooms, onion and garlic in it gently (lid on the pan). When the vegetables begin to soften, stir in the flour, then the stock and milk, or milk and cream. Leave to simmer for a minimum of 10 minutes. Correct seasoning. Whisk in the extra butter, off the heat, just before serving.

Two sauces from Hannah Glasse's Art of Cookery, *1747*

To make mushroom-sauce for white fowls of all sorts

"Take a Pint of Mushrooms, wash and pick them very clean, and put them into a Sauce-pan, with a little Salt, some Nutmeg, a Blade of Mace, a Pint of Cream, and a good piece of Butter roll'd in Flour. Boil these all together, and keep stirring them; then pour your Sauce into your Dish and garnish with Lemon."

N O T E : Slice the mushrooms and cook them in cream with seasonings for 5 minutes. Then add the butter, which is really beurre manié, a tablespoon of butter mashed up with a tablespoon of flour.

Mushroom-sauce for white fowls boil'd

"Take half a Pint of Cream, and a quarter of a Pound of Butter, stir them together one Way till it is thick; then add a Spoonful of Mushroom-pickle, pickled Mushrooms, or fresh, if you have them. Garnish only with Lemon."

NOTE: Use very thick cream; and with fresh mushrooms, cook them lightly first in butter before adding to the sauce. The basic mixture of butter and cream is still very popular in Normandy, where it is served with fish as well as with chicken, and flavoured with herbs and lemon juice. One of the best sauces I know, and the quickest of all to make—use a small frying pan rather than a high-sided saucepan.

Mushroom and sour cream sauce from Russia

A thick but slightly sharp sauce that goes well with fish, chicken, veal and some vegetables (see *Potatoes with mushroom sauce in the Russian style*). The mixture may be made thinner by adding more sour cream and a very little water: or into a creamed mushroom mixture for tartlets, chou cases and so on, by adding more mushrooms. For the best flavour, field mushrooms should be used: they make the flavour outstanding.

1 onion, chopped
¾ pound mushrooms, chopped
1½ ounces (3 tablespoons) butter
1 heaping teaspoon flour
1 cup sour cream
dillweed or fennel, chopped
salt, pepper

Cook onion and mushrooms gently in the butter for about 15 minutes. Stir in the flour and leave for a few moments over the low heat before adding the sour cream gradually. The sauce is done when the cream comes to the boil (don't let it boil). Add dill or fennel to taste, and season with salt and pepper.

Sauce au beurre aux amandes, ou aux pistaches (Butter sauce with almonds, or pistachio nuts)

In his *Gastronomie Pratique*, in the ninth edition of 1928, Ali Bab (the pen name of Henri Babinski) recommends this delicious sauce with several kinds of mushrooms—the cultivated kind obviously, but also field and fairy-ring mushrooms, and young ceps. It is also delicious with fish when it has been fried or baked with mushrooms.

1 ounce (2 tablespoons) clarified butter
1 tablespoon flour
1 cup boiling water
pinch of salt
2 tablespoons heavy cream
2 egg yolks
lemon juice
2 ounces blanched, chopped almonds, or chopped pistachio nuts
3 ounces (6 tablespoons) butter

Put the clarified butter and flour in a pan over a moderate heat. Stir well and cook for a moment or two without allowing the mixture to brown. Pour in the boiling water gradually, and add the. salt. Remove the pan from the fire. Beat cream with the egg yolks, tip in a little of the sauce, then return to the pan; put over a low heat for a moment or two so that the sauce binds and thickens slightly *without boiling*. Sharpen to taste with lemon juice, add the nuts, and finally the remaining butter, which should melt in the sauce without further cooking.

Mushroom sauce with pasta

Mushrooms make a good and unusual sauce for pasta, particularly field mushrooms or ceps which have plenty of flavour. However, even cultivated mushrooms produce quite a good sauce with the help of garlic. This is a French recipe.

SERVES TWO TO THREE
8 ounces mushrooms, sliced
2 tablespoons lemon juice
1 small onion or shallot, chopped
1 large clove garlic, chopped
2 ounces (4 tablespoons) butter
4 tablespoons olive oil
1 bunch parsley, chopped
salt, pepper

Sprinkle the mushrooms with lemon juice. Cook onion or shallot and garlic gently in the butter and oil until they soften, without browning. Add the mushrooms and parsley, raise the heat slightly, and cook for another 10 minutes—the time will depend on the type of mushrooms being used: they should still have a little bite to them, and the mixture should be moist and succulent rather than swilling in juices. Season.

Serve with the egg pasta shells which are called *coquillettes* in France and *conchiglie* in Italy. Put a small onion and a clove of garlic into the cooking water, and remove them when draining the cooked pasta.

Purée de champignons veloutée (Mushroom purée)

The Rohans were in their various branches one of the great families of French history. Nor, as you will see from this recipe and from the one for onions soubise, were they unmindful of good food. The chefs they employed were distinguished in their profession and included Dunan, who later worked for Napoleon, and who passed this recipe on to his friend Carême. He claimed that his employer, the Prince Louis de Rohan, in the days of "la vieille France" before the Revolution, had invented the purée described here. Another friend of Carême's, Laguipiere, who died in the atrocious cold of the retreat from Moscow, made quite a different recipe (which follows) flavoured with ham, tomato and brown *sauce espagnole,* and thickened with ground rice.

This Rohan recipe is particularly good with chicken and white meat, as you would expect from the ingredients.

SERVES FOUR TO SIX
1 pound mushrooms, sliced
juice of ½ lemon
4 ounces (8 tablespoons) butter
3 tablespoons chicken consommé or jellied stock
pepper, grated nutmeg
1 cup fresh white breadcrumbs
heavy cream (see directions)
⅓ cup thick sauce béchamel
chicken drippings (optional)

Slice the mushrooms and blanch for a moment or two in some water and the lemon juice. Drain them well and cook them gently with half the butter; as they begin to soften, add the chicken consommé and seasoning, and continue to cook, with the pan covered for 20 minutes more. Put the purée through a food mill, but do not liquidize in a blender or it will become too smooth. Mix the breadcrumbs to a paste with some cream, and stir in the mushrooms. Put back over the heat so that the mixture dries out to a light purée. Add the béchamel sauce, the remaining butter and, if possible, some chicken essence or drippings (i.e., the rich jelly that accumulates beneath the fat from a roast chicken).

Purée de morilles (de mousserons) à la ravigote

SERVES FOUR TO SIX
Choose twenty fine morels (or field mushrooms), and follow the recipe above. Finish with a bunch of green herbs, as good a mixture as you can make, blanched for a minute in boiling water, then drained and chopped.

Laguipiere's mushroom purée

Laguipiere was one of Carême's masters, and Carême dedicated his first book to his illustrious shade: "Lève-toi, ombre illustre de Laguipiere, entends la voix d'un homme qui fut ton admirateur et ton élève." Carême goes on to recall his career, which was spoilt by the jealousies of lesser men in the profession. Then he goes on to describe the old man's appalling death on the retreat from Moscow in 1812: "Tu as péris misérablement, les pieds et les mains gelées, par l'affreux climat du Nord . . . tu voulus suivre ton Prince"—Napoleon—"en Russie et tu fus témoin de nous désastres dont toi même fus frappé."

SERVES FOUR TO SIX

"Wash and chop four punnets of mushrooms"—allow a pound—"then put them into a pan with a ladleful of consommé, a little lean chopped ham, a tomato from which you have removed the juice and seeds, a spoonful of ground rice, a pinch of pepper and grated nutmeg. Mix everything well together, and simmer gently, stirring from time to time. Twenty minutes later add a ladle of *sauce espagnole*. Allow the sauce to boil up a time or two, then sieve the purée: at the moment of serving add a little fresh butter and some lemon juice."

A purée for beef and veal, with a more robust flavour than the Rohan purée preceding.

White wine sauce for fish

The slightly sweet flavour of wine thins the rich combination of mushrooms, egg yolks and cream, making it a good sauce for fish. This recipe is based on one from *The Russian Cook Book* by Princess Alexandre Gargarine.

SERVES FOUR TO SIX

½ *pound mushrooms, quartered*
2 *ounces (4 tablespoons) butter*
1¼ *cups fish stock*

2 *tablespoons lemon juice*
2 *tablespoons flour*
1 *cup white wine*
2 *egg yolks*
salt, pepper, sugar
⅔ *cup heavy cream*

Cook mushrooms for a few minutes in half the butter. When the juices begin to run, add about half the fish stock and the lemon juice, and leave for 20 minutes to simmer without a lid on the pan. Meanwhile melt the remaining butter in another pan, stir in the flour, then the rest of the fish stock and the wine. Leave to cook down a little. Beat the egg yolks in a bowl, and whisk in the almost boiling wine sauce bit by bit. Clean the cooking pan out, and put an inch of water in it. When simmering, stand the bowl of sauce over it and stir gently until it thickens *without boiling*. Tip in the mushrooms, which should just have a little liquid left with them, but not much, and correct the seasoning. The sugar, just a pinch of it, is a good idea if the wine you are using is very dry. Or not very good. Stir in the cream, and go on cooking until the sauce is very hot again.

White wine sauce for chicken

SERVES FOUR TO SIX
The above sauce is good for a boiling fowl. Substitute chicken for fish stock, and otherwise follow the recipe exactly. Some chopped fresh tarragon can be added at the end.

Madeira and mushroom sauce

This simple recipe for Madeira sauce (to go with steak, ham, kidneys) was given me by the best cook I have ever met. She was a widow, but had been for many years the wife of a director of Cook's Wagons-lits in Paris. Every night of their marriage, Monsieur walked into the house at precisely the same time, hung up his hat and expected to sit down immediately to his meal. For any man who had the luck to share his life with such a cook, this must have been the crowning moment, the desired moment, of the day. Everything Madame touched became, by some magical skill, delicious.

3 tablespoons butter
4 ounces mushrooms, chopped
1 small onion, chopped
2½ tablespoons flour
1¼ cups very hot water
⅔ cup Madeira
salt, pepper
extra knob of butter

Melt butter and cook mushrooms and onion in it gently for 5 minutes, or a little longer, until they soften. Stir in flour, raise heat, and allow the roux to brown lightly. Stir in water to make a sauce. Simmer 20 minutes, then pour in Madeira and simmer for a further 5 or 10 minutes. Season well. Remove from heat and stir in a nice knob of butter—this gives the sauce a specially good flavour, and a shiny appearance.

Sauce périgueux and sauce périgourdine

As you would expect from the names of these two sauces, the essential ingredient is the truffle. The first recipe demands no more than a modest tablespoon of chopped truffles, or even truffle peeling; the second "a generous quantity," cut into half-inch dice. *Sauce périgueux* goes with egg dishes, croquettes, fillet steak and chicken; *sauce périgourdine* with pheasant, quails and feathered game of all kinds. Both sauces are based on *sauce madère*.

3–4 *tablespoons beef drippings*
1 *onion, minced*
2½ *tablespoons flour*
2 *cups beef stock*
4 *tablespoons tomato purée*
1 *pound mushrooms, sliced*
6 *tablespoons butter*
½ *teaspoon salt*
freshly ground pepper
1 *shallot, minced*
⅓ *cup Madeira*
1 *heaping teaspoon chopped parsley*
1 *tablespoon chopped truffles or peelings*
a little liquor from canned truffles
PLUS:
about 2 ounces diced truffle for sauce périgourdine

Melt beef drippings and brown onion in them. Stir in flour and cook the roux until it is a nut-brown colour. Moisten with the beef stock, add tomato purée, and boil down to about a cup.

Meanwhile cook the mushrooms until they are golden brown in all but about a tablespoon of the butter. Season, and turn into the reduced sauce, together with the shallot, Madeira, and parsley. Simmer five minutes; before serving add the chopped truffles and truffle liquor. If making *sauce périgourdine*, add the diced truffle as well. Keep the sauce just below boiling point. Stir in the remaining butter off the heat, just before serving. Correct seasoning.

Red wine sauce

A quickly made sauce for steak or ham. Also a good sauce for roasted game (e.g., hare, venison) which has first been marinated. Substitute the marinade for part of the stock; instead of tomato and Worcestershire sauce, the final flavouring could be red-currant jelly if this seems more appropriate. For duck, use stock made from the giblets, and flavour finally with Seville orange juice and grated peel—the crushed duck liver could also be added with the mushrooms.

1 ounce (2 tablespoons) butter
1 small shallot, chopped
1 ounce mushrooms, chopped
2 teaspoons flour
⅔ cup red wine
⅔ cup beef stock
1 teaspoon tomato paste
1 teaspoon Worcestershire sauce
salt, pepper

Melt butter in a small pan, add the shallot, and as it begins to soften, stir in the mushrooms. After 3 or 4 minutes, mix in the flour, then, gradually, the wine and stock to make a smooth sauce. Simmer for 30 minutes. Flavour to taste with tomato concentrate, Worcestershire sauce, and salt and pepper; start with half the amounts given above, and add the rest if you feel the sauce needs the extra flavour. Strain the sauce before serving.

Carême's sauce hachée

A delicious sauce of chopped piquancies—for pork or beef, or for fish if a velouté is substituted for the *espagnole,* or brown sauce.

4 tablespoons wine vinegar
3 tablespoons chopped mushrooms
1 tablespoon chopped parsley
2 shallots, chopped
½ clove garlic, chopped
1 sprig thyme
½ bay leaf
2 cloves
pinch white pepper
a little grated nutmeg

Simmer the above ingredients until they are reduced to a lightly moistened mixture. Remove the bay, thyme and cloves. Add:

4 tablespoons chicken stock
⅔ cup sauce espagnole, *or good meat sauce from a stew*

Cook gently for another 10 minutes. Meanwhile mash together:

1 tablespoon butter
2 anchovy fillets

Chop together:

2 small pickled gherkins
capers

Add the anchovy butter to the sauce at the last moment, with the gherkins and a few capers.

Walnut and mushroom sauce

One might not expect the combination of walnuts and mushrooms to be successful, but this sauce goes well with poached chicken and white fish of quality. It has richness, tempered with the clear flavour of lemon, and the mealy, slightly dry taste of walnuts. A surprising and delicious mixture which takes the place of vegetables as well.

1 medium onion, chopped
1 large clove garlic, chopped
4 ounces mushrooms, chopped
1 cup chicken or fish stock
juice of ½ lemon
½ glass Madeira, or other fortified wine
4 ounces walnuts, roughly chopped
2 eggs
⅓ cup heavy cream
salt, pepper

Cook onion and garlic in the butter until they begin to soften. Add mushrooms. When they are just cooked, pour in the stock, lemon juice and wine, and simmer for a few moments before adding the walnuts. Beat eggs and cream together, and stir in a little of the hot sauce. Return this mixture to the pan and cook slowly until the sauce thickens (without allowing it to boil). Correct the seasoning.

NOTE : For another walnut and mushroom dish, see *Champignons farcis aux noix;* and *Aubergines (eggplant) à la chinoise* is an unusual mixture of the vegetable with oriental dried mushrooms and nuts.

Sauce chasseur, for roast and pan-fried meat (Huntsman's sauce)

6 ounces mushrooms, quartered
6 shallots, minced
6 tablespoons butter
2½ tablespoons flour
⅔ cup dry white wine
1¼ cups meat stock
¼ cup canned tomato sauce (not *tomato paste*)
meat juices from roasting or frying pan
salt, pepper
chopped parsley, tarragon, chervil

Brown mushrooms and shallots lightly in half the butter. Stir in flour to absorb the fat and juices, then add the wine, stock, and tomato sauce. Cook for 15 to 20 minutes until the flavour and texture are rich. Add more tomato sauce if you like. When the meat has been roasted, or pan-fried, skim off the fat and add the juices to the sauce. Off the heat, whisk in the remaining butter, season to taste, and add the herbs. Serve immediately.

Stuffings

Mushroom forcemeat

A recipe I cut out of the London *Times*, years ago, when we had an abundance of field mushrooms in our parish (see the recipe for *Mushroom pie*). It can be used quite simply as a stuffing for chicken or turkey, but it also makes—and this was the point of the recipe—delicious forcemeat balls for serving with soup. Good, too, with fish, as a stuffing for *paupiettes*.

6 ounces mushrooms
2½ ounces (5 tablespoons) butter
salt
powdered mace
cayenne pepper
1 cup white breadcrumbs
nutmeg
1 large egg yolk

Fry the mushrooms in half the butter, adding salt and mace to taste and a pinch of cayenne pepper. Cool, then chop or mince mushrooms fairly small and mix with the breadcrumbs (include any mushroom juice). Melt the remaining butter without overheating it, and add that. Correct the seasoning, and grate in a little nutmeg. Bind with the egg yolk. (Beat the mixture to a paste, roll into small balls, and fry them, if you wish to serve them with soup.)

Mushroom and olive stuffing

There's a high proportion of interesting bits and pieces in this stuffing—high, that is, in proportion to breadcrumbs—which makes it ideal for spreading on fillet steak when making *boeuf en croûte*.

Or for duck, which is always made more appetising by a sharp contrast of flavour (but don't overdo things by putting olives in the sauce as well). Lamb, chicken and turkey are other candidates. Red mullet baked on this kind of mixture is delicious, too. For steak *en croûte*, halve the quantity of breadcrumbs.

2 ounces (4 tablespoons) butter
1 medium onion, chopped
1 clove garlic, chopped
1 slice bacon, chopped
4 ounces mushrooms, coarsely chopped
1 cup breadcrumbs
2 tablespoons chopped parsley
¼ cup stuffed olives, halved
1 egg
salt, pepper

Melt butter, and cook onion and garlic in it gently until they soften without browning. Add bacon and mushrooms and continue to cook slowly so that the mushroom juices are not evaporated. Stir in breadcrumbs, parsley and olives. Bind with the egg, and season.

Ceps and olive stuffing

The finest stuffing of all, even though you will probably have to use dried ceps. Suitable for the Christmas bird—goose or duck, turkey or capon. The fine flavour permeates the meat.

2-ounce packet dried ceps, or 8–10 ounces fresh ceps
3 shallots, or 1 medium onion, chopped
4 tablespoons olive oil
⅓ cup pitted green olives, quartered
¾ cup chopped parsley
2 cloves garlic, minced
1 goose, duck, or turkey liver—or 2 chicken livers, chopped
4 ounces bread
milk

3 ounces (6 tablespoons) melted butter
4 anchovy fillets, or anchovy paste to taste
salt, pepper

Soak dried ceps according to instructions on the packet (usually for 20 minutes in tepid water). Meanwhile cook shallots or onion gently in the oil for 10 minutes without it colouring. Cut ceps into ½-inch chunks, add them to pan, and fry for another 10 minutes. Put into a bowl with the olives, parsley, garlic, and liver. Squeeze out the bread in a little milk to make a thick paste, and add that to the bowl. Stir in the butter and anchovy fillets or paste (anchovies make an excellent seasoning, not in the least fishy, a good unidentifiable accent).

More bread can be added, but with these fine flavours, a small amount of stuffing is all that's required.

Soups

Cream of mushroom soup I

Here is the basic recipe for mushroom soup. If you can use wild mushrooms, the flavour will be exquisite—field or horse mushrooms, parasols or ceps or fairy-ring mushrooms.

SERVES FOUR TO SIX
1 pound mushrooms
juice of a lemon
3 ounces (6 tablespoons) butter
1 shallot, chopped, or 2 tablespoons chopped onion
1 small clove garlic, chopped
salt, pepper
5 tablespoons flour
4½ cups beef stock
½ cup heavy cream

Chop the mushrooms finely. Sprinkle with lemon juice. Melt one-third of the butter in a pan and cook the shallot or onion and garlic in it until soft and yellow, but not brown. Add the mushrooms and continue cooking until the juices have evaporated, making a duxelles. Season.

Meanwhile, melt the remaining butter in a large saucepan, and stir in the flour and moisten with hot beef stock gradually, whisking all the time to avoid lumps. Simmer 20 minutes. Add the mushroom mixture, and simmer a further 10 minutes. Correct the seasoning and add the cream. Pour into a soup tureen, straining out the bits and pieces if you like: serve very hot.

Cream of mushroom soup II

This recipe comes from *The Gentle Art of Cookery* (1925), by Mrs C. F. Leyel and Miss Olga Hartley. Its unusual ingredient is the Sauterne. Sweetness doesn't seem at all the thing for mushrooms. It can work well, though; another example is the lovely *Délice de champignons*.

SERVES SIX TO EIGHT
8 ounces mushrooms, minced
1 slice of a large onion
4½ cups veal or chicken stock
2 ounces (4 tablespoons) butter
2½ tablespoons flour
⅔ cup heavy cream
⅔ cup milk
salt, pepper
⅓ cup Sauterne

Simmer mushrooms and onion in the stock for 20 minutes. Put them through the vegetable mill or purée in the blender. Melt the butter in a pan, stir in the flour, and after this roux has cooked gently for two minutes, stir in the soup. Add the cream and milk and season. The Sauterne should be poured in at the last moment before serving.

Cream of mushroom soup III

SERVES SIX TO EIGHT

Use the preceding recipe, omitting the Sauterne and adding a seasoning of nutmeg.

Or else sweat the mushrooms and onion in the butter, stir in the flour, and then the stock. Blend or sieve, pour in the cream and milk, and correct the seasoning. A small nib of garlic, cooked with the mushrooms and onions, improves the flavour. No Sauterne.

Clear mushroom soup (and mushroom stock)

A fine clear soup which is full of flavour, and equal in pleasure to any beef consommé. The rich background comes from the slow browning of onion slices in olive oil, and the delicacy from the mushrooms. If you have field mushrooms or woodland ceps, the soup will taste even better. The strained liquid makes an excellent base for sauces and vegetable stews.

SERVES FOUR

4–6 tablespoons olive oil
1 medium onion, sliced
2½ cups water
1 clove garlic, sliced
8 ounces mushrooms, sliced
½ teaspoon mixed dried sage, rosemary and oregano
nutmeg
1 teaspoon salt
black or cayenne pepper
lemon juice

Pour enough olive oil into a saucepan to cover the base. When it is hot, stir in the onion and leave it to cook slowly in the oil until it takes on a rich, appetizing brown colour. This takes time.

Do not be tempted to hurry things along, or the onion will start to blacken.

Now pour in the water, add garlic, mushrooms, herbs, a grating of nutmeg, and salt. Spice it with plenty of freshly ground black pepper or a pinch of cayenne. Leave to simmer for about 20 minutes. Taste and correct the seasoning, using lemon juice to accent the flavour. Strain off the liquid (there should be about 2 cups) into bowls, and serve very hot with a few slices of mushroom in each bowl.

Iced mushroom soup

A beautiful soup, unusual and delicate in flavour, from *Penguin Cordon Bleu Cookery,* by Rosemary Hume and Muriel Downes.

SERVES SIX
6 ounces mushrooms
4½ cups chicken stock
1 tablespoon arrowroot
3 egg yolks
¾ cup light or heavy cream
salt, white pepper
plenty of chopped chives

Push mushrooms through a vegetable mill, or purée in blender with a little of the stock. Dissolve arrowroot with a little of the stock. Bring remaining stock to boil, add mushroom mixture and cook 3 minutes. Remove from heat, and stir in arrowroot. Reboil, then quickly remove from the heat again. Mix yolks and cream, pour into soup, put over a moderate heat, and stir until it thickens to the consistency of cream (*do not let it boil, or the yolks will curdle*). Correct seasoning if necessary. Chill. Serve sprinkled with chives.

Crème de bolets
(Boletus soup)

A good way of using a few ceps: it makes the most of their flavour.

½–1 *pound ceps*
1 *large onion, chopped*
2 *ounces (4 tablespoons) butter or olive oil*
2 *tablespoons flour*
4 *cups water*
milk
salt, pepper
⅓–½ *cup cream*
parsley, chopped

Slice cep caps, chop the stalks. Sweat onion in butter or oil until soft but not browned. Add ceps, and continue to cook slowly for a further 10 to 15 minutes. Stir in flour, and add water gradually. Simmer until ceps are completely soft and done. Sieve or liquidize in blender, keeping a few pieces of cep back to chop roughly and add as a final garnish. Add milk until required consistency is achieved. Reheat, correct seasoning, and add roughly chopped ceps. Stir in the cream, sprinkle with parsley, and serve.

Two mushroom soups, with a garnish of raw mushrooms

We've eaten raw mushrooms as a salad for many years, but I'd never thought of using them with soup until I came across Philip Harben's *Grammar of Cooking* (Penguin, 1962). And then in 1970, Michael Field published a richer version in *All Manner of*

Food (Knopf). Here is a résumé of both recipes with minor adaptations. First the more modest Harben soup:

SERVES FOUR

½ *pound mushroom stalks*
1¼ *cups boiled bacon stock, or veal or chicken stock with a few bacon rinds*
bouquet garni
salt, pepper
2 *ounces (4 tablespoons) butter*
3 *tablespoons flour*
2½ *cups milk*
1–2 *fine large mushrooms*

Simmer the first three ingredients in a covered pan for an hour to extract the maximum flavour from the stalks. Strain off, measure, and either add more stock to bring it up to about a cup or boil down to about a cup (this will depend on how tightly the lid fitted the pan). Season. Melt the butter, and stir in the flour. Stir in the stock and milk. Correct seasoning. Slice the mushrooms very thinly, and float them on the surface of the soup just before it's served.

And now the American version:

SERVES SIX TO EIGHT

4 *ounces (8 tablespoons) butter*
2 *cups finely chopped green onions (about 12 scallions) using 4 inches of green*
2 *level tablespoons flour*
5 *cups chicken stock*
¾ *pound firm, fresh mushrooms*
1–1½ *cups heavy cream*
salt, freshly ground black pepper

Melt butter, add onions, cover, and simmer gently without browning for 15 minutes. Stir in the flour, cook for a minute or two, then add the stock and bring to the boil, stirring until slightly thickened. Chop ½ pound of the mushrooms, and add them to the soup; slice the remaining mushrooms very thinly and put into the soup tureen. Cook the soup for another 10 minutes after the mushrooms have been added, then sieve the soup or put it through a food mill. Do not use a blender—the soup should have a slightly grainy texture. Reheat, add cream, and correct the seasoning. Pour into the tureen and serve at once.

Potage aux champignons à la bressane (Mushroom soup in the Bresse style)

It's difficult to choose between the different mushroom soups—obviously one uses the recipe which coincides with the contents of the store cupboard—but for flavour, I think this is the best. It comes from Elizabeth David's *French Provincial Cooking*.

An interesting thing is the use of breadcrumbs for thickening rather than flour or a final addition of egg yolks and cream. This was the normal style for sauces in the Middle Ages; it persisted into Tudor times, and survives in our own bread sauce.

The district of Bresse in southern Burgundy is famous for its food, in particular its chickens, and also for being the home country of the great gourmet Brillat-Savarin. Recipes from that area have a fine simplicity of flavour, which can be achieved only by using ingredients of the first quality, without skimping.

SERVES FOUR TO FIVE
¾ pound mushrooms, chopped
2 ounces (4 tablespoons) butter
4 tablespoons minced parsley
small piece of garlic, minced
salt, freshly ground black pepper
nutmeg or mace
thick slice of bread
4½ cups chicken, beef, or veal stock
⅓–½ cup cream

Cook mushrooms gently in butter. As the juices start to run, mix in half the parsley, the garlic, and the seasonings to taste. Soak the bread in a little stock, stir it into the mushrooms, then add the remaining stock. Cook for 15 minutes, then purée in a blender or sieve through a vegetable mill. Heat cream to a boil, and add it to soup with remaining parsley. Adjust seasoning. Excellent chilled with extra cream.

Mushroom barley soup, in the Middle-European manner

Another recipe from Michael Field's *All Manner of Food* (Knopf, 1970), quite different from the usual cream of mushroom soup. Mr Field does not specify the exact variety of dried mushroom to be used, but I find that ceps give by far the best flavour. Sometimes one can buy Polish dried ceps, which are good and not too expensive. Otherwise look for an Italian brand; a good one comes from Vicfungo of Costabissara in a bright orange packet labelled *funghi porcini*—you will need two to make up the quantity, as they contain only half an ounce.

SERVES SIX TO EIGHT
8–10 dried mushrooms (about 1 ounce)
8 cups chicken stock
2 ounces (4 tablespoons) butter
1 small onion, finely chopped
½ medium carrot, finely chopped
½ stalk celery, finely chopped
½ cup pearl barley
2 level tablespoons flour
salt, freshly ground black pepper
fresh dill or parsley, chopped (minced)

Put the mushrooms into a small bowl. Heat a ladleful of the stock, and pour it over them. After 20 minutes, or when the mushrooms are pliable, remove and chop them. Reserve their soaking liquid.

Meanwhile, melt half the butter in a large pan. Add the onion, carrot and celery and cook them gently for about 10 minutes. They should not brown. Pour in the stock, add the pearl barley, and the mushrooms and their soaking stock when they are ready. Simmer for 1 hour, or until the pearl barley is cooked.

Melt the remaining butter in another pan, stir in the flour, and cook until it turns a delicate golden brown. Add enough stock from the soup to make a smooth sauce, then tip it into the pan of soup, stirring well until everything is amalgamated. Simmer 20 minutes. If the soup becomes too thick, dilute it with more stock or water. Correct the seasoning. Sprinkle with a few tablespoons of dill or parsley, and have some more in a bowl for people to add extra if they like.

Potage de levraut à l'anglaise (English hare soup)

In the eighteenth century, before the difficult era of the soup kitchen, the English were famous for the abundance and quality of their meat and game, and for dishes made from them, such as pies and soups. Foreign travellers exclaimed, with a tone of priggish shock, that the British working classes ate *meat*, and not just occasionally but often. The unspoken conclusion was that it would all come to no good. But in fact we escaped the excesses of revolution. Can we ascribe this to meat-eating by the lower orders in the eighteenth century?

Here is an excellent version of our hare soup, given, with proper respect, by the greatest of French chefs, Carême. No doubt he first came across it when working for the Prince Regent in England.

The recipe suggests using one young hare: but if you have a more mature animal, use only the head and leg, keeping the saddle aside for another meal.

In the likely event of your not using claret—Carême's *bon vin de Bordeaux*—but some cheaper red wine, a spoonful of red-currant jelly, added towards the end, will improve the flavour. And if your hare was slightly beyond the *levraut* stage, and needed prolonged cooking, add a few extra mushrooms at the end, which have been quickly fried whole in butter.

SERVES FOUR TO SIX
3 ounces (6 tablespoons) butter
1 young hare, cut in pieces
4 ounces salt pork or bacon, diced
2½ tablespoons flour
1½ cups claret or other red wine
2 cups consommé or beef stock
1 large onion, stuck with a clove
8 ounces whole mushrooms
pinch cayenne pepper
½ teaspoon mace
½ teaspoon black pepper
bouquet garni, with 5 extra sprigs parsley, plus a sprig each of basil,
    rosemary, and marjoram
salt

Bring the butter to a boil in a small pan, then pour it through a muslin-lined sieve into a large frying pan. Brown the hare and pork or bacon in the butter. Stir in flour, then wine and stock and remaining ingredients. Simmer until the hare is cooked, skimming off any fat that rises to the surface. Pour soup through a large sieve into a clean pan. Discard onion, bouquet and bones. Separate the meat into small convenient pieces and return to the strained soup with the pork and whole mushrooms. Reheat, correct the seasoning, and serve very hot.

Mussel soup with mushrooms

Chopped mussels and sliced mushrooms give this soup a nourishing but finely flavoured thickness, almost the consistency of a stew. The affinity of mushrooms with shellfish is always a delight; recipes like this and others in the book using shellfish taste far beyond the modest effort one puts into them. To me this is a bonus in cooking. Even after years of experience, I am still surprised by it.

SERVES SIX
3 pounds mussels
⅔ cup water
⅔ cup dry white wine

3 *shallots, chopped*
2 *ounces (4 tablespoons) butter*
4 *ounces mushrooms, sliced*
5 *tablespoons flour*
1¼ *cups fish (or light meat) stock*
⅔ *cup cream*
pepper, salt
4 *tablespoons chopped parsley*

Scrub mussels, and remove barnacles and beard with a knife. Throw away any that are broken, or refuse to close when given a sharp tap. Simmer water, wine and two-thirds of the shallots for 5 minutes. Put in the mussels, cover the pan, and leave over a good heat for a further 5 minutes. By this time most of the mussels will have opened. Remove them to a colander set over a bowl (kitchen tongs are the best implements for this job). Discard all the shells, and any mussels that have not opened. Strain the liquor carefully and reserve. Cut each mussel into three or four bits, according to size. Now melt the butter, and cook the remaining shallots and the mushrooms until the mixture is well moistened with the mushroom juices. Stir in the flour, then the stock and the strained mussel liquor. Cook gently, covered, for 15 minutes. Stir in the cream, adjust the seasoning, and add parsley and chopped mussels. Serve with wholemeal bread and butter.

If you increase the quantity of the various liquids, you would have enough soup for six, but it would not be quite such a nourishing dish. As it is, the recipe makes a pleasant evening meal for four, when followed by cheese and fruit only.

Fish soup in the Mediterranean style

Mediterranean recipes for fish soups often include tomatoes and saffron and a good mixture of fish, including shellfish. Our varieties in the north of Europe and in the United States, too, are different, so we can never hope to produce a bouillabaisse. But we can make a good soup on the same lines, and enjoy it for its own qualities. I have not specified exactly which fish should be used.

Firstly because it doesn't matter precisely, and secondly because fishmongers vary widely in their stock in different parts of the country, and on different days of the week. Generally speaking, you need a cheap fish for background flavour: conger eel is good, but redfish, often sold as bream, will do instead (in the United States anything from ocean perch to porgy would be fine); then a better type of fish to add fineness and an agreeable texture, red mullet, John Dory, brill or turbot (in the States, perhaps red snapper or sea bass would be best); and lastly shellfish for sweetness and piquancy.

When you have made your choice, take them home and prepare them appropriately. Mussels will need to be scrubbed and opened (see preceding recipe) and their liquor should be carefully strained and added to the soup in place of some of the water. Then all the fish should be cut into nice chunks and divided into three piles—10 minutes of cooking (conger), 5 minutes of cooking (most white fish), and 2 minutes of cooking (shellfish). If these times seem short to you, remember that the fish continues to cook in the broth as it is served and brought to the table, and that nothing is worse than soup with a flannel-like mush of overcooked fish.

SERVES SIX TO EIGHT

2 *pounds fish (see above)*
1 *pound mussels or other shellfish*
¼ *cup olive oil*
1 *large onion, sliced*
3 *cloves garlic, minced*
½ *pound fresh tomatoes, peeled, chopped*
½ *pound mushrooms, chopped*
3 *tablespoons rice*
7½ *cups water*
bouquet garni
pinch saffron
salt, freshly ground black pepper, sugar
tomato paste (optional)
6 *thick slices French bread*
extra olive oil
grated Parmesan cheese
basil or parsley, minced

Clean and separate the seafood as described above. Heat olive oil and fry onion and garlic until lightly browned. Add tomatoes, mushrooms and rice, and stir over the heat for a few moments. Pour in water, and add bouquet and saffron. Season with salt, pepper and a little sugar (many commercial tomatoes are tasteless by comparison with French ones—some extra tomato concentrate may also be a good idea). Simmer for about 15 minutes, then add the fish at the intervals described above. Correct the seasoning.

Meanwhile brush the slices of bread with oil and place under grill until lightly browned. Sprinkle one side of each slice with cheese, and return to the grill until it is melted and bubbling. Either place these in the soup tureen or put on a separate plate.

Pour the soup into the tureen, scatter the basil or parsley over the top, and serve boiling hot.

MUSHROOM
DISHES

There can be no doubt about the virtues of mushrooms with meat and fish, or in soups and sauces, but for me this section is the heart of the mushroom feast. The mushroom is the chief character, the hero, demonstrating its versatility in a sequence of recipes that goes from rustic simplicity to the classical solidities of fine cookery. Here you will find the richness of mushrooms in cream, the unexpected piquancies of stuffed mushrooms, the small dishes of the best home cookery, and one or two frivolities like *Délice des champignons,* in which mushrooms are cooked with grapes.

This is the chapter of first courses and supper dishes, of mushrooms in croustades, in vol-au-vent or chou cases, and in tarts, of mushrooms in soufflés or with eggs and anchovies, of mushrooms marinaded or sliced raw into salads. I hope that these recipes will give a hint of the European delight in mushrooms that we seem to miss, that they will convince you that few pleasures can compare with a dish of *cèpes bordelaise* after an autumn afternoon in the woods, or of field mushrooms in cream at the midday meal in summertime.

Some general mushroom recipes

A recipe for all fungi

Now that there is such concern for the environment and the quality of food, books about edible wild plants have become popular. Few of them can compare, for experience and knowledge, with *The Wild Foods of Britain* by Jason Hill, which appeared in 1939. A neurologist in Harley Street, he was prompted to write the book when one of his children remarked that she didn't like "nature." By this she meant school nature study, which was decidedly unproductive. He sympathized with her, and planned his book on the basis that there's no "incentive to knowing the country really well so strong as the prospect of getting something out of it—

there is, too, a deep and rather primitive pleasure in foraging."

Jason Hill included mushrooms among his wild foods, along with hop shoots, nettles, hazel nuts, sorrel, and so on. Some of his suggestions are incorporated in my opening discussion on the best edible mushrooms. Here, though, is his basic recipe for all kinds of mushrooms:

Clean and trim the mushrooms. Put them into an ovenproof dish with butter, oil or fat, and seasoning. Cover and cook at mark 4, 350°F, for 10 to 25 minutes, according to the age and thickness of the mushrooms. Squeeze a little lemon juice over them before serving.

Several variations are possible. For instance, replace the fat with soured cream. Add finely chopped onion and garlic (it's a good idea to soften them in butter first, or they will still be hard when the mushrooms are cooked). Or herbs. Increase the juices with a little hot stock or meat essence. Thicken with breadcrumbs sprinkled over the top, or with egg yolks and cream stirred in last of all.

Eliza Acton's mushrooms au beurre (Delicious)

Eliza Acton may have been a generation younger than Jane Austen—she was born in 1799, before the publication of *Sense and Sensibility*—but her *Modern Cookery* shares something of the atmosphere of the novels, a lightness and grace of tone which is missing by the time one comes to the Victorian Mrs Beeton.

"Cut the stems from some fine meadow mushroom-buttons, and clean them with a bit of new flannel, and some fine salt; then either wipe them dry with a soft cloth, or rinse them in fresh water, drain them quickly, spread them in a clean cloth, fold it over them, and leave them for ten minutes, or more, to dry. For every pint of them thus prepared, put an ounce and a half of fresh butter into a thick iron saucepan, shake it over the fire until it *just* begins to brown, throw in the mushrooms, continue to shake the saucepan over a clear fire that they may not stick to it nor burn, and when they have simmered three or four minutes, strew over them a little salt, some cayenne, and pounded mace; stew them until they are perfectly tender, heap them in a dish, and serve them with their own sauce only, for breakfast, supper, or luncheon. Nothing can be finer than the flavour of the mushrooms thus prepared; and the addition of any liquid is far from an improvement to it. They are very good when drained from the butter, and served cold, and in a cool larder may be kept for several days. The butter in which they are stewed is admirable for flavouring gravies, sauces, or potted meats. Small flaps, freed from the fur and skin, may be stewed in the same way; and either these, or the buttons, served under roast poultry or partridges, will give a dish of very superior relish.

"Meadow mushrooms, 3 pints, fresh butter 4½ oz: 3 to 5 minutes. Salt, 1 small teaspoonful; mace, half as much; cayenne, third of saltspoonful: 10 to 15 mintues. More spices to be added if required—much depending on their quality; but they should not overpower the flavour of the mushrooms.

"*Obs.*—Persons inhabiting parts of the country where mushrooms are abundant, may send them easily, when thus prepared . . . to their friends in cities, or in less productive counties. If poured into jars, with sufficient butter to cover them, they will travel any distance, and can be re-warmed for use."

N O T E : Instead of the spices in the recipe above, use a little thyme or rosemary to make a change of flavour.

Mushrooms, or the Pearl of the Fields

Under this title, in his *Shilling Cookery for the People*, first published in 1845, Alexis Soyer describes a method of cooking field mushrooms which is most delicious. "Being in Devonshire, at the end of September and walking across the fields before breakfast to a small farmhouse, I found three very fine mushrooms, which I thought would be a treat, but on arriving at the house I found it had no oven, a bad gridiron and a smoky coal fire. Necessity, they say, is the mother of Invention; I immediately applied to our grand and universal mamma, how I should dress my precious mushrooms, when a gentle whisper came to my ear. . . ."

He cooked them on toast, on a stand in front of the fire, with a glass tumbler inverted over them. We can of course make use of our ovens, so here is his recipe adapted to our modern circumstances.

Wipe the mushrooms—they should be a fair size—and remove the earthy part. Spread rounds of toast, half an inch thick, with clotted (or very thick) cream. Place mushrooms, stalks up, on the toast, season them, and put a little more cream into the caps. Arrange toast and mushrooms on a baking sheet, and invert pyrex bowls or small custard cups over each piece. Leave for half an hour in a fairly hot oven, mark 5–6, 375°–400°F.

"The sight when the glass is removed, is most inviting, its whiteness rivals the everlasting snows of Mont Blanc, and the taste is worthy of Lucullus. Vitellius would never have dined without it; Apicius would never have gone to Greece to seek for crawfish; and had he only half the fortune left when he committed suicide, he would have preferred to have left proud Rome and retire to some villa or cottage to enjoy such an enticing dish."

Cèpes à la bordelaise (Ceps in the Bordeaux style)

As you drive through the forests in the south-west of France in the summer and autumn, small boys on the side of the road hold up baskets of ceps they have picked, hoping you will stop and buy some. Around Bordeaux ceps are particularly abundant. No wonder the local way of cooking them has become the classic recipe. It's simple to do, yet brings out perfectly the flavour and texture of the best of mushrooms.

SERVES SIX
2 pounds firm ceps
½ cup olive oil
salt and pepper
2 shallots, minced
handful of parsley, minced
juice of a lemon
1 biscotte, crushed (optional)

Clean and slice the caps: chop the stalks and set them aside. Cook the slices in the oil for 5 minutes, season them, and turn them over for another 5 minutes. If they exude a lot of juice, raise the heat so that it evaporates to a modest amount. Stir in the stalks and cook another 5 minutes. Mix shallots and parsley. Put on top of the ceps and cook for 2 or 3 minutes to heat through—the shallots should still be crisp. Slide the panful on to a hot serving dish, trying as best you can to keep the chopped shallot mixture on top. Sprinkle with lemon juice. Some people also add a scattering of *biscotte*, but I prefer to omit this, which is a recent embellishment of the recipe.

Cèpes sur le gril

Although this method can be used to cook any kind of mushroom, it is particularly successful with ceps and much favoured in the central western districts of France. Obviously you need perfect specimens, no worm holes or bruised edges. And as usual, with perfect food, with perfect basic ingredients, the cooking is simplicity itself. The best way of cooking ceps.

Remove the stalks from the ceps and put them aside for another dish, such as *paupiettes forestières* or a poultry stuffing.

Heat the grill (or broiler). Place the caps, underside up, in the grill pan, and pour a spoonful of olive oil into each one. Cook under the heat for 15 minutes. Transfer them to an oven dish, salt and pepper them, and add a knob of butter to each one. Give them 5 minutes in the oven or a little longer, mark 6, 400°F. Serve them very hot with a generous scattering of chopped parsley.

Beignets de champignons, sauce tomate
(Mushroom fritters with tomato sauce)

Mushrooms make good fritters, either raw (which I prefer) or partially cooked in a little white wine and lemon juice. A piquant tomato sauce sets them off well. The batter given here makes a very complete coating: if you want something lighter, use the tempura batter recipe on page 272, which is more of a veiling.

MUSHROOMS:

¾ pound medium mushrooms
2 ounces dry white wine ⎫
squeeze lemon juice ⎬ optional (see directions)
salt, pepper ⎭

BATTER:

1 cup flour
1 large egg yolk
2 tablespoons brandy or other spirits
4 tablespoons melted butter
a pinch of salt
up to ⅔ cup milk
1 egg white, beaten stiff

SAUCE:

6 tablespoons chopped shallots or onion
6 tablespoons olive oil
1½ pounds tomatoes, skinned, chopped
bouquet garni
2 cloves garlic, minced
¼ cup dry white wine
¼ cup black olives, pitted
salt, pepper, sugar

Trim mushrooms neatly. If you like, cook them for 5 minutes or so in a covered pan with wine, lemon juice and seasoning: drain them and leave to cool. Otherwise sprinkle them with lemon juice and a little salt.

Make the batter in the usual way, mixing the batter ingredients in the given order, and folding in the egg white just before you intend to cook the fritters.

To make the sauce, brown the shallots or onion lightly in the oil. Add the tomatoes, bouquet, garlic, and white wine. Cook steadily to a purée. Add the olives, simmer for a few minutes, then correct the seasoning. A little sugar helps if the tomatoes are on the tasteless side.

Keep the sauce hot in a pan while you dip the mushrooms in the batter and deep-fry them at 370°–380°F for about 3 minutes, or more if they are large. As they rise to the surface, golden-brown all over, remove a fritter to see if they are ready. The mushrooms should be juicy inside the crisp batter. Cook them in batches or the pan will become overcrowded. Keep them warm on crumpled kitchen paper in the oven and serve them as quickly as possible.

Mushrooms cooked in vine leaves

At midsummer on the Loire, after the vine flowers have lost their rich sweetness and begun to turn into grapes, we often bring back a handful or two of vine leaves from our walks. At this time they are fully grown but fresh, not fatigued to leathery darkness by the sun. They have flavour, and are good stuffed with a savoury rice and chicken mixture. I sometimes include mushrooms, but the essential is a piquant taste such as lemon juice or anchovies. Then the little rolls are simmered in some stock for about 20 to 30 minutes.

I have always wanted to try the recipe for *cèpes à la génoise*, fresh ceps baked in a swathing of fresh vine leaves, but I've never succeeded. By the time we return to France in the autumn, and find a few ceps in the commune woods, the vine leaves are tough and beginning to blaze with yellow and red. So I was glad to come across an adaptation of this famous recipe to cultivated mushrooms, which are always available. It's from *Summer Cooking* by Elizabeth David, and as she remarks, it makes them taste like field mushrooms.

If you have a vine against the wall of the house, this recipe is simple. Otherwise it means a visit to the delicatessen for a tin or jar of vine leaves, plain *unstuffed* vine leaves.

15 vine leaves
olive oil
about 1 pound medium mushrooms
salt, pepper
4 cloves garlic, minced

Blanch the vine leaves in boiling water for 2 or 3 minutes. Drain them, and put about 10 on the base of a shallow fireproof pot. Brush lightly with oil, and put the mushrooms on top, stalk side up. Season with salt, pepper and garlic, and brush with more oil. Put the remaining leaves over the whole thing, cover it with foil, and bake for 35 to 60 minutes in a slow oven, mark 3, 325°F, until the mushrooms are cooked.

Cèpes à la génoise

Here is the original recipe, briefly summarized, in case you are luckier than I seem to be in the conjunction of season and resources.

Trim the cep stalks so that they are flat, but keep the trimmings. Sprinkle the caps with coarse sea salt and leave them for a while to exude their juice. Then put them in the oven to dry them off for a few minutes.

Meanwhile put a layer of fresh vine leaves in an oblong fireproof pot, and cover them with about ¼ inch of olive oil. Heat them slowly. Then place the ceps on top, stalk side up, cover them with foil, and put into a moderate oven, mark 4–5, 350°–375°F, for half an hour. While they cook, slice the trimmed stalks thinly. Remove the ceps from the oven, put the sliced stalks on top, and in each corner of the dish put a halved clove of garlic. Cook in oven a further 10 minutes. Season well with black pepper and serve.

Basic recipe for mushroom tart (quiche)

The word *quiche* is overused these days. It should really be kept for open tarts originating in the eastern part of France (the word is related to the German *Kuchen*, meaning cake). After all we do have our own words, tart and flan, for similar dishes. The thing about the *quiche*, in particular the *quiche Lorraine*, is that the custard filling is made from cream and eggs. Savoury confections of a similar kind in England are decidedly short on the cream, and often, instead of custard, a floury sauce is used, which sits heavily on top of the pastry. An unpleasing economy which is unfortunately not unknown in French restaurants and cooked food shops these days.

The thing to aim for is crispness, lightness and richness, not always an easy combination. The lightness and richness are achieved by using a cream and egg custard, crispness by pre-baking the pastry case. The main flavouring ingredients should be well spiced and piquant; they can vary according to the taste and skill of the cook. Mushrooms and onion alone make a delicious tart, or mushrooms and prawns or shrimp, or mushrooms and bacon, or mushrooms and other vegetables—young garden peas, cubes of buttered parsnip for instance, or mushrooms and anchovies: allow enough to cover the base of the pastry—obviously you will need a smaller proportion of anchovies, or bacon, or prawns, and a larger proportion of mushrooms. And plenty of pepper.

This kind of dish tastes best when eaten warm rather than piping hot. A green salad goes with it well, if it's the main course at a midday meal.

SERVES SIX

PASTRY:
1 cup flour
pinch salt
2 ounces (4 tablespoons) butter, or butter and lard
1 egg yolk

FILLING:
8 ounces mushrooms, sliced
1 small onion, chopped
2 cloves garlic, minced
2 ounces (4 tablespoons) butter
salt, pepper, nutmeg
3 egg yolks
1¼ cups light cream, or half-and-half
3 tablespoons chopped parsley

To make the pastry, put the flour and salt in a bowl, add the fat, and rub it in lightly. Mix in the egg yolk and a little water if necessary to bind the pastry. Roll out and line a flan tin (8 to 9½ inches) with a removable base. Prick with a fork, or put in a piece of foil weighted down with an even layer of dried beans, and bake for 10 to 15 minutes at mark 6, 400°F, until set and lightly coloured.

Meanwhile prepare the filling. In a frying pan, cook mushrooms, onion and garlic in the butter for about 10 minutes or until the juices are almost entirely evaporated. Season with salt, pepper, and nutmeg and spread evenly over the pastry case. Mix egg yolks, cream, and parsley, and pour over the mushroom mixture. Bake at mark 4, 350°F, for 30 to 40 minutes, until the custard is just firm and a little browned on top.

Mushroom pie

One marvellous summer, years ago, there was a glut of field mushrooms in our part of Wiltshire. Every Sunday morning for several weeks, two girls came to the house with a huge basket of them, at least seven or eight pounds, which they sold for a few shillings In fact we became sick of mushrooms, and, coming from the town, I never thought of drying them (but then neither did anyone else in the village, so far have we lost essential country skills in our suburban country lives). I always associate this recipe with that fruitful summer. It came, I think, from the London *Times*, and we ate it frequently, always with pleasure.

SERVES SIX

6 *tablespoons long-grain rice*
1 *large onion*
2 *sage leaves*
5 *ounces (10 tablespoons) butter*
6–8 *ounces field or cultivated mushrooms (see recipe)*
salt, pepper
3 *hard-boiled eggs, shelled*
4 *ounces shortcrust pastry*
1 *beaten egg*

Boil rice until cooked, then drain. Meanwhile chop onion and sage together, and cook until soft and golden in about a third of the butter. Use half the remaining butter to grease a pie dish liberally. Cover with a layer of mushroom caps, gill side up, pushed closely together (the exact weight required will vary according to the mushrooms). Chop the stalks and scatter them on top. Season well. Spread the rice over the mushrooms, then the onion and sage on top of the rice. Halve the eggs and embed them, cut side down, in the rice. Dab all over with the remaining butter. Cover with pastry, brush with beaten egg, and bake at mark 7, 425°F, for about half an hour. Protect the pastry with paper or foil if it becomes too brown.

Gâteau de champignons à la crème (Mushroom cake with a cream sauce)

This unusual recipe from France is well worth making as a luncheon dish, or as a first course for a dinner party. But don't attempt it without some kind of chopping machine, or it will take up a great deal of your time. One of those hand choppers that you push up and down is quite effective, or the new French electric choppers. A blender could also be used so long as you were careful not to emulsify the mushrooms and ham. They should retain a certain bite, a mild knobbliness of texture, which the cream sauce will complement with its richness.

SERVES SIX

CAKE:
2 pounds small mushrooms
4 ounces (8 tablespoons) butter
juice of 1 lemon
½ pound cooked ham
4 shallots, finely chopped
1 large clove garlic, finely chopped
2 tablespoons chopped parsley
2 tablespoons fine breadcrumbs
¼ cup heavy cream
6 tablespoons brandy
4 large eggs
salt, pepper, nutmeg

SAUCE:
1 generous tablespoon butter
2 tablespoons flour
2 tablespoons tomato paste
⅔ cup light cream
salt, pepper, nutmeg

To make the cake, put the mushrooms, 2 ounces of the butter, and the lemon juice in a large pan over a moderate heat. Cover and cook for 10 minutes, then strain off the juice and set aside for the sauce. Reserve 12 of the best mushrooms for decoration and chop the rest with the ham. Melt 1 ounce of the remaining butter in a small pan and cook the shallots gently for 5 minutes. Mix with the ham and mushrooms, the garlic, parsley, breadcrumbs, cream, and brandy. Beat in 2 whole eggs and 2 egg yolks.

Whisk the 2 spare egg whites until very stiff. Season the mixture with salt, pepper, and nutmeg, then fold in the whites carefully with a metal spoon, as if you were making a soufflé. Butter a 3-pint or, in the U.S., a 2-quart straight-sided mould (a soufflé or charlotte dish is best) with the rest of the butter from the cake ingredients, and put in the mushroom mixture. Stand the dish in a pan of boiling water and bake at mark 5, 375°F, for 30 minutes, then at mark 6, 400°F, for 15 minutes.

While the mushroom cake is cooking, melt the butter from the sauce ingredients, stir in the flour, and cook for 2 minutes without allowing the roux to colour. Stir in the mushroom liquor that was set aside, and the tomato concentrate, then the cream. Simmer for 10 minutes and season well. If the sauce is too thick—which will depend on the quantity of liquid from the mushrooms—add a little milk or more cream.

Unmould cake on to a hot dish, decorate with the reserved mushrooms, and serve with the sauce.

Mushroom croquettes

SERVES FOUR

Turn to the recipe for chicken croquettes on page 242, and substitute 10 ounces of chopped mushrooms for the chicken, ham and smaller amount of mushrooms called for there. Add a couple of cloves of crushed garlic when cooking the mushrooms, and use lemon juice to give the mixture an extra piquancy.

Risotto ai funghi

When the French have a few ceps, they stretch them with potatoes. The northern Italians choose rice; the plump melting grains produced in the Po valley go well with mushrooms. The recipe is simple, the standard risotto with one extra ingredient.

4 ounces (8 tablespoons) butter
1 medium onion, chopped
8–12 ounces ceps, caps sliced, stalks chopped
2 cups Italian rice
1 cup dry white wine
up to 5 cups meat stock
salt, pepper
Parmesan cheese, grated

Melt half the butter, and sweat the onion in it. When it is soft, stir in the ceps and cook for another 5 minutes. Add the rice, and when it becomes translucent, pour in the wine. This will soon be absorbed, so add a quarter of the stock, then another quarter as that disappears. And so on, until the rice is cooked— about 20 minutes. Different kinds of rice, even different brands, need different amounts of liquid, so this is a dish to be watched.

Correct the seasoning and stir in the remaining butter and several tablespoons of cheese. Serve at once, with more grated cheese in a separate bowl.

Risotto con tartufi

SERVES FOUR TO SIX
A good way of using one solitary white truffle. Even a small one makes a homely dish into something special.

Just cook a risotto, as above but without the ceps. Before serving, cover the rice with paper-thin slices of white truffle (use the cucumber blade on a grater). Butter and cheese as above.

Girolles on buttered toast

In spite of undeniably good recipes like the *girolles à la forest-ière* which follows, or the delicious flavour of chicken and girolles together, I still think that the best way of eating them is the simplest one of all. If you choose *biscottes* in preference to toasted bread, you will agree with me, I think, that this recipe combines crispness and a beautifully flavoured chewiness, both set off by butter, black pepper and some parsley.

SERVES FOUR
2–3 pounds girolles
butter
1 clove gárlic, minced
salt, freshly ground black pepper
parsley, chopped
well-buttered biscottes, *or rusks, or toast*

Trim off the earthy part of the girolle stems, then wash the caps quickly but carefully, and drain them well. Cook them in several tablespoons of butter, adding the garlic. Keep the heat high once the mushrooms begin to exude their juice—some people drain off this liquid, and complete the cooking of the mushrooms in some fresh butter. It very much depends on how wet or dry the girolles are, which again depends on the season in which they are picked. The answer is to drain off the liquid if it doesn't evaporate before the mushrooms are cooked; they must not be allowed to stew to leather. Season with salt and pepper, sprinkle with parsley, and serve on *biscottes,* rusks or toast immediately.

Girolles à la crème

Girolles cooked to the preceding recipe make a fine vegetable to go with veal—escalopes, chops or a roast. If they are being served with chicken, it is usual to add some very thick cream just before dishing them up; 5 or 6 tablespoons should be enough, and stir it well into the pan juices so that the sauce is well amalgamated.

Girolles à la crème also make a fine filling for an omelette, or for the whole range of pastry cases. Such recipes stretch a small quantity of girolles in the most economical way possible.

Girolles à la forestière

This French recipe is also a good one for ceps.

SERVES FOUR
3 pounds girolles
4 ounces (8 tablespoons) butter
4 ounces lean smoked bacon, cut in strips
6 ounces new potatoes
salt, black pepper
parsley, chopped

Wash and trim girolles. Cook them in a bare ounce of butter for 5 minutes, then drain off the liquid. Fry the bacon rapidly in the remaining butter for a few moments until it begins to brown, then add the girolles and leave to simmer for 20 minutes. Meanwhile cook the new potatoes and cut them into pieces roughly the size of the girolles. Add to the pan of girolles and bacon, and stir everything about so that the potatoes colour slightly in the juices —this should take 5 minutes. Season to taste. Serve sprinkled with parsley.

Field mushroom stew from Holland

This recipe comes from Justin de Blank, whose provision shops are one of the pleasures of London. It was his Dutch grandmother's way of cooking large field mushrooms, the ones with most flavour, which begin to look a little shaggy at the edges.

4-ounce piece fat bacon, diced
1–1½ pounds field mushrooms
½ cup white wine
½–⅔ cup chicken stock
1 tablespoon cornstarch
salt, pepper

Cook the bacon slowly at first until the fat runs, then raise the heat and brown the mushrooms lightly. Pour in the white wine and stock and complete the cooking to taste. Transfer mushrooms and bacon to a dish, and thicken the pan juices with the starch in the usual way. Correct the seasoning and pour sauce over the mushrooms.

Funghi porcini al tegame
(Ceps with mint)

Mint seems to belong so much to English cookery that it's surprising to find it in an Italian recipe, particularly a recipe for mushrooms. In fact the Romans use mint more widely than we do—Ada Boni uses it with eggs and chicory as well. As you will see from the recipe for mushrooms baked in the Genoese style, a *tegame* is a shallow earthenware dish. Over a modern electric or gas stove, use stoneware or flameproof glass with an asbestos mat for extra security.

SERVES SIX
2 pounds ceps, or field or cultivated mushrooms
½ cup olive oil
4–6 anchovy fillets, chopped
2 cloves garlic, crushed
6 large ripe tomatoes, peeled, seeded, chopped
4 sprigs mint
salt, pepper
slices of French bread, fried in butter

Slice mushrooms; chop the stalks. Heat oil in the cooking pot with the anchovies, stirring until the anchovies dissolve. Add mushrooms, garlic, and tomatoes. Finely chop 3 sprigs of the mint, add them, and season. Cover the pot and cook over a good heat for 15 to 20 minutes. Correct seasoning. Serve in the pot, with the last sprig of mint chopped and sprinkled on top, and the bread tucked round the side.

Cèpes au chester (two recipes)

In France "chester" is the name of a cheese made in Cheshire style. Seeing that we sometimes label their delicious Cantal "French Cheddar," I think we cannot complain.

The recipe is a simple one. Take young, fresh ceps and fry them in olive oil. Place them in an ovenproof dish in a single layer. Make up some velouté sauce (see appendix), and flavour it decisively with grated Cheshire cheese. Pour the sauce over the ceps and brown the whole thing in the oven.

This comes from one of the greatest cookery books of this century, Ali Bab's *Gastronomie Pratique* (the author's real name was Henri Babinski). A rather similar dish, again a French one, is a kind of ceps and Cheshire rarebit. Place the fried young mushrooms on buttered toast, lay slices of the cheese on top, and put it into the oven or under the grill until melted and appetisingly browned.

A good mixture. Be sure to buy your Cheshire from a whole cheese, not a slice of it sweatily sealed into a plastic packet.

Creamed mushroom recipes

Champignons à la crème
(Mushrooms in cream)

Many years ago I saw a film in which Françoise Rosay, playing an elderly and wealthy woman, tempted a young man to live in her house with the combined attractions of *champignons à la crème* and a pretty maid of all work. I am not sure which was the major attraction—probably, being a French film, the mush-rooms—together they were irresistible. In time the young man broke away from the emotional problems of the household, but eventually returned. I can still hear the triumphant voice of Fran-çoise Rosay saying to the maid, on his return, *"Et ce soir, cham-pignons à la crème,"* and the two women smiled at each other.

The recipe is extremely simple, one of the best ways of cooking mushrooms, particularly field mushrooms, those tiny ones with pinkish gills that the French call *petites roses des prés*. They can be served as combined vegetable and sauce with veal or chicken. They can be eaten on their own, as a first course, served up in vol-au-vent cases, in deep-fried boxes (*caissettes*) cut from a loaf of white bread, or in shortcrust tartlets baked blind: all good ways of stretching a small quantity of mushrooms. If you have plenty, serve them with *biscottes*.

The mushrooms are prepared in the usual way, small ones left whole, large ones sliced, large stalks chopped. Then they are cooked in butter. Very heavy cream is added and simmered for a little while to thicken it (if you use light cream, beat it up with a tea-spoon of flour first). The whole thing is seasoned to taste with lemon juice, salt, pepper, parsley and chives. Beautiful.

Hannah Glasse's white fricassey of mushrooms

In the eighteenth century, the mushrooms were boiled up three times with a small quantity of milk and water. Cream enough to make a sauce was then added, with a seasoning of mace, nutmeg, pepper and salt. The whole thing was thickened with beurre manié.

Escoffier's cèpes à la crème

Before cooking 1–2 pounds prepared ceps, sweat a heaped table-spoon of chopped onion in some butter in the pan. As the ceps exude their juice, raise the heat so that by the time they are cooked there is barely a spoonful of liquid. Pour in about ½ pint very thick cream and quickly reduce to a thick coating sauce. Now add enough thin cream to dilute the sauce to a thick but liquid consistency. Season and serve with toast or bread.

Curnonsky's morilles du Jura à la crème

Stew about 1 pound well-washed morels in 3 ounces of butter; as they begin to soften pour in 4 ounces of the yellow vin d'Arbois from the Jura. After 15 minutes' cooking, stir in ¼ pint thick cream. Season with salt, pepper and a squeeze of lemon juice. Serve in small puff pastry cases, baked blind.

The popular interest in French provincial and country cooking didn't occur until the 1920s, although the great chefs had never been so foolish as to despise the good regional dishes and peasant soups of their childhood. Curnonsky, born at Angers in Anjou, a country of fine fruit, vegetables, dairy products, pork and fish, became the leading propagandist of the many writers who began to publish collections of recipes from their parts of France. He drove everyone out of Paris on to the roads of the country districts in search of good food. When one thinks of what they came up with, it seems surprising. The hastiest dip into Henry James's *Little Tour of France*, an account of a journey he made in the 1880s, shows how distressing public food was, once he ventured south of a line drawn from Tours across to Bourg en Bresse. The agricultural and horticultural improvements of the intervening forty years must have been far-reaching.

A flan of mushrooms or morels à la crème

From the *Alice B. Toklas Cook Book*. She and Gertrude Stein had arrived at Senonches, north-west of Chartres. "We were seduced at once by the little town, the hotel and the forest. We not only ordered lunch but engaged rooms to spend the night. While waiting for lunch to be cooked, we walked in the forest where Gertrude Stein, who had a good nose for mushrooms, found quantities of them. The cook would be able to tell us if they were edible. Once more a woman was presiding in the kitchen. She smiled when she saw what Gertrude Stein brought for her inspection and pointed to a large basket of them on the kitchen table, but said she would use those Gertrude Stein had found for what she was preparing for our lunch."

Alice B. Toklas observes that this is a dish that every experienced cook in France prepares in his own way. If morels are used —it must have been morels that Gertrude Stein found in the forest, because they were making their journey in the spring when the fields were "coloured with the first poppies and cornflowers and hedges of blossoming hawthorn"—the cheese is omitted from the sauce, because the flavour of the mushrooms is so fine. Chopped ham may be added to the sauce, or four or five boned and crushed anchovies.

SERVES SIX TO EIGHT

PASTRY:
2 ounces (4 tablespoons) butter
1 generous cup flour
½ tablespoon salt
1 egg
2 tablespoons heavy cream

1 *ounce (2 tablespoons) butter*
1 *medium onion, sliced*
1 *medium carrot, sliced*
1 *stalk celery, sliced*
salt, pepper
1½ *tablespoons flour*
3 *cups hot milk*
3 *tablespoons heavy cream*
½ *cup grated Parmesan (optional)*

MUSHROOMS:

1 *pound small mushrooms, or morels*
½ *ounce (1 tablespoon) butter*
juice of ½ lemon
1 *tablespoon sherry*
salt, pepper, paprika
½ *clove garlic, crushed*

To make the pastry, rub butter into the flour, then add the salt and the egg. Gently knead and roll out. Spread half the cream over it, knead, and roll out again. Add remaining cream, knead, and roll out, then roll into a ball. Leave in the refrigerator for 1 hour, then use pastry to line a flan tin with a removable base, and bake for about 10 minutes in a mark 6, 400°F, oven.

Meanwhile make the *sauce Mornay:* melt butter and fry the vegetables in it until lightly browned. Add seasoning and flour. Cook gently for 5 minutes, then stir in the hot milk. Simmer for half an hour until the sauce is reduced to a rather thicker consistency than normal for a pouring sauce. Strain into a clean bowl, then add cream. Add cheese (unless you are using morels).

To prepare the mushrooms, cook them in butter, lemon juice, sherry, salt, pepper, paprika, and garlic for 8 minutes, covered. Remove mushrooms with a perforated spoon and add to the Mornay sauce. Pour into the baked flan case and place them in a mark 8, 450°F, oven for 12 minutes. Keep an eye on it to make sure it doesn't burn.

Désir des belles dames orléanaises
(Creamed mushroom puffs)

The filling for these puffs comes from *La Vraie Cuisine du Berry et de l'Orléanais,* by Roger Lallemand: the recipe was supplied by a French chef working in New York, who's a native of that area. The recipe for chou paste I have taken from a book of professional baking, and it is far superior to any usually given in books for the housewife.

SERVES EIGHT

CHOU PASTRY:

2 *ounces (4 tablespoons) butter*
⅔ *cup water*
1 *scant teaspoon sugar*
1 *scant cup flour*
8 *ounces eggs (about 4 eggs)*

Heat butter, water and sugar in a pan until boiling. Remove from the heat, tip in the flour all at once, and beat with a wooden spoon or spatula until mixed. Set over the heat again and cook for another 3 minutes or so until the mixture comes completely free of the sides of the pan. Leave for 5 minutes to cool down. Beat in the egg a little at a time.

The reason why choux at a good bakery are so huge and so light is that they are cooked in covered bun tins—i.e., they are cooked in their own steam. To achieve the same effect at home, place a large deep roasting tin over the baking sheet. Or use a self-basting roaster—if you do this you will need to bake the mixture in three lots; with a baking sheet, you will get away with two. Use a tablespoon to put the mixture out into 16 little mounds, and rough up the tops with a fork. The mixture puffs up enormously, so leave plenty of space between each spoonful. Bake for 25 minutes at mark 7, 450°F: this is what suits my oven, but the first time you do it, it would be prudent to raise the lid after 20 minutes to see if they are done. Leave to cool on a wire tray. There is usually no need to slit the sides at this stage. These puffs can be made in advance, though I think they are best eaten the same day. Remember to reheat them in the oven just before they are required.

To make the special *champignons à la crème* filling:

1½–2 *pounds cultivated mushrooms, sliced*
3–4 *ounces (6–8 tablespoons) butter*
⅓ *cup white wine*
juice of a lemon
2 *cups heavy cream, or half-and-half*
salt, freshly ground white pepper
2 *heaping teaspoons arrowroot*
2 *ounces brandy*

Cook mushrooms in 1 ounce of the butter, adding wine and lemon juice. When they are just done, pour in cream and reduce a little by boiling. Season. Dissolve arrowroot in brandy and use to thicken the sauce in the usual way. Remove from heat and whisk in the remaining 2 or 3 ounces of butter. Fill the chou puffs, putting any left-over filling round the edge of the serving dish. Eat immediately, before the pastry has time to become soggy.

N O T E : This version of *champignons à la crème* can be served in a pre-baked pastry case, or vol-au-vent, or simply as a vegetable, like any of the simpler recipes.

Champignons au madère
(Mushrooms in Madeira sauce)

Madeira is a good wine to use in cooking, much better than sherry. The rich sweetness blends well with mushrooms in particular, making this dish a delight to eat on its own, or as a companion to veal, chicken, sweetbreads, turkey and ham. A good recipe for girolles, *pieds de mouton,* or oyster mushrooms.

SERVES SIX AS A SEPARATE COURSE
1 *ounce (2 tablespoons) butter*
1½ *pounds mushrooms, sliced*
3 *tablespoons chopped parsley*
2 *cloves garlic, finely chopped*
2 *tablespoons flour*
¼ *cup meat drippings from roasted veal or beef or chicken, or very concentrated stock*
¼ *cup Madeira*
salt, pepper
2 *egg yolks*
½ *cup cream*
6 *slices bread fried in butter*
   or 6 tartlet cases, baked blind
   or 6 chou puffs (preceding recipe)
   or 6 vol-au-vent

Melt the butter in a large saucepan and add the mushrooms, parsley and garlic. Cook gently for 5 minutes, with a lid on the pan so that the mushrooms exude their juices, then remove the lid and raise the heat so that the juice evaporates almost completely (girolles, for instance, will exude far more juice than cultivated mushrooms). Sprinkle the flour into the pan, and stir in the meat flavouring or stock, and Madeira. Season, particularly with pepper. Beat egg yolks and cream together, then add to the mushrooms and allow the sauce to thicken over a gentle heat, without boiling. Pour on to the bread, or into whichever pastry cases you have chosen, and serve immediately.

Champignons à la dauphinoise
(Mushrooms in the Dauphiné style)

One tends to think of all the southern part of France as olive oil country, which of course it is. But in the mountain districts of the Alps and Pyrenees, food often contains cream from the rich milk of cows grazing on the high pastures. Think of the delicious gratins of potatoes, bathed in cream. Or of sauce Nantua, cream, brandy and crayfish from the uncontaminated streams. Or of the lovely sauces that come with the *lavaret* and *omble chevalier* and trout of Lake Annecy or Bourget.

In this recipe the soft, brownish-white heads of the mushrooms are coated with a rich pink sauce. Very good.

SERVES FOUR

1 *pound white button mushrooms*
3 *ounces fat bacon, chopped*
2 *sprigs each chervil, tarragon, parsley, chopped*
salt, pepper
6 *heaping tablespoons chopped, skinned tomato*
tomato paste (optional)
sugar (optional)
½ *cup heavy cream*
2 *egg yolks*
juice of ½ lemon

Wipe and trim mushrooms. Put bacon over a low heat in a frying pan until the fat runs, then add mushrooms. After 2 minutes, turn them over and cook for another 2 minutes. Season with herbs, salt and pepper. Stir in chopped tomato (adding a little tomato concentrate and sugar if tomatoes are the usual tasteless commercial kind) and cream. Cook 2 minutes. Remove mushrooms to a serving dish, with bacon bits. Whisk some of the sauce with the egg yolks, return to the frying pan, and cook until the sauce is thick *without boiling it*. Add lemon juice. Correct seasoning. Pour over mushrooms and serve.

Mushroom loaves

An excellent recipe, adapted from the 1782 edition of Elizabeth Raffald's *The Experienced English Housekeeper*, for those who like to start a meal with a modest amount of something rich and delicious.

MUSHROOM FILLING:

one of the preceding champignons à la crème *mixtures, made with 12
ounces mushrooms, and other ingredients to scale*
  or *Hannah Glasse's white fricassey on page 84, made with 8–12
  ounces mushrooms*
  or *the mushroom sauce for boiled chicken, from Hannah Glasse's* Art
  of Cookery, *page 37*
  or *Escoffier's* cèpes à la crème, *page 84*

PLUS:

8 brioches, or soft rolls, or miniature cottage loaves
8 bay leaves

Prepare whichever mushroom filling mixture you choose. Remove
the tops from brioches or rolls, and scoop out as much of the
inner crumb as you can (save it for another dish). Plain rolls
can be brushed with melted butter and crisped in the oven, or
they can be left soft; it's all a matter of taste—I like the softness with the mushrooms, as a change from vol-au-vent or chou
paste cases. In either event, have the rolls hot.

Fill them with the mushroom mixture. Place a bay leaf on the
top, so that when the lids are replaced they stick out at an angle.
Serve immediately.

Croûtes aux morilles à la normande
(Morels in the Normandy style)

In France the cream tastes quite different from ours, almost a
little sour. If you buy cream produced by a farmer rather than
a factory, you may get something of the same flavour. But mostly
one has to compensate with a little lemon juice, or a mixture of
cream and sour cream—though in dishes of this kind where
just a modest amount of very rich sauce is required, thick cream
and lemon juice give the best result, closest to the taste of the
French crème fraîche.

SERVES SIX
2 pounds morels
7 ounces (14 tablespoons) butter
1 cup heavy cream, or cream and sour cream
1 cup skinned, seeded, chopped tomato
salt, pepper
lemon juice (optional)
6 slices bread fried in butter

Soak the morels in cold water for an hour, changing it occasionally. Remove them carefully so that the earth can fall out with the water. Split the larger ones down the centre, and leave the small ones whole. Put them into a pan of cold salted water and bring to the boil. Cook for 2 minutes, then drain. Stew the morels in the butter for about 5 minutes, and add the cream. Drain any excess liquid off the tomatoes, pressing them to a solid mass, and add to the morels. Season to taste. Simmer until the morels are cooked and the sauce well thickened. Taste, and add a little lemon juice (especially if you have not used sour cream) if you wish to give the sauce an agreeable edge. Pour into a deep serving dish, and put the bread slices round the edge.

Herrenpilze mit paprika
(Ceps with paprika)

A recipe from Austria, which I have taken from *Viennese Cookery* by Rosl Philpott (Hodder & Stoughton, 1965). It combines the

French *à la crème* methods with the paprika and sour cream of East European cookery. Delicious.

SERVES FOUR
1 *pound ceps*
1 *small onion, chopped*
1 *small clove garlic, minced*
2 *ounces (4 tablespoons) butter*
1 *large tomato, skinned, seeded, chopped*
1 *teaspoon mild paprika*
salt
8 *tablespoons sour cream, room temperature*
lemon juice

If the ceps are large, cut them into convenient-sized pieces. Cook onion and garlic gently in the butter until they are soft and golden. Stir in the tomato, and bubble everything together for a moment or two before adding the paprika, and then the mushrooms. Cover and cook for 3 minutes. Remove from the heat, and add salt to taste. Put the pan back on the stove, and stir in the sour cream. It should be allowed to boil gently and thicken with the sauce. Season with lemon juice to taste, and serve immediately, preferably in the cooking pot.

Stuffed mushroom recipes

Champignons farcis . . .

Large mushrooms, being somewhat older, have had more opportunity to develop flavour than tight little button mushrooms. This means they can be combined with a robust stuffing to make a piquant first course or supper dish. Field mushrooms cooked this way are a great delicacy. Here are two or three recipes from which you can develop your own variations. All can be eaten on their own hot or cold (though I think they are nicest eaten hot, or at least warm). Or they can be served as a vegetable with grilled or roast meat. Or, in the case of the walnut and crab stuffing, with grilled, fried or baked white fish. In the recipes that follow the number of people served will be flexible according to how you are using the stuffed mushrooms.

. . . aux amandes

SERVES FOUR TO SIX

1 *pound large mushrooms*
1 *pound high-meat-content sausage*
6 *tablespoons concentrated meat or poultry juice, or 4 tablespoons port*
  and 1 tablespoon brandy
2 *ounces (⅓ cup) flaked almonds*
freshly ground black pepper
butter
4–6 *tablespoons white wine (optional)*

Wipe mushroom caps with a damp cloth. Remove stalks, chop them, and mix with sausage meat (discard skins). Add meat juice or port and brandy. Set a few flaked almonds aside and stir the rest into the stuffing. Season well with freshly ground black pepper. Fill the caps with this mixture, mounding it up slightly. Put the reserved almonds on top.

Butter a shallow ovenproof dish generously. Pour in white wine if no alcohol has gone into the stuffing. Lay the mushrooms on top in a single layer, stuffing side up. Bake for 20 to 30 minutes at mark 7, 425°F, until the sausage meat is cooked through and the almonds are nicely browned on top.

Serve hot or cold. Bread, toast or *biscottes* go well with this dish.

. . . aux noix

A slightly different method, useful when the stuffing ingredients need no more than reheating, and when the mushrooms are very large. If you have to make do with smaller caps, they will not need the preliminary cooking in butter and white wine: just add them to the dish before putting into the oven. The recipe is slightly adapted from *J'aime les noix,* by Huguette Couffignal (Robert Morel).

SERVES SIX
16 *large mushrooms (1¼ pounds)*
butter
⅓ *cup white wine*
2–3 *ounces (about ½ cup) walnuts, chopped*
12 *ounces crabmeat (1 medium crab)*
juice of 1 lemon
1 *cup thick béchamel sauce*
salt, pepper
breadcrumbs
parsley, minced

Remove mushroom stalks and chop them. Cook mushroom caps in a little butter for 3 minutes, then add white wine and cook for another 3 minutes. Reserve cooking liquid, and place mushrooms in a buttered ovenproof dish. Mix chopped stalks with walnuts, crabmeat, lemon juice and sauce. Season to taste. Fill the caps, mix the breadcrumbs and parsley, and sprinkle on top. Put into a hot oven, mark 6–7, 400°–425°F, for 10 to 20 minutes, basting with the butter and wine from the first cooking of the mushrooms.

NOTE: ¼ pound of chopped ham may be used instead of crabmeat; in this case, the lemon will not be needed. Either mixture can also be used for filling chou or puff pastry cases.

. . . aux oeufs durs

SERVES THREE TO SIX
12 *large mushrooms*
1 *ounce (2 tablespoons) butter, or 3 tablespoons olive oil*
4 *hard-boiled eggs*

creamy milk or light cream
1 *cup white breadcrumbs*
2 *cloves garlic, minced*
salt, pepper
grated Gruyère or Lancashire cheese (optional)

Remove stalks from the mushrooms, chop them, and cook in butter or oil. Shell the hard-boiled eggs, and fork them to crumbs. Add just enough milk or cream to the breadcrumbs to moisten them, without sloppiness. Mix chopped stalks, eggs, breadcrumbs and garlic. Season well. Stuff the mushroom caps and place in a buttered ovenproof dish. Scatter with cheese if you like. Bake at mark 6–7, 400°–425°F, for about 20 minutes.

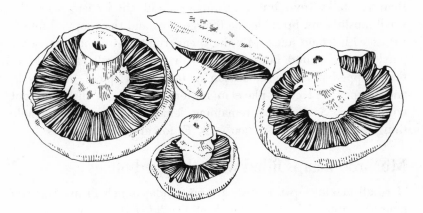

. . . aux champignons

This recipe, without onion, garlic or shallots, comes from *Gastronomie Pratique* by Ali Bab, the pen name of Henri Babinski. The book was first published in 1907, but was extensively revised for subsequent editions. Luckily for cooks who cannot afford £20 or more for an occasional secondhand copy, it was reprinted two or three years ago by Flammarion, and is now available in an English translation, too. His introduction to the chapter on mushrooms, giving a general résumé of the best way to cook most of the edible mushrooms, is full of information.

6 *huge mushrooms, 2 ounces each*
4–5 ounces small mushrooms
juice of a lemon
1 *cup breadcrumbs*
meat jelly (drippings) from roast beef, chicken, or game
parsley, chopped
2 *ounces (4 tablespoons) butter, melted*
1 *egg yolk*
quatre épices (7 parts pepper to one part each nutmeg, cloves, cinnamon)
curry powder
salt and pepper
extra butter

Remove stalks from huge mushrooms, and chop them with the small mushrooms. Sprinkle the 6 large caps and the chopped mushrooms with lemon juice. Mix the breadcrumbs with the meat jelly, parsley, and melted butter. Bind with the egg yolk, and fold in the chopped mushrooms. Season to taste with spices, curry, salt, and pepper. Fill caps, place in buttered ovenproof dish and dot with butter. Scatter any remaining lemon juice over the whole thing. Bake at mark 6–7, 400°–425°F, for about 20 minutes.

Mushroom caps filled with chopped olives

"I recall making up this dish at one Sunday lunch in my lakeside house," wrote Albert Stockli in *Splendid Fare* (Knopf, 1970), "when I had available only the ingredients listed below." Perhaps these things are better managed in America, but no one in England, apart from Mrs Bones the Butcher's Wife, is likely to have beef marrow handy. It is the one ingredient for this delicious recipe which needs organization. Ask the butcher to chop two or three shin bones into thick pieces for you. Use them to make a good stock in the usual way, for other dishes, and carefully scoop out the marrow from the bones for this one. You could leave the marrow out, but this makes the recipe less delicious; poached brains (or soft roes) could be used instead, but they lack the rich fatness of marrow.

12 *large mushrooms*
juice of 2 lemons
25 *large green olives, minced*
4 *cloves garlic, minced*
2 *anchovy fillets, minced*
½ *cup diced beef marrow*
1 *teaspoon salt*
¼ *teaspoon pepper*

Clean mushrooms and remove stems (use for another dish). Have ready a pan half full of boiling water, add the lemon juice, and then the mushrooms: remove them after 4 minutes. Drain, and keep warm.

Combine the remaining ingredients, fill the mushroom caps and put into a shallow ovenproof dish. Bake at mark 8, 450°F, for 10 minutes, to heat through. Serve on their own with bread and butter, or on pieces of fried bread, or as a vegetable with veal or steak.

Champignons à la bordelaise
(Mushrooms in the style of Bordeaux)
A recipe for really large cultivated mushrooms, or field mushrooms, or ceps.

SERVES FOUR
12 *large mushrooms*
parsley, minced
1 *shallot, sliced*
1 *clove garlic, minced*
4 *ounces (8 tablespoons) butter*
salt, pepper, nutmeg
4 *tablespoons* sauce espagnole, *or rich gravy from a stew*
⅓ *cup Sauterne*
breadcrumbs

Remove the stalks from the mushrooms and chop them fine. Weigh them and add half the weight of chopped parsley. Cook them gently with the shallot and garlic in half the butter. Season with salt, pepper and nutmeg, and bind the mixture with a little of the *sauce espagnole:* it should be coherent but not sloppy. Divide this mixture among the 12 mushroom caps.

Grease a shallow oven dish with half the remaining butter and arrange the mushrooms on it, close together, with the filling upwards. Pour the wine in carefully *around* the mushrooms. Sprinkle breadcrumbs evenly over the filling, and dot the mushrooms with the remaining butter. Bake for 30 minutes in a moderately hot oven, mark 5–6, 375°–400°F. Arrange them on a serving dish, and stir the remaining *sauce espagnole* into the mushroom juices: when the mixture is hot and slightly thick, pour round the mushrooms and serve immediately.

Funghi ripieni
(Italian stuffed mushrooms)

Ceps are the ideal mushroom for this dish, but large field or cultivated mushrooms can be used instead.

SERVES FOUR TO SIX
13 *large mushrooms*
1 *medium onion, chopped*
1 *small clove garlic, crushed*
olive oil
4 *anchovy fillets, chopped*
2 *heaping tablespoons minced parsley*
salt, pepper
½-*inch slice of bread, crusts removed*
1 *egg*
breadcrumbs

Remove mushroom stalks and chop them up with one of the mushrooms. Stew onion and garlic in a couple of tablespoons of olive oil until they begin to soften. Add chopped mushrooms, raise heat, and cook for 5 minutes. Stir in anchovies and parsley, and cook for another 5 minutes. Remove from heat and correct seasoning. Meanwhile squeeze bread to a thick paste with a little water.

Mix with fried mushroom mixture and bind with the egg. Fill the caps. Pour a little oil into a shallow ovenproof dish, and arrange the stuffed mushrooms in it close together. Sprinkle with breadcrumbs and olive oil. Bake in a fairly hot oven, mark 6, 400°F, for about 20 minutes—field and cultivated mushrooms will not need quite so long, so keep an eye on them after 10 minutes.

Funghi al tegame alla genovese
(Mushrooms baked in the Genoese style)

Ceps are the right mushrooms for this dish. Other kinds can be used, but part of the exquisite flavour will be lost. The recipe comes from the bible of Italian cookery, *Il Talismano della Felicità*, by Ada Boni. She says that ceps should always be cooked in an earthenware pot, a *tegame*. This type of dish is more suitable for the thick fleshiness of ceps, because it heats through more slowly than a metal pan. When cooking ceps directly over electric rings or gas burners, be careful to use a flameproof pot, or stoneware with an asbestos mat. For this oven-cooked recipe, though, earthenware is perfectly suitable.

SERVES SIX
12 large ceps
¾ pound brains, or 6 ounces each brains and sweetbreads
milk
olive oil
small clove garlic, crushed
salt, pepper, marjoram
2 tablespoons grated Parmesan cheese
2 egg yolks

Remove the stalks from the ceps and chop them. Soak the brains in salted water for an hour, remove the fine skin with the blood vessels, and parboil the brains in milk. If sweetbreads are used, prepare them in the usual way (see page 211). Slice the brains, and sweetbreads if used.

Fry cep stalks lightly in a little olive oil with the garlic. As they begin to brown, add brains and sweetbreads if used. Cook for 5 minutes, stirring about. Season with salt, pepper and marjoram. Chop finely, then add the cheese and egg yolks. Fill the caps, place them in a shallow earthenware dish, sprinkle with olive oil and bake at mark 5, 375°F, for 30 to 40 minutes until cooked.

Cèpes farcies

Ceps are so good, so full of flavour, that they do not need the more elaborate stuffings used with cultivated mushrooms. The simplest recipe of all is to mix some good-quality—by which I mean high meat content—sausages with chopped garlic, parsley, salt and pepper according to your taste. You must remove the sausage skins first. The chopped stalks of the ceps may also be added. Fill the caps with this mixture, stand them close together in a buttered gratin dish, dot them with butter, and bake at mark 7, 425°F, for 20 to 30 minutes, until the sausage is cooked through.

If you live within reach of Cumberland sausage, this is ideal. The coarsely chopped meat much resembles French *chair à saucisses*. The lack of rusk and artificial colouring is another similarity between the two.

Cèpes Brimaud

A year or two ago the French and Belgians produced an encyclopaedia of recipes which came out in parts, every month for a couple of years or so. As well as the classics of the French repertoire, there was an abundance of less usual recipes, based on less usual ingredients such as ceps. Here is one of them.

SERVES SIX

12 fine large ceps

2 shallots, minced

2 cloves garlic, minced

⅔ cup olive oil

8–12 tomatoes, according to size (about 2 pounds)

2 ounces (4 tablespoons) butter

salt, pepper
1 teaspoon curry powder
1 cup breadcrumbs
parsley, minced

Set aside the cep caps. Chop the stalks, and cook them with the shallots and garlic in a few tablespoons of oil. Meanwhile pour boiling water over the tomatoes and skin and chop them roughly. Set them cooking in the butter. Now add seasoning, curry powder, about a third of the breadcrumbs, and a tablespoonful or thereabouts of parsley to the cep stalk mixture. Let this mixture colour slightly, and use to stuff the cep caps.

When the tomatoes have reduced slightly after cooking about 10 minutes, season them and spread them over the base of an ovenproof dish. Place the cep caps on top. Pour the remaining oil over the ceps and sprinkle with remaining crumbs. Bake in a moderate oven, mark 4–5, 350°–375°F, for 15 minutes, or longer if the ceps are really large and thick.

Morilles farcies, en cocottes
(Stuffed morels en cocottes)

This recipe is best made with large morels, which can easily be stuffed from the stalk end. An alternative would be to use parasol mushrooms, which can be moulded round the stuffing and then placed upright in the little pots.

SERVES SIX
1 pound morels
4 ounces (8 tablespoons) butter
2 cups white breadcrumbs
7 ounces grated Parmesan cheese
2 tablespoons minced parsley
salt, pepper

Clean the morels carefully under the cold tap, and remove the stalks carefully from the largest ones. Chop the stalks with the smaller morels to make about 5 ounces. Melt three-quarters of the butter in a pan, stir in the chopped morels, the breadcrumbs and 5 ounces of the Parmesan. When everything is well mixed, add the parsley and seasoning. Stuff the morels with this mixture, using a teaspoon. Stand them upright in six small pots. Sprinkle the remaining cheese on top of them, and dot with the remaining butter. Cover with foil, and stand them in a roasting pan half full of boiling water. Leave them in a moderate oven, mark 4–5, 350°– 375°F, for an hour. Remove the foil covers and serve immediately.

Cold mushroom dishes and hors d'oeuvres

Mushroom caviare from Russia

The Russians are great mushroom gatherers—think of the mushroom parties in *Anna Karenina*—and have many delicious ways of cooking them. Here is one that is simple and particularly good. It can be served on its own, or as part of a mixed hors d'oeuvre. The finer you chop the mushrooms, the more the greenish grey speckled mixture will *look* like the finest-flavoured Osetr caviare: of course it won't taste the same. Use ceps if you possibly can, otherwise cultivated mushrooms.

SERVES FOUR
1 *medium onion, minced*
2 *tablespoons olive oil*
½ *pound firm mushrooms*
salt, freshly ground black pepper
juice of ½ *lemon*
2 *generous tablespoons sour cream*
chives, chopped

Cook onion gently in the oil until almost cooked, without allowing it to brown. Meanwhile chop the mushrooms, stalks and all. Add to the pan and cook for 8 to 12 minutes—if the mushrooms exude a lot of juice turn up the heat; the final result should be moist but not wet, the mushrooms cooked but not too soft. Season, remove from the heat, and add lemon juice, sour cream and chives to taste. Serve well chilled, sprinkled with more chives. Toast should be served as well.

See *Mushroom croutons for roast meat* for a hot version of this kind of dish from France.

Mushroom sandwiches

Alice B. Toklas says in her cookbook: "Mushroom sandwiches have been my specialty for years. They were made with mushrooms cooked in butter with a little juice of lemon. After 8 minutes' cooking, they were removed from heat, chopped, and then pounded into a paste in the mortar. Salt, pepper, a pinch of cayenne, and an equal volume of butter were thoroughly amalgamated with them. Well and good. But here is a considerable improvement over them, also called mushroom sandwiches:

"The method is the same as above up to a certain point. These are the proportions. For ¼ pound mushrooms cooked in 2 tablespoons butter add 2 scrambled eggs and 3 tablespoons grated Parmesan cheese and mix well. The recipe ends with: This makes a delicious sandwich which tastes like chicken. A Frenchman can say no more."

A blender cuts out hard work with a pestle and mortar, but keep the mixtures a little grainy if you can. In the second one, add the cheese gradually to taste. With the British tablespoon two level ones will probably be quite enough. Either mixture makes a good first course to a meal when served with toast. For sandwiches, use a good wholemeal bread.

English mushroom sandwiches

Dorothy Hartley, in *Food in England,* says: "Country people make delicious sandwiches of brown bread and butter and finely sliced up mushrooms (raw), the mushrooms being sprinkled with lemon juice. Similarly, thin slices laid on beef in sandwiches are much enjoyed by most folk in the fields. They keep the sandwiches nice and moist."

Mushroom paste

A recipe from a small pamphlet entitled *Pottery* (see page 32). The mixture is excellent with toast, as a first course.

1 *small onion, chopped*
2 *ounces (4 tablespoons) butter*
2 *slices bacon, chopped*
1 *cup skinned, chopped tomatoes*
1 *pound mushrooms, sliced*
2 *eggs beaten*
1 *teaspoon salt*
dash of cayenne pepper

Brown the onion lightly in a little of the butter. Add the rest, and immediately stir in the bacon, tomatoes and mushrooms. When everything is well cooked, put it through a vegetable mill, or liquidize in a blender. Mix with the eggs and stir over a low heat until the mixture thickens (do not let it boil). Season with salt and cayenne. "This can be put in a jar and will keep some time. It is, however, so good that it can never be kept."

Champignons à la grecque I

SERVES FOUR TO EIGHT

This popular French dish is best served as part of a mixed hors d'oeuvre. When serving mushrooms like this on their own, the recipes which include tomato or tomato and orange are to be preferred on account of their extra piquant flavour (see recipes following this). Be careful not to overcook the mushrooms: they should still be crisp in the centre.

MARINADE:

½ *cup olive oil*
1¼ *cups water*
juice of ½ lemon
¼ *teaspoon peppercorns, crushed*
¼ *teaspoon coriander seeds, crushed*
salt to taste
bouquet of ½ small bay leaf, sprig each of parsley, thyme, and fennel,
plus 1 celery leaf
1 *pound small mushrooms*

Boil all the ingredients except the mushrooms together for 10 to 15 minutes to make a marinade. Add mushrooms, and boil for about 3 minutes, then leave to cool. Serve with a little of the marinade, well chilled.

Champignons à la grecque II

SERVES FOUR TO EIGHT

Prepare the marinade and boil the mushrooms in it as directed in preceding recipe. Remove mushrooms, and reduce sauce until it is thick. Skin and chop 3 large tomatoes, add to sauce, and boil for a few minutes. Pour boiling sauce over mushrooms. Serve chilled, sprinkled with a little chopped parsley.

Mushrooms with tomato and orange sauce

A variation of *champignons à la grecque* above. Avoid overcooking the mushrooms.

SERVES FOUR TO SIX
1 *pound tiny button mushrooms*
1 *lemon quarter*
⅓ *cup olive oil*
¼ *cup water*
1 *pound tomatoes, skinned, chopped*
1 *large clove garlic, chopped*
1 *bay leaf*
2 *sprigs thyme*
1 *sprig parsley*
thin peel of ½ orange
juice of 1 orange
salt, pepper, sugar

Rub mushrooms with lemon quarter. Simmer remaining ingredients for 10 minutes. Add mushrooms and cook 3 minutes, then remove them to a serving dish. Boil down the sauce to a strong-flavoured purée, adjust the seasonings to your liking, and fish out the thyme and parsley stalks (leave the bay leaf, or replace with a new one). Pour sauce over the mushrooms. Serve well chilled.

Champignons au vin blanc

Another variation of the *à la grecque* method.

SERVES FOUR TO SIX
1 *pound small button mushrooms*
lemon quarter
¼ *cup olive oil*
⅔ *cup dry white wine*
⅔ *cup water*
bouquet garni
3 *tablespoons finely chopped onion*
juice of 1 lemon

salt, freshly ground black pepper
3 tablespoons minced parsley

Rub cleaned mushrooms over with the lemon quarter. Bring remaining ingredients, except parsley, to the boil. Simmer for 5 minutes. Add mushrooms, boil for 3 minutes, and leave to cool. Serve chilled with some of the marinade, and scattered with parsley.

Coriander mushrooms

A recipe from Elizabeth David's *Spices, Salt and Aromatics in the English Kitchen* (Penguin). Mrs David remarks that the flavourings are the same as those which are used for *champignons à la grecque,* "but the method is simpler, and the result even better."

SERVES TWO TO THREE
6 ounces firm, white, very fresh mushrooms
lemon juice
olive oil
1 teaspoon coriander seeds, crushed
1 or 2 bay leaves
salt, pepper

Clean the mushrooms, and quarter them if they are on the large side. Trim the stalks. Brush them with a little lemon juice.

Heat olive oil to cover bottom of a frying pan and cook the coriander seeds for a few seconds over a low heat. Add mushrooms and bay leaves. Season. After a minute, cover the pan and cook for another 3 to 5 minutes—but no longer.

Pour the mushrooms with their cooking juices into a serving dish and sprinkle them with fresh oil and lemon juice. Serve chilled; or hot with veal or chicken.

Les champignons aux aromates I
(Marinaded mushrooms I)

A fine and useful item for the store cupboard. In flavour they are not unlike *champignons à la grecque,* but they can be prepared days, even weeks, in advance of being eaten. Leave them in a cool place for four or five days, then transfer them to the refrigerator if you like. Do not put them immediately into the fridge, or the oil will solidify rapidly before the mushrooms have a chance to become really impregnated with the aromatic flavours. If you are keeping the mushrooms for any length of time, you must be sure they are well covered with olive oil. If they are going to be eaten within twenty-four hours, this is not so important. As with all preserves, the basic ingredient must be in perfect condition. Choose small, nicely closed, firm ceps or cultivated or field mushrooms.

As you will see from the title, this and the following recipe are French. In England we have the unpleasant habit of dowsing delicately flavoured mushrooms with malt vinegar and water, which I cannot recommend. And the oil must be *olive*, not tasteless corn oil.

SERVES FOUR TO EIGHT
1 *pound mushrooms*
1 *lemon*
8 *ounces pickling onions, peeled*
5 *cloves garlic, peeled*
5 *shallots, peeled*
1 *teaspoon cumin seeds*
1 *teaspoon peppercorns*
1 *teaspoon juniper berries*
3 *good sprigs of thyme*
3 *bay leaves*
wine vinegar
salt, pepper
olive oil

Clean the mushrooms with a damp cloth, only if necessary. Cut off protruding stems and slice them. Cut the caps in two, or four if they are on the larger side. Remove the peel of the lemon in thin strips, and sprinkle the mushroom caps and stems with lemon juice. Place lemon peel in a saucepan with about a quart of water. Add whole, peeled onions, garlic, and shallots, then cumin, peppercorns, juniper berries, thyme, bay leaves, a few tablespoons of vinegar, and about a teaspoon of salt. Simmer uncovered for 10 minutes, then raise the heat, tip in the mushrooms, and boil for 2 *minutes only*. Pour into a sieve held over the sink. Pick out the thyme stalks and bay leaves, and put remaining ingredients into one or two jars. Add salt and pepper, and cover with olive oil. After an hour or two, stir everything up, taste, and add vinegar if necessary to sharpen the flavour a little more. This last addition is very much a matter of personal taste. Serve chilled.

Les champignons aux aromates II (Marinaded mushrooms II)

SERVES FOUR TO EIGHT

1 pound small, firm ceps or cultivated mushrooms
wine vinegar
1 heaping teaspoon salt
olive oil
8 whole peppercorns
bouquet garni
thinly cut peel of a lemon
3 large cloves garlic, minced
4 tablespoons minced parsley

Prepare mushrooms as in preceding recipe. Bring about a quart of water, a few teaspoons of vinegar, and salt to a rolling boil. Tip in the mushrooms and cook for 2 minutes only. Drain well in a sieve. Put into a jar, or on a serving dish, and keep warm. Simmer 3 ounces (about ⅓ cup) olive oil, 4 teaspoons vinegar, peppercorns, bouquet, and lemon peel together for 5 minutes, then strain liquid, boiling, over the mushrooms. If you wish to keep them for any length of time, you will need to add more oil and vinegar proportionately, and do not strain out the peppercorns and lemon peel. Scatter with garlic and parsley, and chill before serving.

Uncooked mushroom salads

Cultivated mushrooms are often described as tasteless—the implied comparison being made with field mushrooms. But this is not altogether fair. How can one expect immaturity—and the mushrooms we buy are immature, or mainly so—to have a pronounced character? Surely one should be looking for freshness, for an engaging but gentle crispness which has its own pleasures and purposes. For instance, raw sliced mushrooms contribute their own note to a salad, which is quite unlike any other. The small pink and cream slices have a deliciously soft bite.

If you are after strong flavour, buy the large mushrooms, the ones measuring four inches across. I wish we had the chance to buy enormous ones. Sometimes in the mushroom caves, one or two are left to swell up undisturbed, and they grow to a pound in weight. Then, I'm told, their flavour is equal to the finest field mushroom's.

Basic mushroom salad

SERVES FOUR
4 ounces button mushrooms
6 tablespoons olive oil
2 tablespoons lemon juice
freshly ground black pepper
½ clove garlic, crushed
salt
parsley and chives, minced

Trim off the mushroom stalks, then slice the mushrooms thinly and place in a bowl. Mix in oil, lemon juice, plenty of pepper, and the garlic. The salad can now be left for a while. Just before serving, drain away the moisture, season with salt, and put on a serving dish. Sprinkle with the herbs and serve well chilled.

Lobster salad

Shellfish and mushrooms make a delicious partnership, as you will see from this and the following recipe. The texture of the mushroom sets off perfectly the sweetness of lobster, scallops and prawns.

Using 8 ounces of mushrooms, make the preceding *Basic mushroom salad*. Drain it well, then mix it with the flesh, roughly chopped, of a cooked lobster. Fold in about 1 cup of mayonnaise flavoured with a spoonful of pastis Ricard or other anise-flavoured drink. Some chopped Florentine fennel can also be added, but not too much.

Shellfish salad

Double the ingredients for *Basic mushroom salad*. Combine with 4 to 6 poached scallops, and 4 ounces of shelled prawns or shrimp. Sprinkle with parsley.

N O T E : Always buy prawns or shrimp in their shells, as the flavour is much better. Frozen packages are useless. Buy a generous 8 ounces to give you about 4 ounces shelled weight—use the debris to make some stock for a fish soup or sauce.

Smoked salmon and mushrooms

When you arrange slices of smoked salmon on plates or on pieces of buttered brown bread, put a line of neatly cut mushroom slices down each one, and sprinkle with lemon juice.

Sometimes one can buy the trimmings of a side of smoked salmon comparatively cheaply. Roll the pieces round button mushrooms and spear three or four onto cocktail sticks. Again, sprinkle with lemon juice.

Mushroom salad with lemon and herbs

SERVES FOUR
4 ounces medium-sized mushrooms
juice of 1 large lemon
6–8 leaves basil
6–8 leaves marjoram
large sprig parsley
6 tablespoons olive oil
salt, pepper, nutmeg

Quarter the mushrooms and sprinkle them with the lemon juice. Leave them for about an hour. Put the remaining ingredients— seasonings to taste—into a blender and liquidize to a smooth sauce. Bear in mind that quantities of herbs are always difficult to state categorically—their strength of flavour will depend on the warmth of the season, so be prepared to add more, if you think it a good idea. Drain the mushrooms, and mix them with the sauce.

Mushroom salad with smoked sausage

Mushrooms and smoked sausage from the delicatessen make a good combination—choose any sausage you like, from salami to cervelat or one of the boiling rings which can be eaten without further cooking. Large slices of sausage should be quartered; and the skins should be removed, whichever kind you use.

SERVES FOUR
8 ounces mushrooms
juice of 1 large lemon
1 small onion, chopped
½ stalk celery, chopped
4 tablespoons minced parsley
⅓ cup olive oil
¼ pound smoked sausage, sliced thinly

Slice the mushrooms, and immediately sprinkle them with lemon juice. Add remaining ingredients and mix well. Serve chilled.

Broad bean and mushroom salad

SERVES FOUR TO SIX

6 ounces mushrooms, sliced
½ cup olive oil
3 tablespoons wine vinegar
freshly ground black pepper
1 small clove garlic, crushed
1¼ cups broad beans, shelled
4 slices bacon, or 4 ounces Gruyère cheese
salt

Combine the first five ingredients. Boil the broad beans in the usual way, drain, and remove the white skins. This may be a little boring, but it makes all the difference to the final flavour. Cook the bacon until crisp, crush it to pieces, and mix with the vegetables, or dice the cheese and mix that in instead. Season with salt. Serve chilled.

If you like sage with broad beans, sprinkle the salad with one or two leaves finely chopped. Frozen broad beans also do very well for this recipe.

Les crudités

A favourite French hors d'oeuvre of variation and crispness, which depends above all on the fresh quality of the vegetables. And on the skill of the cook in preparing and arranging them—this does not mean cutting radish roses and tomato waterlilies, but grouping the different vegetables together in a bold gaiety of colour and form. Although the name of the salad implies that the vegetables are raw, it is usual to soften cauliflower, French beans and beetroot by cooking them in salted boiling water, but they should still have plenty of bite. Piquancy makes the salad even more delicious—olives, for instance, or anchovies. The sauce can be vinaigrette, either sprinkled on the salad or in a bowl, or mayonnaise. It's very much a spring and summer salad for the gardener (the ideal is two hours from ground to table). If you have a first-class greengrocer, though, and tell him what you are planning, you can do almost as well.

Another point: it is better to have three or four vegetables in perfection than twenty which have seen better days.

RAW VEGETABLES:
lettuce hearts
cress
watercress
celery
radishes
grated carrot
cucumber
peppers
young sweetcorn
mushrooms, sprinkled with lemon juice
onions, or spring onions
tomatoes
avocado pear slices
young shelled peas
young shelled broad beans

COOKED VEGETABLES:
green beans, 15 minutes in boiling water, rinse in cold
pieces of cauliflower, 15 minutes in boiling water, rinse in cold
small boiled beetroot

PIQUANCY AND SAUCES:
anchovies
capers
olives
hard-boiled eggs
vinaigrette with chopped herbs
mayonnaise, flavoured with lemon juice
mayonnaise, flavoured with tomato concentrate
mayonnaise, flavoured with chopped fresh herbs

Oignons à l'orientale
(Onions with sultanas and mushrooms)

Escoffier's *oignons à l'orientale* is one of my favourite recipes. It makes a good first course on its own. In half quantities, it can be served as part of a large hors d'oeuvre. This variation, which includes mushrooms, comes from a French newspaper, and I think it is an improvement on the original dish. The tomato flavouring can be fresh tomatoes of real quality, or concentrate, or tomato ketchup (the French cook's latest discovery).

SERVES SIX TO EIGHT
2½ pounds small pickling onions, peeled
2½ cups water
⅔ cup white wine vinegar
⅔ cup dry white wine
6 ounces (1½ cups) sultanas (seedless raisins)
1 cup sugar
⅓ cup olive oil
½ cup chopped tomatoes,
  or 4 tablespoons tomato paste,
  or ⅓ cup tomato ketchup
3 small bay leaves
3 sprigs thyme
1 teaspoon salt
plenty of freshly ground black pepper
pinch of cayenne pepper
generous 6 ounces button mushrooms
parsley, chopped

Put all ingredients, except mushrooms and parsley, into a large pan. Boil steadily, uncovered, about 30 minutes, until the sauce is thick and the mixture rather like a runny chutney. The onions should still be recognizably whole. When you judge that the onions are almost cooked, add the mushrooms, which should be left unsliced. Cook 5 to 10 more minutes. Taste and correct seasoning, remove thyme stalks but not the bay leaves. Serve chilled in a shallow dish, sprinkled with parsley.

Mushrooms cooked with other vegetables (and fruit)

Gratin de pommes de terre aux champignons (Potatoes gratin with mushrooms)

The affinity between potatoes and mushrooms is remarkable, as you will see if you try this or any of the next three recipes. Obviously the higher the quality of both, the better the dish will be, but even with cultivated mushrooms and the humdrum potatoes which are all we can usually buy, this dish is worth eating. I think, though, that it is worth searching for Désirée or some other waxy variety of potatoes and *large* cultivated mushrooms. The addition of water to this kind of recipe stops the cream curdling to wateriness and white blobs: it was the brainwave of Monsieur Dumaine, the great chef-patron of the Côte d'Or at Saulieu in Burgundy, and it makes all the difference.

SERVES FOUR

1 *pound potatoes*
½ *pound mushrooms*
butter
1 *clove garlic, finely chopped*
salt, pepper
⅔ *cup each light and heavy cream*
¼ *cup water*
4 *tablespoons grated Parmesan, or pecorino, or hard, mature Cheddar*

Peel the potatoes and slice them thinly. Slice the mushrooms. Grease an oval *shallow* gratin dish generously with butter and sprinkle the garlic over it. Arrange half the potatoes, the slices overlapping, in the bottom of the dish, season, and put in the mushrooms. Season again and finish off with a final layer of potatoes. Mix the cream and water and pour over the whole thing. Sprinkle the cheese on top, dot with butter, and bake for 1½ hours at mark 3-4, 325°–350°F: the top of the dish will turn a crisp-looking golden brown with the cream bubbling up round the edges.

Although the next two recipes come from parts of France, the Savoy and Périgord, where ceps are found by the basketful, don't pass them over if you have only a few. It is surprising how strongly they will flavour a dish of potatoes when cooked in this way. If you have less than a pound of ceps, scale the potatoes down to roughly twice their weight.

Gratin de pommes de terre aux cèpes (Potatoes gratin with ceps)

SERVES SIX TO EIGHT

2¼ *pounds waxy potatoes, peeled or scraped*
1-2 *pounds ceps*
salt, pepper
1 *clove garlic*
butter
½ *cup finely chopped onion*
½ *cup chopped parsley*
¾ *cup grated Gruyère cheese*
1¼ *cups heavy or light cream*

Slice the potatoes thinly (cucumber blade of the grater does this well). Slice the ceps not quite so thinly. Season both with salt and pepper. Rub an oval gratin dish with garlic and butter. Alternate layers of potatoes and ceps, sprinkling each one with onion, parsley, and cheese, reserving a few tablespoons of cheese for the top. Pour on the cream, scatter remaining cheese over the whole thing, and dot with butter. Cook in a low oven, mark 3, 325°F, for 1¾ hours, lowering the temperature when the dish begins to bubble hard. Serve in the cooking pot.

N O T E : See *Leg of lamb with gratin of ceps and potatoes*.

Pommes de terre aux cèpes (Potatoes fried with ceps)

This is a delicious and fragrant mixture. It can be served with sirloin steak. Or, like many of the poorer families in the Dordogne, you can eat it with a green salad only, and a glass of wine. Cut enough potatoes into cubes to fill your frying pan comfortably. Brown them quickly on all sides in lard, or in goose or duck fat if you can. Season them, add such ceps as you've collected, cut into pieces, and put on the lid or a covering of foil. Cook for half an hour.

Meanwhile chop up a clove of garlic with a small bunch of parsley, and tip into the pan as soon as possible. Leave for the remaining time, giving an occasional stir to make sure the potatoes cook evenly.

Potatoes with mushroom sauce in the Russian style

Fattening, and worth it. Particularly in summer if you can find field mushrooms and fine waxy new potatoes. In winter, use large cultivated mushrooms (because they have a lot of flavour, far more than the tiny buttons) and make an effort to get hold of firm potatoes.

If you have no dillweed or fennel in your back yard or garden, use chives or a mixture of chives and parsley. But dill is the true flavour.

S E R V E S   S I X   T O   E I G H T
3 *pounds potatoes*
mushroom and sour cream sauce from Russia (*page 38*)

4–6 ounces extra mushrooms
⅓–½ cup extra sour cream
extra dillweed or fennel, minced

Scrub and boil the potatoes, or, if you have the time, steam them. As they cook, make the mushroom sauce, using the extra mushrooms and cream. When the potatoes are cooked, strip off the peels and slice them as tidily as possible on to a hot serving dish. Spread the mushroom sauce evenly over the top, sprinkling a little extra dillweed or fennel as garnish.

Concombres farcis
(Stuffed cucumbers)

This is the kind of French recipe I like—and often make for supper to follow the soup. Everyday ingredients are assembled with style and surprise.

SERVES FOUR
2 medium cucumbers
¾ cup rice
salt
1 large onion, minced
4 ounces (8 tablespoons) butter
6 ounces mushrooms, sliced
pepper
3 slices smoked bacon
2 eggs
pinch of sugar
parsley, chopped

Cut both cucumbers in half lengthwise, then across so that you have eight pieces to make "boats." Scrape out the seeds. Boil cucumbers in salted water for 10 minutes, and meanwhile boil rice until cooked. Cook onion gently in half the butter: when soft, add mushrooms and season. Cut bacon into short strips (discarding any rind); stir into the mushroom mixture, and cook for a few seconds more. Remove pan from heat. Beat eggs with a good pinch of sugar: make two omelettes in the usual way and roll them up, then slice like a jam roll. Drain rice, add with the strips of omelette to the mushroom mixture, and correct seasoning. Pile into the cucumber boats. Sprinkle parsley on top. Serve very hot.

Concombres aux champignons et à la crème (Creamed cucumbers with mushrooms)

Another good combination of cucumber and mushroom, this time a recipe which I have adapted from *Mastering the Art of French Cooking, Volume I,* by Simone Beck, Louisette Bertholle, and Julia Child (Knopf, 1961; Penguin, 1966). Both vegetables retain a certain crispness, each different in its kind but complementary, and set off by the cream and herb sauce.

SERVES SIX

6 cucumbers, about 8 inches long (or equivalent)
2 tablespoons wine vinegar
salt
⅛ teaspoon sugar
3 tablespoons melted butter
½ teaspoon dill or basil
3–4 tablespoons minced green onions
pepper
½ pound mushrooms, quartered
1 cup heavy cream
1 teaspoon cornstarch, mixed with 1 teaspoon water
2 tablespoons minced parsley

Peel and cut each cucumber into four pieces so that the seeds can be removed with a teaspoon. Then cut cucumbers into strips, roughly ½ inch wide and 2 inches long. Mix with vinegar, 1½ teaspoons of salt, and sugar, and leave for at least 30 minutes—several hours if more convenient. Drain and pat dry.

To bake the cucumbers, mix the butter, dill or basil, onions, and ⅛ teaspoon of pepper in a baking dish, and stir the cucumber pieces about in it. Leave in a mark 5, 375°F, oven for about an hour, but stir the cucumbers about two or three times as they cook. (This part of the recipe can be done in advance.)

When you are ready to eat the meal, toss the mushrooms about in an ungreased frying pan over a moderate heat for 5 minutes. Add cream and starch mixture. Cook gently for a further 5 minutes to reduce and thicken the sauce. Check seasoning. Heat the cucumbers, and fold them into the sauce. Sprinkle with parsley and serve.

Aubergines (eggplant) farcies duxelles

Although this dish is full of flavour, and fairly rich, it is not so overwhelming as the better-known *Imam Bayeldi*. For this reason it makes a good first course at dinner, or a supper dish. Or serve it with lamb and chicken. This recipe is also adapted from *Mastering the Art of French Cooking, Volume I*, by Simone Beck, Louisette Bertholle and Julia Child (Knopf, 1961; Penguin, 1966).

SERVES SIX

3 *large aubergines (eggplants)*
1 *tablespoon salt*
2 *tablespoons olive oil*

STUFFING:

1 *cup minced onions*
2 *tablespoons olive oil*
1 *pound mushrooms, minced*
1½ *ounces (3 tablespoons) butter*
4½ *ounces (1½ packages) cream cheese*
4 *tablespoons minced parsley*
½ *teaspoon basil or ¼ teaspoon thyme*

GRATIN:

3 *tablespoons grated Gruyère cheese*
3 *tablespoons dry white breadcrumbs*
extra butter

Halve the aubergines lengthwise, removing the stalks. Make cuts down into the flesh, stopping within about ¼ inch of the skin.

Sprinkle with salt, and lay, cut side down, on a cloth for at least half an hour. Press them gently from time to time to get rid of as much moisture as possible. Dry them, pour the olive oil over them, and grill them, flesh side up, under a moderate heat for about 15 minutes. When they are tender and slightly browned, scoop out the flesh, leaving a firm "shell" within the skin, and put the flesh into a bowl. This is the basis of the stuffing, and the remaining ingredients are added to it.

Cook the onions until soft but not brown in 1 tablespoon of the olive oil. Add to the bowl. Cook mushrooms rather more quickly in remaining oil plus the butter: they should be golden brown and as dry as possible. Add to the bowl. Fork the cream cheese to a soft paste and mix it in with the herbs. Season the whole thing, and fill the "shells."

Mix cheese and breadcrumbs and sprinkle over the top. Dot with extra butter and arrange in a roasting tin. Pour water round the aubergines to a depth of ⅛ inch. Bake in the top of the oven, at mark 5, 375°F, for about 30 minutes to heat the stuffed aubergines through and brown the tops.

Aubergines (eggplant) with mushrooms

This dish is full of flavour, with an interesting contrast of textures. The essential thing is to buy large mushrooms, the kind that measure 3 inches across and taste almost like a field mushroom. Or use field mushrooms.

SERVES FOUR

2 *large aubergines (eggplants)*
salt
8 *large mushrooms*
8 *slices smoked Canadian bacon*
olive oil
pepper
parsley, minced

Cut aubergines into 16 thick slices, sprinkle with salt, and leave to drain in a colander for an hour. Wipe them dry. Clean mushrooms and chop the bacon. First fry the aubergine slices in oil over a moderate heat, until they are golden brown outside, and soft inside: put them on kitchen paper to drain, and keep warm. Raise the heat, and quickly cook the mushrooms. Put them to one side and fry the bacon for a few seconds only in the oil remaining in the pan.

To assemble the dish, put the aubergines in a ring round the edge, with the mushrooms in the middle, under side up. Divide the bacon evenly among the mushroom cups. Sprinkle with pepper and parsley. Serve with plenty of good bread to mop up the juices.

This dish can be eaten with grilled meat, but is best on its own.

Mushrooms soubise

The combination of mushrooms and onion is such an essential part of cooking that we take it for granted. Here is an unusual way of putting the two together: it makes a good first course or supper dish.

SERVES SIX
purée soubise (see appendix)
1½ pounds mushrooms, sliced
2 ounces (4 tablespoons) butter
⅓ cup Madeira, sherry or port
nutmeg, salt, pepper
stock (see recipe)
5 tablespoons grated Gruyère cheese
12 triangles bread, fried in butter

Prepare the soubise purée (this can be done in advance, and reheated).

Cook the mushrooms in the butter, and when they are ready but not too soft, stir in the wine. Bubble for a few moments, adding stock if the mixture seems on the dry side—there should be a small amount of liquid, that is all. Season with nutmeg, salt and pepper to taste.

Put the soubise purée into a dish, and place the mushrooms in the centre. Keep warm. Put the grated cheese on top of the fried bread, and place under the grill for a few moments to melt it. Tuck these croutons round the edge of the dish, and serve.

Délice de champignons

One doesn't think usually of combining mushrooms with fruit—always excepting tomatoes—but here is an exceptionally good dish whether eaten hot or cold. It comes from a vegetarian cookery book by Sally and Lucian Berg, *New Food for All Palates*, and I do recommend it. If you have no medium-sweet white wine, use a dry one and increase sugar to taste.

SERVES TWO TO THREE
6 *ounces button mushrooms*
20 *lightly crushed coriander seeds*
⅓ *cup olive oil*
15 *large green grapes, peeled, seeded*
juice of 1 orange
small piece of bay leaf
1 *small clove garlic, crushed*
⅓ *cup medium-sweet white wine*
pinch sea salt
1 *teaspoon Demerara (raw) sugar*
squeeze lemon juice

If any mushrooms are on the large side, cut them in half. Cook coriander in oil gently for 2 minutes, then add mushrooms and cook 2 minutes more. Put in the rest of the ingredients, and simmer for 5 minutes. Remove mushrooms and grapes to a heated serving dish. Reduce sauce to a concentrated flavour, then pour it over mushrooms. Serve hot with rice, or chilled with bread and butter, and glasses of white wine in either case.

Stewed horse "buttons" with red fruit

Dorothy Hartley, in *Food in England,* presents this recipe: "The rounded 'button-shaped' horse mushrooms may be quite large. These are best stewed in milk, with a suspicion of *mace* (nutmeg is too strong); when soft, drain, pack the rounded mushrooms into a deep dish, and use the milk to make a thick coating sauce (using as much butter as possible). Pour over the hot mushrooms and garnish the white dishful with sprigs of barberries, made hot, to bursting point, in the oven, or a spoonful each of butter and red-currant jelly, that will melt in combined yellow and red sauce. The slight garnish of tart fruit brings out the smooth aromatic delicacy of the mushroom sauce."

If you are using bought red-currant jelly, melt it first and sieve it, otherwise it will not liquify in the heat of the sauce but stay in a lump. The illustration of this dish adds a garnish of bright green cress or parsley.

Mushroom and egg dishes

La Varenne's scrambled eggs with mushrooms

I have already mentioned that La Varenne's *Cuisinier français* of 1651 was the first modern cookery book in arrangement and method. Here is a deliciously simple recipe from it for eggs scrambled with mushrooms, and, if you like, some cooked asparagus. La Varenne may not give the exact quantities for the vegetables, and obviously they can be varied according to what you have in the larder, but he does cover the essential point of the recipe, which is that the vegetables must be cooked and ready before the beaten eggs are added, otherwise you will end up with a dry, overscrambled mess.

We were given a similar dish last year by a French friend, as the first course of a superb dinner party. She used artichokes, or rather the base of the artichokes, instead of mushrooms, and she had added a little thought or two of her own (fines herbes, mustard and cream), but essentially her recipe was La Varenne's, and all of 321 years old.

"Season some cultivated or field mushrooms well, and cook them [in butter], adding some chopped asparagus if you like, and when the cultivated or field mushrooms are ready to serve, break three or four eggs, and scramble them, and cook them with the other things so that they are nicely bound together."

Three or four ounces of mushrooms and two to four stalks (depending on size and thickness) of cooked asparagus should be plenty for four eggs. Serve triangles of fried bread, buttered *biscottes,* or some really good bread with the dish.

Anchovy and mushroom eggs

A Scandinavian recipe which first led me to the delicious combination of mushrooms with anchovy. The sauce described here makes a piquant filling for vol-au-vent, or large puffs of chou pastry (see page 88): it is also a great help to the plainer white fish such as cod and halibut, and a good filling for omelettes.

SERVES SIX
¾ *pound mushrooms, sliced*
2–3 *ounces (4–6 tablespoons) butter*
⅔ *cup each light and heavy cream, or 1¼ cups béchamel sauce (see*
    appendix)
1 *tin anchovies, drained, chopped*
freshly ground black pepper
6 *eggs*

salt
dill or parsley, minced

Cook mushrooms in butter. Pour on cream or béchamel: simmer until thick. Add anchovies gradually, stopping when the flavour is piquant to your taste. Season with freshly ground black pepper. Spread out in a greased fireproof dish. Make 6 hollows in it with the back of a tablespoon, and break an egg into each. Sprinkle with salt and pepper. Bake at mark 6, 400°F, until the egg whites are just set. Sprinkle with dill or parsley, and serve immediately with toast.

These two recipes, which I came across in a book of Viennese cookery first, are very similar to the recipes on pages 137–8, which Raymond Oliver recommends for truffles.

Girolles with scrambled eggs

A shining tawny dish, with the yellow eggs and the orange girolles.

SERVES FOUR
1 *pound girolles*
1 *medium onion, chopped finely*
4 *ounces (8 tablespoons) butter*
8 *eggs*
salt, pepper
lemon juice
parsley, minced

Clean and divide the larger girolles into pieces. Cook the onion gently in the butter, then add the mushrooms and cook them over a high heat so that their liquid evaporates and only a small amount of juice is left. Beat the eggs lightly, season, and pour over the girolles. Do not overcook (it's important to have the girolles exactly right before the eggs are added). Season with some lemon juice, turn into a heated serving dish, and sprinkle with parsley.

Girolles with oeufs mollets

Again a beautiful dish. Cook the same amount of girolles in the same way as in preceding recipe. Meanwhile cook 4 (or 8) eggs for exactly 6 minutes if they are large, 5 if they are medium size. Run them immediately under the cold tap, crack the shells with a teaspoon and remove them carefully. Put the mushrooms into a dish and place the eggs on top with some parsley. Serve immediately. The idea is for each person to break his eggs over the mushrooms—the soft yolks will form a sauce.

Oeufs en meurette
(Eggs in a red wine sauce)

A meurette, originally a Burgundian dish, is usually a wine stew containing fresh-water fish, much the same kind of thing as a matelote. It's one of those stew-soup dishes that I find very restoring in the evening after a hard day. The method is very similar to *boeuf à la bourguignonne,* in that the essential flavouring ingredients are onions and mushrooms with, of course, the red wine. It's a counsel of perfection to advise you to use a good Beaujolais—a Fleurie, a Juliénas, or a Saint-Amour: cheaper wine makes a good dish, so long as you add a little sugar to the seasonings. Because eggs, like fish, need only minutes to cook, the sauce is prepared first, and only when the flavour and thickness are right do you cook the main ingredient in it.

SERVES SIX

8–10 ounces pork belly slices
6 ounces mushrooms
2½ ounces (5 tablespoons) butter
1 large onion, finely chopped
1 medium carrot, diced small
4 cloves garlic, minced
2½ tablespoons flour
3 cups red wine

1¼ *cups beef or chicken stock*
bouquet garni
salt, freshly ground black pepper
sugar (optional)
12 *eggs*
parsley, chopped
12–24 *small triangles of fried bread*

Remove skin and bone from the pork, and cut meat into match-stick strips. Halve the mushrooms if they are medium-sized, then brown them lightly in about half of the butter. In a large saucepan, lightly brown the pork, onion, carrot, and garlic in the remaining butter. Stir in the flour, and when the roux begins to colour, moisten with the wine and stock. Add the bouquet and seasonings, and leave to cook down, with the lid off the pan, for 45 minutes or longer, until the sauce is thick and rich. Correct the seasoning, adding sugar to taste, and tip in the mushrooms. Simmer gently for 10 minutes.

Strain the sauce into a wide frying pan; discard the bouquet, but treasure all the little bits of vegetable and pork, and keep them warm. Poach the eggs in the sauce for 4 minutes (the yolks should remain soft) and divide them among 6 individual pots or soup bowls, with a share of the sauce and the bits of vegetable and meat. Sprinkle with parsley, and tuck the croutons of bread round the edge. Serve immediately.

N O T E : The sauce and croutons can all be prepared in advance of the meal and reheated, but the eggs should be cooked only at the last minute.

Omelette à la provençale
(Omelette in the style of Provence)

Try to get salted anchovies for this recipe. They will need to be soaked for an hour or two in water, before being filletted and chopped.

1 *large onion, chopped*
8 *fine morels, sliced*
olive oil
12 *anchovies, soaked, chopped,*
  or 1 *tin anchovies in oil, chopped*
12 *black olives, pitted and chopped*
2 *ounces (4 tablespoons) butter, softened*
salt, cayenne pepper
grated nutmeg
2 *tablespoons chopped parsley*
12 *eggs*

Cook the onion and morels in enough oil to cover bottom of pan until soft, without allowing them to colour. Drain and put them in a bowl with the anchovies, olives, butter, salt, cayenne, nutmeg, and parsley. Mix everything together well.

Beat the eggs, season them, and cook one large or two to four small omelettes according to your convenience (and the size of your omelette pan). Use olive oil instead of butter to grease the pan. In the centre, put the filling. Roll the omelette(s) over and serve immediately on a very hot plate.

Soufflé aux champignons
(Mushroom soufflé)

I once asked a friend, a biochemist, about her work. She replied that it was really a kind of cooking. And certainly cooking is a kind of chemistry, or perhaps one should say a kind of alchemy. One doesn't always realize this because so many dishes can be made in a somewhat casual way, within generously defined principles. A little bit more, a little bit less—it doesn't really matter. But there are dishes which require exactness, and soufflés are a good example. They are not difficult, quite the contrary—so long as certain rules are obeyed in a certain sequence. I like this kind of cooking. It has the dignity and security of order about it. You know it will work, and yet there is delight in the result.

FLAVOURING:
1 ounce (2 tablespoons) butter
1 small onion, minced
6 ounces mushrooms, minced
salt, pepper

SOUFFLÉ:
2½ tablespoons butter
3 tablespoons flour
1 cup milk
½ teaspoon salt
¼ teaspoon pepper
pinch cayenne pepper
⅛ teaspoon grated nutmeg
4 egg yolks
1 tablespoon grated Parmesan
5 egg whites

FOR SOUFFLÉ MOULD:
butter
breadcrumbs

First attend to the mushroom mixture: melt the butter and cook the onion in it gently. When it begins to soften, without browning, add the mushrooms and seasoning. When everything is just cooked, set the pan aside.

To make the soufflé, melt the butter and stir in the flour. Let it bubble without colouring for 2 minutes. Meanwhile bring the milk to the boil. Remove the flour-and-butter pan from the heat, and when the mixture stops boiling, pour in the milk all in one lot. Whisk with a wire beater until smooth. Add the seasonings and the mushroom mixture. Put back over the stove and stir over a high heat for 1 minute. The mixture will be very thick.

Take the pan from the heat, and stir in the yolks one by one. Stir in the Parmesan and more seasoning if necessary. Whisk the egg whites until they are stiff and stand in points. Stir a large spoonful into the mushroom sauce until it is thoroughly amalgamated. Then fold in the rest of the egg whites gently, with a rubber spatula or metal spoon. Turn the mixture carefully, so that it remains as light and foamy as possible. One minute should be enough.

Preheat the oven to mark 6, 400°F. Heavily butter a 2½-pint (U.S., 6-cup) soufflé dish or charlotte mould. (Tie on a collar of foil so that it comes about 2 inches above the rim if the dish is of smaller capacity.) Put in the breadcrumbs and shake them about so that they coat the entire inside. This helps to give a brown crust to the soufflé. Turn the soufflé mixture into the dish, put it on a baking sheet, and place it in the centre of the preheated oven. Lower the heat immediately to mark 5, 375°F (don't open oven door for 20 minutes). In 25 to 30 minutes the top of the soufflé should be nicely browned and puffed over the rim of the dish. Bake 4 to 5 minutes more to firm it up. Eat it immediately.

Truffles, and some Roman recipes

The apparently magical growth of truffles underground, coupled with their exquisite flavour, has attracted a lively collection of facts and legends during the last 2,500 years. Pliny described them as "callosities of earth," or "lumps of earthy substance balled together." He reported that the Roman Minister of Justice in Cartagena, Lartïus Licinius, had recently cracked his teeth on a denarius which was embedded in the centre of a truffle. There is the whole business of truffle pigs and truffle hounds (pigs are better at scenting the prize, but they incline to rootle it up and eat it themselves: dogs are more biddable), the truffle school for dogs at Alba in Piedmont, and the night hunts that take place in the darkness with maps that are secretly handed down in families. There are the swarms of yellowish flies that dance in the scented sunlight above a ripe truffle, and the cracks in the ground exuding a wonderful odour as they open up with the swelling below. And did you know that the last of the truffle hunters in England, Alfred Collins of Winterslow in Wiltshire, gave up only in 1935? Though the English truffle does not have as high a reputation with chefs as the Périgord truffle, I think most of us would be prepared to overlook the difference if we ever came across one under a beech tree on Salisbury Plain, or on any other of the chalklands of southern England.

In his book *Mushrooms and Truffles,* Professor R. Singer describes the development of truffle growing in France, as opposed to truffle hunting. The method was invented, or rather discovered, in 1810—a date can be put on it, which is unusual in such matters—by Joseph Talon. He was a peasant in the Vaucluse, the countryside of Petrarch and Laura, and one day he planted some acorns in a small patch of stony waste ground. About six years later he noticed that truffles were growing in the plantation. He bought up waste land, planted acorns from his original oaks, and began to make money from truffles. He confided his secret to a friend, who sent the first lot of cultivated truffles to Paris in 1851. Others followed the Talon method—they still do—which has not so far been improved on. The principle is to plant your tiny oak trees in an area where truffles are known to occur: there is no inoculation of spawn or spreading of prepared mycelium as in other cultivated mushroom industries. The waiting period can be as long as ten years. Nonetheless by the end of the century, according to one authority, two million kilos of truffles a year were being sold in France: this figure includes wild truffles. No wonder Escoffier used them with such an abundant hand, partnering them with that other winter luxury, foie gras (see the recipe for *poularde Derby*). Nowadays the figures are much reduced, and the nearest one gets to them is a sliver of tasteless blackness in the centre of a tin of liver pâté—unless one is in Paris or Périgord at Christmastime. There is no better celebration of the virtues of truffles than the following passage from *Prisons et Paradis*.

The truffle and how to cook it, by Colette
"At least I did learn—in the truffle country of Puisaye, whose soil produces a gray truffle with a good smell but no taste whatever —how to treat the true truffle, the black truffle, the truffle of Périgord. The most capricious, the most revered of all those black princesses. People will pay its own weight in gold for the truffle of Périgord, for the most part in order to put it to some paltry use. They insert it in glutinous masses of foie gras, they bury it in poultry overlarded with grease, they submerge it, chopped to pieces, in brown sauce, they combine it with vegetables covered in mayonnaise. . . . Away with all this slicing, this dicing, this grating, this peeling of truffles! Can they not love it for itself? If you do love it, then pay its ransom royally—or keep away from it altogether. But once having bought it, eat it on its own, scented and grainy-skinned, eat it like the vegetable it is, hot, and served in munificent quantities. Once scraped, it won't give you much trouble; its sovereign flavour disdains all complications and complicities. Bathed in a good, very dry white wine—keep the champagne for your banquets, the truffle can do without it—salted without extravagance, peppered with discretion, they can then be cooked in a simple, black, cast-iron stewpan with the lid on. For twenty-five minutes, they must dance in the constant flow of bubbles, drawing with them through the eddies and the foam—like Tritons

playing around some darker Amphitrite—a score or so of smallish strips of bacon, fat, but not too fat, which will give body to the stock. No other herbs or spices! And a pestilence upon your rolled napkin, with its taste and odour of lye, last resting place of the cooked truffle! Your truffles must come to the table in their own stock. Do not stint when you serve yourself: the truffle is an appetite creator, an aid to digestion. And as you break open this jewel sprung from a poverty-stricken soil, imagine—if you have never visited it—the desolate kingdom where it rules. For it kills the dog rose, drains life from the oak, and ripens beneath an ungrateful bed of pebbles. . . .

"Do not eat the truffle without wine. If you have no great Burgundy of impeccable ancestry to hand, then drink some wine from Mercurey, full-bodied and velvety at the same time. . . ."

Along with this loving and practical celebration of the truffle, I like to remember Maurice Goudeket's description of Colette preparing truffles every year for the Réveillon dinner at Christmastime. The pleasure the task gave her, the anticipation of the evening's delight. Colette on food and drink is very much to be trusted: her responses to such things, to cheese or to a pear, for instance, as to truffles, were robust and sensuous, total and yet discreet.

Truffles as an aphrodisiac

A number of rare or newly experienced foods have been claimed to be aphrodisiacs. At one time this quality was even ascribed to the tomato. Reflect on that when you are next preparing the family salad. Raymond Oliver, of the great Paris restaurant Le Grand Véfour, says firmly that all mushrooms are aphrodisiac, but particularly the truffle, which should be eaten raw and very fresh (for the purpose he had in mind).

It could quite reasonably be argued that any finely prepared meal, well-chosen dishes, beautifully cooked, discreetly served, with the right wines and so on, has a softening effect. Certainly I would expect the provider of truffles to gain his point more rapidly—all other things being equal—than the provider of panhaggerty or shepherd's pie. Or of haggis and bashed neeps, however abundant the whisky. More than that cannot be claimed, I think, for any food. But if you wish to make the experiment, here are some of Monsieur Oliver's suggestions from his chapter on aphrodisiac cookery in *The French at Table* (Wine and Food Society, 1967).

"It is evident that the best way in which to employ truffles is to scrape them, wash them, soak them in Cognac and eat them raw with a little salt.

"Rosy salt is especially suitable and this is made by mixing a soup spoon of fine salt with a tablespoonful of paprika and a coffeespoonful of Cayenne. Blend the mixture well. Initiates pinch this mixture (like snuff) between the thumb and index finger of the left hand and sprinkle as much as they require on the truffle (or on a peewit's egg)."

If this method is thought to be too direct, he suggests that you mix oil, freshly ground black pepper, salt and a little wine vinegar in a bowl. Mix in the hearts of two fine lettuces, then 7 ounces of finely sliced uncooked truffle. No other seasonings.

Eggs come into Monsieur Oliver's chapter, though, rather as restoratives than aphrodisiacs. To make the best use of them they should be lightly scrambled with truffles. Alternatively, put them into cold water, bring it to the boil, and then remove the eggs promptly. Shell them carefully, or rather break them into a warm bowl, scooping out the whites if necessary. Season and add a truffle cut into thin strips.

Oeufs en cocotte aux truffes
(Eggs in cocotte with truffles)

A favourite French way of using small amounts of truffle—amorous inclinations apart—is to combine it with egg. One trick is to leave a (cleaned) fresh truffle overnight in the middle of a basket of eggs: next day they are all wonderfully flavoured and the truffle can be used for another dish. Here's another, which is as good a way as any of using a tiny tin of truffles or truffle peelings. Naturally all the other ingredients must be of first-class quality— genuinely fresh farm eggs, the best unsalted butter from Normandy, freshly ground black pepper, and if possible cream with a slight tang from a farm producer rather than one of the large factory-dairies. This particular version of the recipe comes from the Hôtel de Cro-Magnon at the prehistoric village of Les Eyzies in the Dordogne: Meursault is the wine recommended, in other words a not too dry white Burgundy.

SERVES FOUR
4 eggs
melted butter
⅓ cup heavy cream
4 teaspoons chopped fresh truffle,
  or 1 small tin of truffles, chopped
salt, freshly ground pepper

Break the eggs carefully into 4 saucers, without spoiling the yolks. Brush four ramekins or small soufflé dishes generously with melted butter. Put a tablespoon of cream in each one, and then an egg. Scatter the truffle on top, season, and cover with a foil lid. Place the ramekins in a bain-marie (or use the bottom of a self-basting roaster or deep roasting tin), and pour in water to come halfway up. Bring to the boil, then simmer steadily for about 8 minutes so that the egg whites are set and the yolks still runny—the time will depend on the size of the eggs. Serve immediately, with good bread.

Oeufs brouillés aux truffes
(Scrambled eggs with truffles)

An even simpler way of using a tiny tin of truffles or truffle peelings to good effect.

SERVES FOUR AS A FIRST COURSE

6 eggs
1 small tin of truffles
salt, freshly ground pepper
4 circles of toast or bread fried in butter
butter
4 tablespoons heavy cream

Beat the eggs. Open the tin of truffles, and chop them: put with the juices from the tin into the bowl of eggs. Season, cover, and leave for several hours.

Prepare the bread as desired, and keep it hot while cooking the eggs. Melt a generous knob of butter in a small thick pan and tip in the egg and truffle mixture. Turn it with a wooden spoon over a low heat until it begins to thicken—do not allow the eggs to become dry. Beat in the cream lightly and divide among the four pieces of hot toast or fried bread. Serve immediately.

Omelette aux truffes

Another simple egg and truffle dish, which can be prepared in one of two ways.

SERVES TWO

5–6 eggs
1 small tin truffles, chopped, or 1 truffle, cleaned and chopped
1 teaspoon Madeira
4 tablespoons heavy cream (optional)
salt, pepper
butter

For the first method of preparation, separate the eggs, and mix the yolks with the truffles, truffle juice and Madeira. Beat the egg whites until stiff, then fold into mixture.

Alternately, beat the eggs for an omelette in the usual way, adding the truffles, truffle juice, and wine, and the cream if you like.

Season to taste. Then cook in the usual way in butter so that the pan side of the omelette is firm and the upper side creamy: this takes about half a minute. Roll and slide onto a hot serving dish. Eat immediately.

White truffles with cheese

White truffles should be cleaned with a soft brush first, then a damp cloth. They can then be sliced thinly on the cucumber blade of a grater (the Italians have a special cutter), before being heated through—they are never cooked in the normal sense of the word—or sprinkled raw on top of pasta or egg dishes and so on. If you are lucky enough to be in north Italy, and can afford several white truffles, you can layer the slices with thin pieces of Parmesan cheese. Season each layer and brush it with olive oil. Ten minutes in a hot oven—mark 7, 425°F—is enough to melt the cheese and marry the two flavours. Serve with lemon quarters.

A more economical dish is the *fonduta* or *fondua* of Piedmont. Although there is a resemblance to Swiss fondue, there are important differences. Here is Ada Boni's recipe from *Italian Regional Cooking:*

SERVES FOUR
¾ *pound Fontina cheese*
milk
6 *egg yolks, beaten*
4 *ounces (8 tablespoons) butter*
white pepper
1 *white truffle, thinly sliced*

Remove Fontina rind, and dice cheese. Put into a bowl, cover with milk, and leave for 8 hours or overnight. To cook, place the bowl over a pan of just simmering water, and beat in the egg yolks and pieces of the butter gradually, using a wooden spoon.

When everything has blended to a smooth cream, pour on to a hot serving dish, season with pepper, and cover with slices of truffle. Provide fingers of toast to be dipped into the *fonduta*.

White truffle with egg

The French way of putting a black truffle into a basket of eggs to scent them reminds me of a story I heard recently. It was last autumn. A friend of ours who goes to Milan sometimes on business decided to bring back a white truffle, a fresh one. At the shop he went to, it was most tenderly wrapped up to keep in the exquisite scented flavour. And he, too, had taken precautions, adding a couple of plastic bags, a number of clean socks and two or three layers of miscellaneous underclothing, until it looked ready for a game of pass-the-parcel. When his wife opened the case a few hours later in London, the wonderful smell poured out into the room, even through all the swaddling clothes. They ate it shaved in thin slices on to a bowl of egg noodles—home-made in its honour—because white truffles must never be cooked. The most you should do is to heat them gently for a few minutes—otherwise the magic disappears. In this respect they are quite unlike black truffles: the flavour is not at all the same either. My feeling is that they do not can as well as black truffles. No doubt the heat of the processing drives out the flavour.

Although white truffles are different from black ones, they have a similar affinity with eggs. A dish of scrambled eggs becomes a feast if you cover it with thinly shaved slices of white truffle. For an omelette, take enough slices from a truffle to make a line down the finished result, and chop the rest, which should then be heated in an omelette pan with some butter. Remove the chopped truffle and keep it warm while you cook the omelette. When it's ready, put the chopped truffle down the middle, fold and slide the omelette on to a heated dish and decorate with the slices of truffle.

Bagna cauda

Bagna cauda—the name means hot bath—is a rich sauce of anchovies, oil and garlic, seasoned with a white truffle. Usually it comes in a small pot, standing on a spirit burner, and surrounded by piles of raw vegetables with perhaps some boiled potatoes as well. Each person dips the pieces he likes into the sauce, fondue fashion. The first time I encountered this magnificent if stomach-testing sauce was at the Belvedere Restaurant at La Morra in Piedmont. There it was served to each person individually in green peppers, which had been boiled before the sauce was put into them.

Ada Boni, the author of the grand Italian cookery book, *Il Talismano della Felicità* (a title which I think needs no translating), gives half a pound of butter, heated with about 3 ounces of olive oil and 4 finely chopped cloves of garlic, 6 anchovy fillets and a little salt. The anchovy will soon dissolve with a little encouragement from a wooden spoon. Finally a thinly sliced truffle is added.

Elizabeth David, in *Italian Food,* provides a robuster set of quantities—3 ounces each of olive oil, butter, anchovies and garlic. With sliced white truffle as well. She remarks that cream is also sometimes added.

Whichever recipe you choose, be sure not to cook the truffle. It should be heated through, and not boiled.

Some Roman recipes for cooking mushrooms

In the packed jumble of his *Natural History,* Pliny sometimes allows himself—and his readers—the indulgence of a few vivid sentences from his own experience. His description, for instance, of the Emperor Tiberius' cherished cucumbers, which were grown in beds mounted on wheels, so that they could be rolled out into the sun; when the weather turned chilly, they were moved under frames covered with sheets of stone cut so thinly that they were transparent. Or his allusion to the dried ceps from Bithynia which arrived in Rome still threaded on their rushes. Or his ironic picture of Roman gentlemen preparing mushrooms with their own hands—the only cooking they ever condescended to do. One can see them prodding the panful of tree fungi or truffles with special amber and silver implements (in case they were poisonous, a useless precaution), hardly able to wait until they were cooked, their mouths watering in anticipation. He doesn't, at this point in the book at least, mention his older contemporary, Apicius, the celebrated first-century gourmet whose excesses were notorious in his own day, but no doubt he was one of the "exquisites" that Pliny had in mind. Certainly Apicius, in the *De re coquinaria*, echoes Pliny's description by inference at least, because his recipes for mushrooms are some of the simplest in the book, with the least number of flavouring ingredients. Quite within the capacity of an inexperienced aristocratic cook, who had no wish to make a fool of himself in front of his reclining visitors.

There has been some argument about the exact identification of the mushrooms the Romans ate. One might gather, from Pliny's preoccupation with antidotes for poisonous fungi, that they were not always wise in their choice, but he may only be reflecting the ancient fear of mushrooms which still persists. It seems, though, that the Romans, like the Chinese and Japanese, were fond of tree mushrooms as well as ceps and the prized truffle.

Tree mushroom recipes, from Apicius

Cook them in water first, drain them well, and finish them in one of the following sauces:

1. Pepper pounded with garum (a favourite Roman condiment, made from small fish and fish entrails rotted down in salt, a preparation similar to modern Indonesian fish sauces, and a forerunner of our anchovy paste).

2. Salt, olive oil, wine and chopped fresh coriander.

3. Pepper, olive oil and wine vinegar, with carenum, which was made by boiling down sweet wine to a concentrated essence.

Cep recipes, from Apicius

1. Cook the ceps with carenum and a bouquet of fresh coriander; remove the coriander before serving.

2. Serve the cep caps (presumably after grilling or boiling) sprinkled with garum or salt.

3. Chop the stalks (as one does with many modern cep recipes) and cook them with the caps, in a clean pan, with pepper, lovage and a little honey. Moisten with garum, and add a little oil. Again the instructions suggest that the ceps were first cooked in some other way, as a preliminary.

Truffle recipes, from Apicius

Peel and simmer the truffles in water. Put them on skewers, sprinkle them with salt, and grill them lightly. Prick them with a fork and give them a few minutes in one of the following sauces:

1. Olive oil, garum, carenum, wine pepper and honey. Remove from the skewer and serve with the sauce, slightly thickened with starch.

2. Garum, green olive oil (one can still buy green olive oil, with a pronounced olive flavour, from Tuscany on occasion), carenum, a little wine, crushed pepper and some honey. Thicken with starch. If you like, the truffles can be wrapped in pieces of caul fat before being skewered and grilled.

3. Pepper, lovage, coriander, rue, garum, honey, wine and a little oil.

4. Pepper, mint, rue, honey, oil and a little wine.

5. Add some leek to the water when cooking the truffles. Serve with salt, pepper, chopped coriander mixed with wine and a little olive oil.

Although one may recoil at first from such mixtures, on reflection they do not seem quite so disgusting. Think of mushrooms flavoured deliciously with anchovy (see index), of the soups and sauces which contain Madeira, Sauterne, or sherry, of a recipe like the one for mushrooms with grapes on page 126, or of the Chinese dish of silvery "cloud ears" cooked in syrup (cloud ears belong to the same family as the "Jew's ear," which grows on elder trees and has been eaten for centuries in Europe). Then the use of garum, carenum and even honey seems perfectly reasonable. Wine, wine vinegar, olive oil, pepper and fresh green herbs are still part of our mushroom tradition—and, as you will see on page 82, the Italians put mint into their cep recipes just as their ancestors did.

As far as truffles are concerned, I think we should prefer Colette's simple way of cooking and eating them, on page 136, without the addition of Roman sauces. But the idea of wrapping them up in caul fat before grilling them on skewers is something I should much like to try.

MUSHROOMS
WITH FISH

After writing this book, and an earlier book on fish, I have come to the conclusion that there is a special affinity between mushrooms and fish. And this affinity works at every level, from cultivated mushrooms to ceps, from the cheapest fish on the slab to sole and turbot. In such recipes as *Truites aux cèpes*, the result is so good that one never forgets the flavour of the occasion. Of course one can rarely combine freshly caught trout with ceps from a nearby forest—this is not an experience which happens to many people unless they live in certain blessed corners of the world—but *sole meunière* with ceps is possible. The fine flavour of field mushrooms works well with the baked and stuffed fish recipes, or in a kulebiaka of smoked haddock or salmon, or in a creamy sauce to be served with grilled fish or *paupiettes*.

At a homelier level, a daily level, try cooking deep-frozen cod or halibut in clarified butter with cultivated mushrooms and a little garlic. The juices intermingle so satisfactorily, with such mutual assistance, that both main ingredients become far more delicious than they ever could be on their own.

When it comes to cooking shellfish, cultivated mushrooms play a more satisfactory role than they do in many dishes. Their mild subtlety and fresh soft-crisp texture set off the sweetness of prawns or shrimp, lobster and crab, and scallops, too. For the same reason, uncooked mushrooms are a good addition to shellfish salads. With oysters or mussels, which provide a point of flavour, a strong moment of flavour, try field mushrooms, so long as they are firm and in their prime.

Truffles do not play such an important part in fish recipes as they do in meat recipes. They are an important garnish in some of the classic lobster and sole cookery, but unless you have the facilities of a first-class French restaurant such dishes are a burden to prepare. I have included two recipes, though, which are simple enough to make at home, enjoyably so: the first is *Filets de sole Walewska*, sole with a rich sauce and a little lobster and truffle; the second, *Brandade de morue truffée*. I particularly like the second recipe for its irreverent combination of the cheapest, most despised fish of all (despised at least by some cookery writers and many English people), salt cod, with the most expensive of all fungi, truffles.

General fish and mushroom recipes

Fish baked in foil with mushrooms

This is a method for every kind of fish, because the foil prevents the juices from evaporating and keeps the dryest halibut moist. (My own personal exception is sea bass—I find both flavour and texture almost unpleasant when cooked in this way: bass, to me at any rate, needs the crispness that only baking in an open dish can give.)

Here is a general method, which is easily varied to your own tastes.

SERVES FOUR
2 pounds fish fillets,
  or 4 whole fish,
  or 4 thick fish steaks
salt and pepper
1 cup chopped shallots or onions
butter
8 ounces mushrooms, chopped or sliced
2 tablespoons minced parsley or mixed herbs
flour

Put fish on a plate, season and set aside. Cook shallots or onions gently in a few tablespoons of butter, covered, until soft and golden. Add mushrooms, turning up the heat a little so that the mixture is not too wet—on the other hand, it should not be dry like a duxelles. Stir in the herbs, season, and remove from the heat.

Cut four pieces of foil, each one large enough to contain a fish or pieces of fish. Melt enough butter to brush over foil, and spread the mushroom mixture over the centres of buttered foil. Dip the fish quickly in flour, shaking off any surplus, and lay it on top. Fasten the parcels in the usual way. Place on a baking sheet and cook for about 25 minutes at mark 5, 375°F.

If, instead of four fish, you are dealing with one large one, or one large piece, you will make one parcel. Bake it for an hour at mark 1–2, 275°–300°F.

Remember that with fish, it is thickness that counts when reckoning cooking time, not total weight. For instance, a whole salmon will take no longer to cook than a large piece cut from its centre. Once you are over the 5-pound mark, reckon 12 minutes to the pound at the lower temperature: but this does not often happen to most cooks. Remember also to increase the quantities of mushroom mixture in proportion.

When the fish is cooked, it can be served as it is, in the foil. Each person opens his own package.

Alternatively, you could place the fish on a serving plate with the mushrooms, and use the delicious juices to make a velouté sauce, enriched with cream and egg yolks if you like.

A quick method is to concentrate the fish juices by sharp boiling until they taste really strong, then beat them up into a sauce by adding cream and a final knob of butter. Extravagant, but worth it with the finest fish such as trout.

Or you could have ready half a pint of cream or béchamel sauce, and add the juices to that.

Be guided by the fish and the circumstances. The only thing to avoid is insipidity of flavour.

Truite, mulet, rouget-barbet aux champignons
(Trout, mullet, or red mullet baked with mushrooms)

Baking is one of the most appetising ways of cooking fish, particularly small, whole fish—trout, for instance, of the size that the French call *truite-portion*, grey or red mullet, herring or mackerel. And when such fish are laid on a bed of delicious things, they work to mutual advantage. Obviously this method is best for the

moist, fat fish. Whiting, gurnard, and so on need more liquid sur-
roundings, though you can cherish them with a buttered paper or
a foil lid. But again, if you do this, the result loses its crisp edges.

SERVES FOUR
1 cup chopped shallots or onions
1 clove garlic, minced
butter
½ pound mushrooms, coarsely chopped
½ cup breadcrumbs
4 tablespoons minced parsley
4 fish, cleaned
salt, pepper
lemon quarters

Cook shallots or onions and garlic very slowly in a few tablespoons of butter, then add the mushrooms and continue to cook
at only a moderate heat so that the vegetables exude their juices.
Off the heat, stir in the breadcrumbs and parsley.

Season the fish with salt and pepper to taste. Butter an oval or
other shallow ovenproof dish generously, and spread the mushroom mixture evenly in it. Lay the fish on top, pressing them down
slightly. Bake in a moderately hot oven, mark 5–6, 375°–400°F,
until cooked (about 20 minutes). If the fish brown rapidly, protect
them with buttered paper. Serve with lemon quarters.

Baked fish with mushroom sauce

A good French recipe for a large fish, sea bream, bass or grey mullet. The fine stuffing is flavoured with almonds, and the sauce with mushrooms.

SERVES SIX
3½–4-pound fish
salt, pepper
butter

STUFFING:
½ cup breadcrumbs
½ cup cream
3 tablespoons ground almonds
4 ounces fish fillets
1 egg
2 tablespoons minced parsley

SAUCE:
1 cup minced shallots or onions
8 ounces mushrooms, sliced
1¼ cups dry white wine
2 tablespoons lemon juice
3 tablespoons minced parsley

Ask the fishmonger to clean out the fish by the gills, without slitting the belly. Scale fish, and season it inside and out.

Mix the first three stuffing ingredients thoroughly together. Mince the fish fillets twice, reducing to a purée, or use a blender and liquidize fish with the egg. Mix with the stuffing mixture, add the parsley, and seasoning to taste. Add the egg if it has not yet been used. Stuff the fish.

Generously grease a large ovenproof serving dish with butter. Put in the shallots or onions and mushrooms, then the stuffed fish. Pour the wine over it, add extra seasoning and lemon juice, and bake for up to 50 minutes in a moderate oven, mark 5, 375°F. Drain cooking liquid from the fish, beat in a few tablespoons of butter, correct the seasoning, pour over the fish, and sprinkle with parsley. Serve with bread or new potatoes to mop up the juices.

Darnes de poisson à la Bréval
(Slices of fish à la Bréval)

I translated and adapted this recipe from an excellent French book, *Les Recettes secrètes des meuilleurs restaurants de la France*, selected and edited by Louisette Bertholle, which came out in 1972, from Albin Michel. It gives an ideal method of baking dryer fish, such as turbot (as suggested in the original recipe), or halibut, or some fine fresh cod. The combination of mushrooms with tomato and shallot is most successful.

SERVES SIX
fish steaks, or thick fillets, for 6 people
salt, pepper
4 ounces (8 tablespoons) unsalted butter
6 tablespoons minced shallots or onions
½ pound mushrooms, sliced
6 medium tomatoes, peeled, seeded, diced
⅔ cup fish stock (or light meat stock)
⅔ cup dry white wine
1¼ cups heavy cream
lemon juice
6 crescents of puff pastry (optional)

Season the fish with salt and pepper. Butter an oval flameproof dish with 1 ounce of the butter. On it place the shallots or onion, mushrooms, and tomatoes, then the fish. Pour in stock and wine. Bring to the boil on top of the stove, then transfer to the oven, mark 3, 325°F, and bake for about 20 minutes. When the fish is *just* done, pour off everything else in the pan into a saucepan. Tidy up the cooking dish with some kitchen paper, put buttered paper over the fish, and return to the oven (heat off, door shut) to keep warm. Now reduce the mush in the saucepan with the cream until you have a thick, concentrated mixture, more like a purée than a sauce. Off the heat, beat in the remaining butter, correct the seasoning, and add lemon juice to taste. Serve, if you wish, with tiny crescents of puff pastry arranged decoratively on top of the fish, which should be surrounded by the sauce.

Gratin de poissons à la bourgeoise (Fish gratin in the housewife's style)

Fish cooked with mushrooms, tomato and wine makes a good dish, as you will see if you try the preceding Bréval recipe for steaks and fillets. When it comes to dealing with whole fish, with the one- to two-pounders, a slightly different method and balance of ingredients is required. This recipe is a homely affair—which accounts for the title—without the finer restaurant touches of the previous one, but it is most appetizing. Use it for grey or red mullet, sea bream, sea bass, snappers, John Dory, gurnard and so on.

SERVES SIX
2–3 *whole fish (about 3½ pounds)*
⅔ *cup chopped shallots*
2 *pounds mushrooms, thinly sliced*
1 *pound tomatoes, skinned, seeded, chopped*
salt, pepper
butter
1 *cup dry white wine*
breadcrumbs
parsley, minced
lemon quarters

Clean and scale the fish if necessary. Mix the shallots, mushrooms, and tomatoes, and season them well. Lightly butter an ovenproof serving dish, and spread about half the vegetable mixture in it. Place the fish on top, head to tail, and put the remaining vegetable mixture round them. Pour in the wine, and scatter breadcrumbs evenly over the fish. Melt a few tablespoons of butter and dribble it over the crumbs. Bake at mark 7, 425°F, for 30 to 40 minutes, according to the thickness of the fish. (If the crumbs become brown too soon, protect them with buttered paper.) Sprinkle fish with parsley, tuck in the lemon quarters, and serve in the cooking dish.

Fillets of fish with cream and mushroom sauce

This recipe is suitable for almost all fillets of white fish—obviously with sole, turbot and John Dory or monkfish it will be better than with sea bream or cod. I make it often with fillets of chicken halibut, really fresh inshore fish, which is firm and not as dry as the huge halibut one sees occupying five feet of the counter. The recipe is variable—if you have no time to make some fish stock, use light chicken or veal stock. Instead of using parsley, you could flavour the sauce with nutmeg or mace.

SERVES SIX
2–3 pounds fish fillets or steaks
salt, pepper
⅔ cup minced shallots or onions
8 ounces mushrooms, sliced
parsley minced
butter
1 cup dry white wine
1 cup fish stock
½ cup heavy cream
lemon quarters

Season the fish with salt and pepper. Put the shallots or onion, mushrooms and some parsley into a buttered ovenproof dish, season, and place the fish fillets on top. Pour on the wine and stock, and dab small amounts of butter over the fish. Bake at mark 5, 375°F, for about 20 minutes, but check after 15 minutes—the length of time required will depend on the fish's texture and the thickness of the pieces. Transfer the cooked fish to a warm serving plate. Pour everything else into a pan, and reduce by hard boiling to a strongly flavoured concentrated sauce. Stir in the cream, and boil again for a few moments. Correct the seasoning, beat in a few tablespoons of butter, and pour over the fish. Sprinkle with parsley, tuck lemon quarters round the edges, and serve.

Paupiettes de poisson aux champignons
(*Paupiettes* of fish with mushrooms)

Although this recipe is generally used for sole, other firm fish can be substituted; chicken turbot or halibut, John Dory, or particularly fine large herring can all be cooked this way. The general principle is to roll the fillets around a little piquantly flavoured stuffing, then to bake them in white wine and stock. The reduced cooking liquid is added finally to a thick cream sauce, which is poured over the fish.

SERVES FOUR
8 fillets of sole or other firm fish
salt and pepper
about 1 cup stuffing (pages 49–51)
2 teaspoons butter
1 glass dry white wine
up to 2 cups fish or chicken stock

EITHER:
1¼ cups béchamel sauce (page 304)
12 ounces mushrooms, sliced and fried in butter

OR:
1¼ cups mushroom sauce (page 36)

Season the fillets with salt and pepper. Spread each one with a tablespoon of stuffing and roll it up, skin side inside. Spear with a wooden cocktail stick. Arrange upright in a small baking dish, as closely together as possible. Put a dab of butter on top of each *paupiette*. Pour the wine into the dish, then enough stock to come two-thirds of the way up the dish. Bake for 10 to 15 minutes at mark 7, 425°F.

Remove the *paupiettes* to a serving dish and keep warm. Reduce the cooking liquid to a concentrated flavour, and add to the cream or mushroom sauce. Pour it over the fish. If mushrooms are used, arrange them around the edge. Serve immediately.

Fish meunière aux cèpes, aux morilles, etc.

This recipe shows how easy the cook's job is when the basic ingredients are of the highest quality and the best flavour. For a dish of this kind, one does not need too many mushrooms. They are a flavouring rather than a vegetable. Fry them rather fast but not for too long.

Turn the fish—small whole fish, or fillets, from salt or fresh water—in seasoned flour. Melt 2 to 4 ounces of butter in a pan, the amount depending on the number of fish to be cooked, and when it froths white, pour it through a damp muslin into a frying pan. Cook the fish in this on both sides until a golden brown. Keep warm. Clean out the pan with kitchen paper, melt some fresh butter in it, and fry sliced ceps or morels. Put them round the fish on a hot serving plate, squeeze a little lemon juice over the fish, and serve immediately.

Fish cooked with cream and mushrooms

The good thing about this rich, simple way of cooking fish is the piquant finish added by the overheat of the grill. It makes all the difference.

SERVES FOUR

4 whole fish (trout, whiting, etc.)
  or 4 thick fillets (halibut, sole, flounder)
seasoned flour
3 ounces (6 tablespoons) butter
8 ounces mushrooms, sliced
salt, pepper
lemon juice
2 cups heavy cream
cayenne pepper

Turn the fish in seasoned flour. Clarify the butter: bring it to a boil in a small pan, then pour it through a muslin-lined sieve into a frying pan. Brown the fish on both sides over high heat in the butter. Transfer fish to a dish, and cook the mushrooms in the fish juices. Season to taste, sprinkle with lemon juice and put the fish back into the pan. Pour the cream over the fish, add a pinch of cayenne pepper, and bring to the boil. When the cream is bubbling gently, place the dish under a hot grill and leave it there for about 8 minutes so that a golden crusty skin forms on top. Keep an eye on the fish when they are under the grill and adjust the heat if necessary. Serve immediately in the cooking dish.

Deep-frozen fish (cod, haddock, trout) with mushrooms

Deep-frozen fish is greatly improved by being fried in clarified butter (see preceding recipe) with sliced mushrooms, field mushrooms in particular, all in the same pan. Before you start, turn the fillets or steaks or trout in seasoned flour. (A small clove of garlic, crushed, and cooked with the fish and mushrooms, also improves the flavour.) Take the cooking slowly, so that the lovely flavour of the mushrooms has a chance to permeate the fish.

When everything is cooked, transfer it to a serving dish and keep warm. Clean out the pan with kitchen paper, and quickly melt some butter over a high heat. Pour it foaming over the fish and mushrooms, and serve immediately with boiled potatoes and lemon quarters.

Surprisingly good, and simple to do.

Scalloped fish with mushrooms

A most useful recipe which is always successful, whether you use cod or turbot or salmon or shellfish. It's also good with cured fish such as salt cod or smoked finnan haddock. Then again, you can use a mixture of fish—cod with mussels, turbot and prawns or shrimp, smoked haddock with cod and prawns, and so on. The only ingredients that must not be left out are the mushrooms and the cheese: they add subtlety and piquancy, which turn this simply prepared dish into a real pleasure.

There are two more ways of adding extra piquancy to this dish —it's a good idea to choose one of them, if your fish is on the dull side and you have no cream for the sauce. The easiest thing to do is to add some good mustard to the mixture just before putting it into shells or pots—e.g., mild Dijon mustard, *moutarde de Meaux*, or one of the Urchfont mustards from Wiltshire. The amount depends on your own tastes, but it's wise to start with a teaspoonful and work upwards. The other alternative is to add a few tablespoons of white wine and the juice of half a lemon to the mushrooms and onions when they are cooking: allow this extra moisture to evaporate so that only the essence is left behind.

SERVES FOUR

1–1¼ *pounds cooked fish fillets, cut in pieces*
1¼ *cups* sauce à la crème, *or béchamel (see appendix)*
2 *ounces (4 tablespoons) butter*
3 *tablespoons minced onion or shallots*
½ *pound mushrooms, chopped finely*
salt, pepper
3½ *ounces grated Gruyère or Cheddar cheese*

Mix the fish—make sure there are no bones in it—with the sauce. Melt the butter, and cook the onion or shallots gently for 5 minutes. Add the mushrooms, and continue to cook until the mixture is dry. Stir into the sauce and turn everything over until well mixed. Correct seasoning. Divide among four deep scallop shells or fireproof pots (or turn into a gratin dish or a cooked pastry case). Sprinkle with cheese. Reheat in a hot oven, mark 7, 425°F, and flash under the grill to brown. Alternatively, you can reheat under the grill at a moderately high temperature. Whichever you choose, the dish should come to the table nicely browned and bubbling.

Crêpes de poisson aux champignons
(Pancakes stuffed with creamed fish and mushrooms)

Another, more filling way of serving the creamed fish mixture in the preceding recipe.

FILLING:
creamed fish and mushroom mixture as in preceding recipe

PANCAKES:
1 cup flour
2 large eggs
4 tablespoons oil or melted butter
pinch salt
1 cup milk

TOPPING:
⅔ cup heavy cream
3½ ounces grated Gruyère or Cheddar cheese

Prepare the filling mixture, omitting the cheese. Keep hot while you mix the pancake ingredients in the given order, and make 12 pancakes in the usual way. Either fill them with the fish and mushroom mixture, roll them up, and place them close together in a fireproof dish, or stack them like a cake, layered with the creamed fish. Pour the cream over them, sprinkle with cheese, and brown under the grill.

Vol-au-vent à la normande

A fine dish which can be adjusted to suit the resources of your fishmonger. Turbot, brill or John Dory could be used instead of sole. Prawns instead of oysters (include their shells when making stock for the *sauce normande*).

SERVES SIX
1–1½ pounds sole or other white fish
dry cider or dry white wine
12 oysters, or 18 cooked prawns or shrimp
2 pounds mussels
sauce normande (*page 35*), *made very thick*
½ pound mushrooms
2 ounces (4 tablespoons) butter

parsley, minced
1 large or 12 small baked vol-au-vent cases

Poach the sole or other fish in just enough cider or wine to cover them.

Open the oysters and mussels in the usual way (see page 174), add juice with the sole juices to the *sauce normande*. Cook the mushrooms gently in the butter: strain off the juice and add it to the sauce.

Divide the cooked sole or white fish into suitably small pieces. Reheat in the completed sauce with the oysters or prawns, and the mussels and mushrooms. Lastly mix in some parsley. Pour into the reheated vol-au-vent case(s) and serve immediately.

This is a recipe which can be prepared entirely in advance, apart from the final reheating.

Salt-water fish and mushroom recipes

Smoked haddock kulebiaka

This recipe, based on the Russian kulebiaka, makes a fine main course for a luncheon party. It's a rich, magnificent affair, so the rest of the meal should be light.

SERVES EIGHT GENEROUSLY, OR TEN

PASTRY:
1 pound (about 3½ cups) flour
8 ounces (16 tablespoons) unsalted butter, chilled
3 ounces (6 tablespoons) lard, chilled
1 teaspoon sea salt
iced water

Put flour in a bowl, cut butter in small pieces, and put with lard into the flour. Add salt. Rub to a crumbly mixture, then bind with iced water. Divide in two, one part a little larger than the other, and refrigerate for at least 2 hours. Meanwhile prepare the filling:

FILLING:
1½–2 pounds finnan haddock (smoked haddock)
2 cups milk
⅔ cup water
¾ cup long-grain rice or kasha
1¼ cups chicken stock
½ pound mushrooms, sliced
4 ounces (8 tablespoons) butter
lemon juice, salt, pepper
2 cups chopped onion
3 teaspoons dried dillweed,
  or 2 teaspoons curry powder
3 large hard-boiled eggs, chopped

GLAZE:
1 egg yolk
2 tablespoons cream

TO FINISH:
½ cup sour cream
8 ounces (16 tablespoons) butter
lemon juice

Cut haddock into several large pieces, and place in a saucepan. Bring milk and water to the boil, and pour over the fish. Stand it over a very low heat for 10 minutes: the liquid should not even simmer, just keep very hot. Remove skin and bone from drained, cooked fish and separate into large flakes (use cooking liquid for making a fish soup).

Cook rice or kasha (i.e., buckwheat, obtainable from health food shops—this is the correct cereal for kulebiaka, but I find the flavour a little strong and prefer rice) in the chicken stock and drain it.

Fry mushrooms in 1 ounce of the butter. Season with lemon juice, salt and pepper. In a separate pan, cook onion until tender in 2 ounces of butter: keep the lid on the pan, and the heat low, so that the onion does not brown. Season.

To assemble the pie, roll out the smaller piece of pastry to an oblong approximately 8 by 16 inches. Place it on a baking sheet which has been buttered or lined with paper. Place half the rice on top, leaving a 1-inch border free, and sprinkle half the dill or curry powder over it. Mix the glaze ingredients together and brush the free rim of pastry with it. On top of the rice put half the mushrooms, half the onions, half the hard-boiled eggs, and all the haddock. Then use up the remaining filling ingredients in reverse order, so that you finish with rice. Melt remaining ounce of butter and pour over.

Roll out the second sheet of pastry and drape it over the whole thing, pressing it down at the edges. Trim, then roll the edge into a piping effect, so that the whole kulebiaka looks like a pillow. Make a central hole, decorate top with leaves cut from the trimmings, and brush over to glaze with the egg yolk and cream. Bake 45 minutes, starting at mark 7, 425°F, then at mark 6, 400°F, as the pastry begins to brown.

Just before serving, bring sour cream to the boil and pour into the pie through a funnel placed in the central hole. Melt the butter, flavour it with lemon juice, and pour into a heated sauceboat. Have everything—serving dish, plates, and sauce—very hot.

N O T E : If you can lay your hand on some ceps, use them instead of mushrooms, allowing ¾ pound. The flavour will be even better.

Salmon kulebiaka

SERVES EIGHT GENEROUSLY, OR TEN
Substitute a generous pound of salmon for the smoked haddock in the preceding recipe. Slice it fairly thinly, and firm the slices in a little butter, but do not cook them right through.

Turbot (or sole) can also be used. The point is to have a fish of good texture and fine flavour.

Sole à la bonne femme

Although this and the following are two of the classic recipes for sole as given by Escoffier, they can equally well be used for other firm fish of quality. By this I mean turbot, or chicken halibut, or John Dory, which all have something of the firm, well-divided flesh which makes the sole such a desirable fish. Always keep a look-out for John Dory. Its large lugubrious head, and the black "fingerprints" of Saint Peter, one on either side, where he picked the fish up, make it easy to recognize. Although the big ones are best, the two-pounders, the small ones, are not to be despised, and the price is ridiculously low for such an exquisite fish. In January of 1973, when there was a fuss about high fish (and meat) prices, I was buying inshore John Dory from Cornwall at 20 pence the pound, in Oxford market; and in spite of the large heads of the fish, 50 pence bought enough for four people.

Naturally these recipes can be used for lesser lights, lemon sole, flounders, brill and so on, but there is always something disappointing in the unresistant softness of their flesh.

SERVES TWO

1 *chopped shallot*
½ *teaspoon minced parsley*
2 *ounces mushrooms, chopped*
1 *large sole, cleaned and skinned*
¼ *cup dry white wine*
¼ *cup hot water*
salt, pepper
juice of ½ *lemon*
4 *tablespoons butter*
1½ *tablespoons flour*

Rub an ovenproof oval dish with buttered paper. Put shallot, parsley, and mushrooms over the base in an even layer and lay the sole on top. Pour the wine and water over it, and season with salt, pepper and lemon juice. Cover with foil, and bake in a moderate oven, mark 4, 350°F, for 5 minutes. Meanwhile mash up one-third of the butter with the flour, to make a paste, and add it in little pieces to the sole liquor. Return to the oven until the sole is cooked—about 10 minutes, or a little longer.

Transfer the sole to a warm serving dish. Whisk the remaining butter into the cooking juices and pour over the sole. Put under a hot grill for a few minutes to brown lightly.

Sole à la fermière
(Sole in the style of the farmer's wife) ·

Fish cooked in red wine—another myth tumbles to the ground. Drink the rest of the bottle with the sole.

SERVES TWO

1 *shallot, chopped*
½ *teaspoon minced parsley*
sprig thyme
half a bay leaf
6 *ounces mushrooms*
1 *large sole*
¾ *cup red wine*
salt, pepper
2½ *ounces (5 tablespoons) butter*
1 *teaspoon flour*

Grease an oval flameproof dish, and put in the shallot, thyme and bay leaf. Chop 2 ounces of the mushrooms, and add them. Lay the sole on top, pour in the wine, and add seasoning. Cover and cook gently on top of the stove until the sole is cooked. Meanwhile slice the remaining mushrooms neatly and cook them in 1 ounce of the butter, tossing them about so that they are golden but still firm and in no danger of being overcooked. Arrange them round the edge of an oval serving dish, and place the cooked sole in the middle. Keep warm while you finish the sauce. Boil it down to half quantity. Mash together the flour with an equal amount of butter, and add it to the sauce in pieces. When the sauce is ready, whisk in the remaining butter off the heat, and strain it over the fish. Place under a hot grill for a moment or two to glaze.

Sole à la rouennaise
(Sole in the Rouen style)

Here is another exception to the rule of white wine with fish. As in the preceding recipe, the robust flavour of red wine does not at all spoil the delicate sole and shellfish.

SERVES TWO

1 *large sole, skinned*
½ *cup red wine*
2 *shallots, minced*
4 *ounces (8 tablespoons) butter*
12 *large mussels*
12 *oysters (if possible)*
12 *cooked prawns or shrimp in their shells*
4 *ounces button mushrooms*
1 *egg yolk*
salt, pepper

Put the sole into a shallow pan. Add wine, shallots and 1 ounce of butter. Simmer until cooked.

Meanwhile open the mussels in the usual way (see page 174). Discard their shells, and strain their cooking liquor into a bowl. Open the oysters; simmer them in their own liquor for a few moments until their edges just start to curl. Strain the cooking juice into the mussel liquor. Peel 8 of the prawns or shrimp. Cook the mushrooms in 1 ounce of the butter. These mussels, oysters, prawns, or shrimp and mushrooms are the garnishes for the sole. Keep them warm. The mussel and oyster juice will be required for the sauce.

Remove the cooked sole to a hot serving dish. (Pour its cooking juices into the mussel and oyster juices.) Arrange the garnishes around the sole and keep everything warm.

Pour the fish juices into a pan and reduce to a fairly strong-flavoured liquid. Beat the egg yolk with a little of this liquid, then tip it back into the pan and stir over a low heat until the sauce thickens (*do not boil, or it will curdle*). Off the heat, whisk in the remaining butter, and strain the sauce over the sole. Place the 4 unshelled prawns in the centre, and serve.

Sole, turbot, John Dory, monkfish, or whiting à la dieppoise
(Sole, turbot, John Dory, monkfish, or whiting in the style of Dieppe)

The Dieppe garnish of mushrooms, mussels and prawns in a creamy sauce is a perfect accompaniment to good white fish. The mushroom juices colour the sauce a delicate grey, which makes a beautiful background for the pink prawns and orange mussels. If you are one of the lucky people who live where oysters are cheap, they can be used instead of mussels: open them in the usual way, and simmer them for a minute in their own liquor.

SERVES SIX

5 ounces (10 tablespoons) butter
fish fillets or steaks for 6 people
12 ounces cooked prawns or shrimp in their shells
1¼ cups dry white wine
2 pounds mussels, scrubbed and scraped
12 ounces mushrooms, sliced
lemon juice
salt, pepper
1 tablespoon arrowroot or cornstarch
½ cup heavy cream
parsley, chopped

Grease a flameproof pan with 1 ounce of butter, and place fish in it in a single layer. Remove shells from most of the prawns, and simmer shells with wine for 15 minutes. Then remove the shells. Meanwhile put mussels into a large pan over a high heat, cover, and shake gently until they open: discard shells and any mussels that refuse to open, keep mussels warm, and strain their liquor into the wine pan. Cook mushrooms, not too fiercely, in 2 ounces of butter and some lemon juice, so that they exude a certain amount of juice: when they are done, keep them warm and strain the juice into the wine pan. Pour all these liquids over the fish, taste for seasoning, and simmer the fish until *just* done: remove to a serving dish, surround with shelled prawns, mussels and mushrooms, and keep warm. Thicken cooking juices first by boiling down to a strong flavour, then beat up the starch with the cream and stir that in bit by bit until the sauce is thickened. Off the heat, stir in remaining butter, and pour over fish; add remaining prawns in their shells, sprinkle with parsley, and serve.

Cabillaud à la paysanne normande (Cod in the Normandy peasant style)

A simplified version of the fine Normandy style of cooking fish, more suitable for cod. Buy the tailpiece of a reasonably small fish if you can, and ask the fishmonger not to remove the skin and bones.

SERVES SIX
3 ounces (6 tablespoons) butter
3-pound piece cod
⅔ cup cider
¾ pound mushrooms, sliced
3 shallots, minced
salt, pepper
1¼ cups heavy cream
3 pounds mussels
4 ounces cooked and shelled shrimp
parsley, minced

Grease an ovenproof dish about the size of the cod with half the butter and place the cod in it. Pour cider over fish. Push mushrooms and shallots into the gaps. Season well and pour half the cream over. Open the mussels in the usual way (see page 174); discard their shells, and if mussels are very large, cut them into quarters. Strain the mussel liquor over the cod. Put the cod into a fairly hot oven, mark 6, 400°F, until the liquid begins to boil, then lower the heat to mark 5, 375°F, cover with foil, and leave for 20 minutes until the cod is cooked. Just before serving, bring shrimps and mussels to the boil in the remaining cream and pour over the cod. Correct the seasoning of the sauce. Sprinkle with parsley and serve in cooking dish with boiled potatoes, or good bread.

Filets de sole Walewska
(Fillets of sole Walewska)

This dish—invented, I believe, by Escoffier—is named after Napoleon's Polish mistress, Marie Walewska. It is simple to prepare, but expensive on account of the lobster and truffles. Dublin Bay prawns could be used instead, or crawfish tails.

SERVES FOUR

8 fillets of sole (or other firm fish)
2 cups fish stock (see appendix)
3 cups béchamel sauce (see appendix)
2 tablespoons grated Parmesan cheese
2 tablespoons butter
8 slices truffle
8–12 slices cooked lobster, or cooked prawns or shrimp

Poach the sole in the fish stock. When just cooked, transfer it to a serving dish and keep warm. Boil the stock down vigorously until it has a strong concentrated flavour. Heat the béchamel sauce, add stock to it, and boil them both together for a few moments. Off the heat, stir the cheese and butter into the sauce. Arrange the truffle slices and lobster or prawns on top of the sole, pour the sauce over them, and place under a very hot grill for a few moments to glaze.

Brandade de morue truffée
(Truffled brandade of salt cod)

The Good Friday dish of southern France, and a great speciality of Nîmes. Apart from the final delicious result, I enjoy making this recipe for the satisfaction of turning what looks like a kite-shaped piece of yellowing, greyish leather into a creamy rich emulsion.

Cod à la paysanne normande / **169**

SERVES SIX
2-pound piece salt cod
2½ cups olive oil
1 large clove garlic, crushed
1¼ cups light cream
salt, pepper, nutmeg
2 tablespoons minced parsley
4 ounces raw truffle, chopped
triangles of bread fried in butter,
  or vol-au-vent case(s)

Soak the cod for between 24 and 48 hours, changing the water three times. Cut into large pieces, put into a pan, cover with water, and bring to the boil; simmer for 10 minutes—the cod is not fully cooked, but it can easily be removed from the skin and bones Put the cod flakes into a clean pan. Warm one-fourth of the oil, and add it and the garlic to the fish. Stir vigorously with a wooden spoon to crush the cod and amalgamate it with the oil. Set over a low to moderate heat. Warm the rest of the oil and cream, and add them alternately, in small amounts, until the cod is reduced to a creamy purée. Season with salt, pepper and nutmeg, and stir in the parsley and truffle. Serve very hot with the croutons or in puff pastry—the *brandade* can be prepared in advance and reheated, but do not add the final seasonings or the truffle until the last minute.

Ragoût de laitances aux morilles
(Ragout of soft roes with morels)

A recipe of Carême's, from his *Art de la cuisine française aux dix-neuvième siècle* (1833–35). A ragout was used to garnish a large entrée, as a kind of super-sauce. Nowadays we eat such things at the beginning of a meal on their own, or for supper, as a rule. But whether you do this, or whether you follow Carême's system and use the ragout to set off a poached chicken turbot or something of the kind, try to get hold of very large, well-separated pairs of soft roes. So often they are all messed up together in a plastic bowl, which does nothing for the final appearance of the dish.

SERVES FOUR

1 pound soft mackerel or herring roes
3 ounces (6 tablespoons) butter
juice of 1 lemon
1¼ cups boiling water
salt
½ pound morels
1¼ cups cream sauce (see appendix)

Cook the roes on both sides in half the butter until they begin to turn opaque. Add the lemon and boiling water with some salt, and simmer until cooked. Drain them (the liquid can be kept for soup), and keep them warm.

Meanwhile fry the morels in the remaining butter. Heat the cream sauce, add the morels, and correct the seasoning. Arrange the roes on a serving dish, pour the sauce over, and serve. A few croutons of fried bread, or *biscottes,* go well with this dish: it can also be used to fill vol-au-vent cases, or chou puffs.

Herring roe and mushroom flan

For the best results, choose well-separated herring roes, even if this means an effort of character. Too many fishmongers paw a horrible-looking muddle on to a little bit of greaseproof paper. One answer is to buy large soft-roed herrings for lunch one day, and keep their roes to make this delicious flan for a dinner party next day.

SERVES FOUR TO SIX
6 ounces shortcrust pastry
about 12 ounces soft herring roes
6 ounces mushrooms
1 ounce (2 tablespoons) butter
salt, pepper
⅔ cup heavy cream ⎫
⅓ cup sour cream ⎬ or 1 cup sour cream
2 eggs ⎭
3 tablespoons minced parsley

Line a flan tin, 8 to 9 inches, with a removable base, with the pastry. Bake blind for 15 minutes, at mark 5, 375°F.

Meanwhile pour boiling water over the roes, leave for 5 minutes to firm up, then drain and cut them in roughly half-inch pieces. In a small pan, cook the mushrooms in the butter. Season. Mix cream, eggs, and parsley and beat well. Season this mixture, too.

Take the pastry out of the oven. Lay the mushrooms evenly over the base, then the soft roes. Pour the cream mixture over that. Bake at the same temperature for about 30 to 35 minutes, until set. Serve hot or warm, with a green salad to follow if it is to be the main course of a meal.

Kipper or matjes herring salad with mushrooms

A good hors d'oeuvre if served really cold.

SERVES FOUR
3 large kippers (not frozen fillets),
  or 6 nice matjes fillets
4 ounces young, fresh mushrooms
chopped chives, or thin onion rings

DRESSING:

well-sweetened vinaigrette made with corn oil and wine vinegar
  or *an olive oil and lemon dressing with a little sugar*
  or *sour cream*
  or *heavy cream, seasoned with lemon juice*

Kippers can be used without further cooking, if they are of high quality: discard the skin and bones with the aid of a sharp knife, and cut the fillets into half-inch slices. The alternative is to put the kippers tail down in a large container and pour boiling water over them: remove after 2 or 3 minutes before they soften too much, then discard skin and bone. Matjes fillets may need soaking. Taste a tiny corner to see. (If you can get hold of a packet of French *harengs saurs* fillets, they are the best of all: they don't usually need soaking.)

Place the fish pieces in a serving dish, and slice the mushrooms, then fit them between the fish pieces. Pour over whichever dressing you have chosen—keep vinaigrette to a minimum or else the dish will be too wet and lose crispness. Top with chives or onion rings. Chill well.

Gratin de pommes de terre aux anchois
(Potatoes gratin with anchovies)

SERVES FOUR

Turn to the recipe on page 118 for *gratin de pommes de terre aux champignons*, and add 2 tins of anchovies and 1 onion finely sliced to the ingredients. Place these two extra items in a single layer in the centre of the gratin, and complete according to the recipe.

This is a version of the Swedish "Jansson's temptation," a dish of admirable piquancy.

Shellfish and mushroom recipes

Moules à la poulette

A favourite French dish. The yellowish white sauce looks most appetizing with the navy blue shells and orange flesh of the mussels: the flavour is wonderful, even better than the appearance of the dish.

SERVES SIX
4 quarts mussels (about 6 pounds)
ingredients for sauce poulette *(page 35), using only 4 ounces sliced mushrooms*

Scrub and scrape mussels, discarding any that are broken. Open them in a large pan over high heat, and discard any that do not open. There is no need to put any wine or water with them: just keep the pan closed and they will open in their own steam after about 5 minutes. Remove them with tongs to a strainer set over a bowl. Throw away the half-shells, place the mussels in a large bowl, and keep them warm. Strain the mussel liquor carefully and use in making the sauce.

Pour the sauce over the bowl of mussels and serve immediately with plenty of good bread to mop up the plates.

Moules (huîtres, praires) farcies
(Stuffed mussels, or oysters, or clams)

There are few things I'd rather eat than small shellfish cooked in this way. To be honest, oysters would be my first choice because they have that delicate sharpness that makes them one of the best things it's possible to eat. But clams and mussels provide a starred dish too; and mussels, big, sweet orange mussels, are one of the cheapest pleasures of food in England. This recipe is the best way of showing them off—the crispness of the bread makes just the right foil for the buttery juices. Buy more than the 6 dozen mussels, oysters or clams you need for this recipe, to allow for those that must be discarded because they do not open.

SERVES SIX
about 7 pounds large mussels (or oysters or clams)
1–2 round or cottage bread loaves
lemon wedges (optional)

MUSHROOM BUTTER:
1 pound unsalted butter
4-ounce bunch parsley, minced
2 ounces mushrooms, chopped
8–12 cloves garlic, minced
1 slice cooked ham, chopped
freshly ground black pepper
sea salt

GRATIN:
1 cup breadcrumbs
2 ounces mushrooms, minced

Clean and open the mussels (or oysters or clams) in the usual way (see preceding recipe). Leave the mussels (you need 6 dozen of them) on the half-shell to cool, and discard the remaining shells. Strain the shellfish liquor and keep it for another recipe.

Meanwhile cut six "trenchers" of bread across the loaves. Using an apple corer, make 12 holes in each one so that the shells can rest in them without wobbling. One needs to make a double hole in each case, of a blunted oval shape.

To make the mushroom butter, all you have to do is mash the ingredients together. I find it saves time to chop the parsley, mushroom, garlic and ham all together in a food mill or in a blender. Mash this mixture up with the butter and season it to taste.

Preheat the oven to mark 8, 450°F. Spread a nice knob of the butter on top of each mussel, and round the sides. The mussel will probably show through in the centre, but it doesn't matter. Arrange the mussels as evenly as you can on their trenchers of bread; put them on baking sheets. Mix the gratin ingredients and scatter them over the mussels. Put the trays in the preheated oven, and immediately reduce the heat to mark 4, 350°F. Leave them for 10 minutes for the butter to melt and bubble, and the tops of the mussels and the edges of the bread to brown and crisp.

Serve with wedges of lemon, if you like, but they are not really necessary.

Coquilles Saint-Jacques sautées aux champignons (Scallops fried with mushrooms)

The French are particularly good at this kind of fried mixture, which really makes one's mouth water. It's the kind of dish I like to eat in the evening, because the smell and flavour immediately rouse one's tired appetite. And because of this deliciousness, the small quantity is completely satisfying.

SERVES SIX
20–24 scallops
small bunch parsley
1 large clove garlic
3 shallots, or 5 tablespoons chopped onion
½ pound button mushrooms
juice of ½ lemon
4 ounces (8 tablespoons) butter
4 tablespoons oil
salt, freshly ground black pepper
6 lemon slices

Separate the coral part of the scallops from the central white disc. Throw away the black part and the piece of hard skin. Cut the white disc into dice; chop coral finely to reduce it to a rough purée. Chop parsley, garlic, and shallots or onion together, and add the coral.

Sprinkle mushrooms with lemon juice (if they are on the large side, halve or quarter them). Fry in 1 ounce of butter in a small pan, then keep them warm. Meanwhile heat another ounce of butter in a separate pan with the oil. Colour the diced scallop in this, stirring it about, for 3 or 4 minutes: the temperature should be fairly high, but the fat must not burn or the flavour will be spoilt. Stir in the coral and parsley hash, and cook for another few minutes until well heated. Add mushrooms and remaining butter. Season, being especially generous with the pepper. Divide among six deep scallop shells, or six individual pots, place a slice of lemon on top of each one, and serve very hot.

Mushrooms with oysters

Like many expensive dishes, this one has the compensation of being simple to prepare. It's from *The Gentle Art of Cookery*, by Mrs C. F. Leyel and Miss Olga Hartley (1925).

SERVES TWO
12 oysters
12 medium mushrooms
butter
salt, pepper

Open the oysters. Clean the mushrooms and remove their stalks (use for another dish). Fry the mushroom caps lightly in some butter, then place them, gill side up, in one layer in a buttered ovenproof dish. Slip an oyster into each cap, and put a dab of butter on top, with some salt and pepper. Bake in a hot oven (mark 7, 425°F), until the oysters are opaque but not overcooked.

If you like, a good béchamel sauce can be served with the dish, but it isn't necessary.

Croissants aux crevettes
(Croissants with prawn and mushroom filling)

The first croissants are said to have been made in Budapest. The Turks were laying siege to the city in 1686. They had tunnelled to the centre, when the bakers, who as usual were working at night, heard noises beneath their feet, and raised the alarm. As a reward they were given permission to make a special pastry, shaped like a crescent, the emblem of the frustrated Turks. Sadly—like many other cookery stories—there is no evidence for this: the tale is also told of Vienna. But whatever the truth of its origin, the croissant soon became popular right across Europe from the Austrian Empire to Switzerland and France.

One thing, though, is sure—croissants vary enormously in kind and quality wherever you buy them. In our small town in France, and in many others, the bakers produce a bread-like croissant; the *pâtissiers* go for a puff pastry crispness.

If you have any choice in the matter, it's the puff pastry type you should use for this recipe (you could always use puff pastry dough, rolled up in the right manner). Not being blessed with a first-class baker in our part of Wiltshire, I always buy rolls of crescent dough which are now on sale all over Britain, and bake them myself. These rolls are an honest "convenience" food. The results are not up to the highest Parisian or Viennese standard, but they compare favourably with many croissants on sale in France and Austria. And they compare even more favourably with the croissants I make myself—quite apart from the saving in time and energy.

You could fill croissants with many of the mushroom recipes in this book, using them as a substitute for other pastry cases such as vol-au-vent, but this is a particularly successful dish. The prawns, mushrooms and cheese (which must be Gruyère) are a piquant combination well set off by the cream sauce and the crisp brownness of the croissants.

SERVES SIX

1 *pound prawns or shrimp in their shells*
2 *cups thick béchamel sauce (see appendix)*
2 *egg yolks*
4 *tablespoons cream*
1 *cup grated Gruyère*
salt, pepper
3 *ounces (6 tablespoons) butter*
3–4 *ounces mushrooms, chopped*
1 *small clove garlic, minced*
6 *croissants, or 1 roll crescent dough*
beaten egg to glaze

Shell prawns, and simmer their *shells* in the béchamel sauce, covered, for 15 minutes, then sieve energetically. You will have a pinkish sauce, of delicious flavour: it's surprising how much the shells can contribute. Add the egg yolks, the cream and half the cheese, then reheat over a moderate flame until very thick, but don't boil. Season and beat in half the butter. In remaining butter, cook the mushrooms and garlic briskly, so that the juices evaporate to a concentrated essence. Stir into the sauce, with the prawn or shrimp *meat*. Set aside, while the croissants are baked: give them 15 minutes for extra crispness and remember to brush them over with beaten egg. Ready-made croissants will only need reheating.

To assemble the dish, slit the croissants from the back and remove any soft bits of dough from the interior. Put a good spoonful of the reheated prawn filling into each croissant and arrange on a fireproof serving dish: any filling left over can be put in the middle. Put the remaining Gruyère cheese on top of the croissants and place under a hot grill for a few moments, so that the cheese begins to melt.

Croissants aux crevettes / **179**

Omelette du Baron de Barante

This recipe comes from a small booklet produced by François Minot, chef-patron at the famous Hôtel du Côte d'Or at Saulieu. One of his grandfathers—he is fifth in a line of chefs—spent some time in Russia, as did the famous chef Edouard de Nignon, who invented this recipe. The Baron de Barante was one of the greatest gourmets of his time.

SERVES SIX TO EIGHT

salt
1 pound mushrooms, sliced
butter
⅓ cup good port
about 1¼ cups heavy cream
12 thick slices cooked lobster tail
18 eggs
1½ cups Mornay sauce
grated Parmesan cheese

Season mushrooms and cook in some butter. Add port and reduce liquid by half. Pour the cream in, stir it well, and add the lobster. Cover and cook very gently, so as not to make the lobster tough and tasteless.

Make one or more omelettes with the eggs, seasoned in the usual way. Put the lobster filling inside, and roll the omelette(s) over. Pour some Mornay sauce over, sprinkle with grated cheese, and put under a hot grill until the cheese turns a fine golden glaze.

Omelette normande

SERVES FOUR TO SIX
½ pound shelled prawns or shrimp
¾ pound mushrooms, cooked in butter
18 oysters or mussels, shelled
about 2 cups sauce normande (page 35)
12 eggs
butter

salt, pepper
black truffle slices (optional)

Mix shrimps, mushrooms and oysters or mussels: use about half the *sauce normande* to bind them together, and reheat gently.

Make the omelette(s) in the usual way with eggs, butter and seasoning, and put the filling in the centre. Pour the remaining sauce, which should also be hot, round the omelette, and, if possible, decorate with slices of black truffle. Serve immediately.

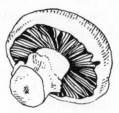

Fresh-water fish and mushroom recipes

Truite au pastis
(Trout with pastis)

One of my favourite recipes, though I would not use it for freshly caught trout (they need the simplest cooking *à la meunière*, with a final sanding of black pepper on their crisp skin). This recipe is for frozen trout, and it turns them into a most presentable dish. The use of anise flavourings (from the Chinese star anise, *badiane* in French, not from aniseed) is common in fish cookery in the south and south-west of France. Pastis country. The recipe can be used also for good salt-water fish—turbot, John Dory, sole and so on.

SERVES SIX

6 *trout*
seasoned flour
6 *ounces* (12 *tablespoons*) *butter*
1 *pound sliced mushrooms, preferably ceps*
3 *cloves garlic, minced*
salt, pepper
½ *cup pastis Ricard or Pernod*
1 *cup heavy cream*

Turn trout in seasoned flour. Clarify butter by bringing it to a boil in a small pan, then pouring it through a muslin-lined sieve into a frying pan. Fry trout in the butter at a moderate heat, allowing 6 minutes a side if frozen, and 4 to 5 minutes if thawed. Remove and keep warm. Raise the heat and cook mushrooms in the pan juices with the garlic. Season and pour in the pastis. After a few moments of hard bubbling, stir in cream and continue to cook for a little longer until the sauce is well amalgamated and thick. Check seasoning, pour sauce round trout, and serve.

Truites aux cèpes
(Trout with ceps)

Another recipe for this excellent combination of trout and ceps.

SERVES FOUR

4 *trout*
1¼ *cups white wine*
salt
12–16 *ounces ceps* (*or field mushrooms*)
⅓ *cup chopped onion*
2 *ounces* (4 *tablespoons*) *butter*
2½ *tablespoons flour*
1 *cup light stock*
3 *tablespoons tomato purée*
parsley, chopped

Poach trout in the white wine, with a little salt. When cooked, pour off the juices, strain, and reserve. Cover the fish with buttered paper and keep warm.

Meanwhile slice the mushroom caps and chop the stalks. Cook onion until soft but not browned in the butter. Stir in the flour, then the stock and the wine reserved from cooking the trout. Add the mushrooms, stalks and all, and the tomato purée, and simmer for 20 minutes. Correct the seasoning. Pour over the trout, and flash under the grill to brown lightly. Scatter parsley on top and serve.

Tanches à la poulette
(Tench [or other river fish] with sauce poulette)

A recipe from the great chef Carême, from his book on the art of French cooking in the nineteenth century.

SERVES SIX

3 *fine tench or catfish, or 6 small (8-ounce) fish*
2 *onions, minced*
2 *tablespoons minced parsley*
½ *large clove garlic, minced*
bouquet garni
1 *large leaf of basil*
2 *cloves*
grated nutmeg
salt, pepper
2 *ounces (4 tablespoons) melted butter*
1 *bottle Chablis*

SAUCE:

3 *ounces (6 tablespoons) butter*
⅓ *cup flour*
8–12 *ounces mushrooms*
3 *egg yolks*

PLUS:

12 *slices bread*
butter

Clean the tench, and cut each one into four pieces. If using smaller fish, clean but leave whole. In a shallow ovenproof baking dish, make a bed of the next eight ingredients. Put the fish on top, then pour the melted butter and Chablis over them. Bake in a moderate oven, or cook on top of the stove, until the fish is firm to the touch, and just cooked. Strain off the cooking liquor and keep the fish warm while you make the sauce.

To make the sauce, melt 2 ounces of the butter, stir in the flour, cook for 2 minutes, then stir in the strained fish cooking liquor. Clean and trim the mushrooms, and add their trimmings to the sauce. Reduce sauce to a good consistency. Meanwhile cook mushroom caps separately in remaining ounce of butter. Strain sauce, add a little of it to the egg yolks, then slowly thicken sauce with this mixture, without boiling. Add mushroom caps, and correct the seasoning.

Cut the bread into heart shapes. Clarify some butter by bringing it to a boil in a small pan, then pouring it through a muslin-lined sieve into a frying pan. Fry the bread in the butter.

Now assemble the dish for serving. Place the pieces of fish on a warm plate, alternating with the croutons. Pour the sauce over, and serve.

Matelote of eel (and other fish)

Matelote, as its name implies, is a fish stew, a sailors' stew. I always think of it as a red wine stew, containing a sumptuous miscellany of eel, mushrooms, glazed onions, prunes, and tiny bits of fried bread. But that is because I spend my time in the country of the Loir. If I lived in Normandy, I should expect to eat sea fish, hopefully sole, with some mussels, and the whole thing would be cooked in cider and thickened with cream. But the mushrooms would still be there, and the little triangles of bread. The whole thing would be more like the *bouilleture* which comes next.

But I shall stick to my own experience of what a matelote should be, and you can alter it to suit your resources, too. The one thing that matters is to get the sauce right first, the long simmering over, before the fish is cooked: the opposite in fact to a meat stew such as *boeuf à la bourguignonne*. To avoid overcooking, which is the besetting sin when dealing with fish, divide a mixed bag of fish into three different piles—on one plate, the thick close-textured fish such as turbot or halibut, on the next the middle fish such as cod, and finally the flatfish and mussels or cooked prawns which will need to cook no more than three or four minutes. Remember that they will all continue to cook in the heat of the sauce as you bring the matelote to table. Which is why you should never keep it waiting around.

SERVES SIX
3 pounds eel, or mixed fish
brandy (optional)
24 prunes
4½ cups red wine
1 large onion, sliced
1 stalk celery, sliced
1 medium carrot, chopped
1 leek
bouquet garni
½ teaspoon peppercorns
24 button mushrooms
4 ounces (8 tablespoons) butter
24 small onions (pickling size), peeled
sugar
1½ tablespoons flour
salt, pepper
18 triangles bread fried in butter
parsley, chopped

Trim and cut up all the eel or fish. Pour the brandy over it, if used, and leave to marinate. Soak the prunes, if they are the kind that need it, in half the wine. Put the rest of the wine into a large pan with the sliced onion, celery, carrot, leek, bouquet, peppercorns and garlic. Simmer for an hour.

Arrange the eel, or thickest pieces of fish, in a pan with the prunes and any soaking liquor. Strain the wine over them. Bring to simmering point and leave for 20 minutes, until the eel is cooked. (With other kinds of fish, add the middle-sized pieces when the thick ones have been cooking for 5 minutes, and the last lot 5 minutes later.)

While the eel is cooking, fry the mushrooms in 2 ounces of the butter, fairly rapidly so that the mushrooms turn a nice golden brown without being overcooked. Set aside. Place onions in a single layer in a large pan. Cover them with water, and add another ounce of the butter and about a tablespoon of sugar. Boil hard until the water is reduced to a syrupy glaze. Now go carefully and watch the pan so that the syrup doesn't burn: it should cook to a beautiful golden brown colour. Turn the onions about in it to coat them nicely, and remove from the fire.

The eel (or fish) should now be finished cooking. Remove it along with the prunes to a serving dish. Thicken its cooking liquid by mashing the remaining of the butter with the flour and add the mixture in small bits so that the sauce thickens gradually. Taste it and adjust the seasoning if need be. A hint of sugar is a good idea if the wine was on the ordinary side, but remember that the onions will be sweet, so go easy. Arrange the mushrooms and onions with the fish and prunes in the serving dish. Tuck the bread triangles round the edge, pour the sauce over the fish (if the sauce is too abundant, serve the surplus in a sauceboat), and sprinkle with parsley.

This sounds a long, complicated recipe, but it's simple enough once you understand how a matelote is constructed, and the reasons for the various stages. Obviously you could cook the small onions and mushrooms in the general mêlée, but richness and the beautiful contrast and balance of textures and flavours would be lost. At each step of this dish, you can control and adjust the recipe. And if, for instance, at the end you think the sauce is on the thin-flavoured side, boil it down hard until you like it better, before thickening with the beurre manié.

Bouilleture d'anguilles
(Eel stew)

This dish from Anjou is a kind of matelote, but it's made from "white" ingredients. It is, in consequence, a mild dish, more what one expects from *le douceur angevin*. The correct wine to use is a Saumur, but price and availability are likely to make this impossible, and you will have to substitute an ordinary dry white wine.

SERVES SIX
3 pounds eels
juice of a lemon
4 ounces (8 tablespoons) butter
¼ cup brandy
½ pound button mushrooms
2 cups dry white wine
1 bay leaf
salt, pepper
1 large egg yolk
¼ cup heavy cream
parsley, chopped
½ pound prunes, soaked and simmered in tea (optional)

Ask the fishmonger to skin and cut up the eel for you. Before cooking it, sprinkle with lemon juice, leave for 20 minutes or so, then pat dry. Melt half the butter in a large heavy frying pan, and fry the eel until it is lightly coloured. Warm the brandy, set it alight, and pour over the eel. Turn the pieces about in the flames. Add the mushrooms, cover, and cook gently for 10 minutes. Now pour in the wine and tuck bay leaf into the centre. Season. Raise the heat and cook vigorously, without a lid on the pan, for a further 10 minutes. By now the eel should be done, but check the thickest piece to see—the flesh should be just parting from the bone. Remove to a serving dish with the mushrooms and keep warm. Throw away the bay leaf. Beat the egg yolk and cream together, and add a little of the sauce. Return this mixture to the sauce slowly: keep the heat low so that it can thicken without boiling. Allow 5 minutes. Correct the seasoning and, off the heat, stir in the remaining butter. Pour sauce over the eel and mushrooms, sprinkle with parsley, and serve very hot.

If you like the idea of the cooked prunes with eel in a creamy sauce—though to my mind they go better with the red wine matelote—drain them and put them round the eel with the mushrooms. Keep everything warm while you finish the sauce as above.

N O T E : Other fish can be used instead of eel. Sole, for instance, or turbot, or any good fresh white fish. Cook rather more gently than the eel, and reduce the liquid by hard boiling when the fish has been safely removed to the serving plate to keep warm.

MUSHROOMS WITH MEAT, POULTRY, AND GAME

Boeuf à la bourguignonne
(Beef in the Burgundy style)

This is the stew of stews, an apotheosis of stew, which has nothing whatever to do with the watery, stringy mixture served up in British institutions. It's a rich, carefully cooked recipe which is served up on special occasions in French homes, and which appears without shame on the menus of high-class restaurants. The *bourguignonne* garnish is mushrooms, small button mushrooms fried in butter, glazed small onions and triangles of fried bread: these should all be cooked separately and amalgamated with the main part of the dish just before it comes to table. The method can be used for topside, chuck or shin of beef, or for ox tail, also for venison or for a good roasting or boiling fowl (*coq au vin*): the cooking time will vary, that is all. The same ingredients are also used for matelote of eel, but as the method is different I have given that recipe separately.

The dish can be prepared in two stages; the main cooking can be completed a day in advance (this means that any fat rising to the top can easily be removed when the dish has cooled down, a great advantage when preparing ox tail). On the day you intend to eat the dish, reheat it thoroughly, prepare the garnish, and serve. If you use a cheap red wine, rather than a Burgundy, compensate for the thinner flavour by adding a tablespoon of sugar. If you have no brandy, use another spirit—whisky, gin, Calvados, vodka, whatever you may have to hand.

SERVES SIX

2–3 *pounds round roast, chuck steak or shin of beef*
  or *2 oxtails*
  or *1 large roasting chicken*

MARINADE:
2½–3 *cups red wine*
⅓ *cup brandy*
1 *large onion, sliced*
bouquet garni

sprig rosemary (optional)
12 peppercorns
1 teaspoon salt

SAUCE:

2 ounces (4 tablespoons) beef drippings or butter
½ pound piece of bacon, cut in strips
2 large onions, chopped
2 large carrots, diced
3 cloves garlic, crushed
2½ tablespoons flour
beef or chicken stock
bouquet garni
2 tablespoons sugar (optional)
salt, freshly ground black pepper

GARNISH:

1½ pounds small or pickling onions, peeled
2 tablespoons sugar
4 ounces (8 tablespoons) butter
salt, pepper
½–¾ pound tiny button mushrooms
6 slices bread, cut in triangles, crusts removed
2 tablespoons oil
parsley, minced

Cut up meat into cubes or pieces as appropriate. Mix marinade ingredients together and leave the meat in it at least 6 hours, then strain off liquid and reserve.

Heat the drippings or butter, and brown the bacon strips lightly. Transfer to a casserole. Pat meat dry, and brown it next, then onions, carrots, and garlic, transferring them to the casserole in their turn. Sprinkle flour into the pan juices, cook for a moment, then add the strained marinade to make a smooth sauce. Pour into casserole, adding enough beef or chicken stock to cover the meat, plus bouquet and the sugar if you wish. Season. Put on lid and simmer either on top of the stove or in the oven at a low temperature until meat is cooked—about 2 to 3 hours, possibly longer with ox tail (the meat should be parting from the bone).

About 45 minutes before the end of cooking time, prepare the garnish. Put onions in a closely packed single layer in a large pan, add sugar and 1 ounce of butter, plus a good pinch of salt and some black pepper. Boil hard, without covering the pan, until the onions are cooked and a little syrupy brown juice remains. Shake the pan so that the onions are thoroughly coated and become an appetizing brown. Watch this, or the whole thing will suddenly burn to a nasty black colour. Meanwhile cook the mushrooms in another ounce of butter. Fry bread in remaining butter and oil. Keep everything hot.

When the meat is cooked, it will appeal more to stew-haters if you remove it from the casserole and place it on a large shallow dish with the garnish tucked round it. Keep warm while you reduce the sauce by boiling to a very rich concentrated flavour. This is really the whole point of success with stews. Pour this sauce over the meat, stopping before the dish becomes sloppy, sprinkle with parsley, and serve.

Paupiettes forestières
(Stuffed veal rolls forestières)

This recipe from Berry, the area around Bourges, is a variation of a popular French dish, which is sometimes called *alouettes sans têtes*—birds without heads. If you make it with beef instead of veal, some butchers can be persuaded to cut the thin slices necessary on their bacon-slicing machines. The following recipe has been slightly adapted from *La Vraie Cuisine du Berry et de l'Orléanais*, by Roger Lallemand. There are plenty of chestnuts and mushrooms in the Berrichon woods, and the white wines of Sancerre and Quincy are famous.

SERVES SIX TO EIGHT
24 chestnuts, peeled
1¼ cups beef or veal stock
6 ounces high-meat-content sausage
1 onion, chopped

1 large clove garlic, crushed
butter
milk
1 cup breadcrumbs
1 egg
cep stalks, chopped
salt, pepper
16 slices round steak or veal scallops, about 1 ounce each
3-ounce piece pork or bacon fat, or some pork skin
1 onion, sliced
1 carrot, sliced
1¼ cups dry white wine
flour
handful ceps or girolles

Put the chestnuts to simmer in the stock until just cooked. Drain off the stock and reserve for later. Set chestnuts aside.

To make the stuffing, remove skins from sausage. Cook the chopped onion with garlic until soft but not browned in 2 ounces of butter. Add just enough milk to the breadcrumbs to moisten slightly. Mix with sausage, cooked onion and garlic, egg, and cep stalks. Season well, divide among the slices of meat, and roll each slice up, turning the sides over to enclose the stuffing. Tie each *paupiette* twice with button thread.

In a heatproof pan, cook the pork or bacon fat gently until the fat runs. Put in the sliced onion and carrot and simmer for about 10 minutes, before adding the *paupiettes*. Raise the heat slightly, so that they brown a little but not much. Remove the pork or bacon fat and pour in the stock in which the chestnuts cooked. Mix the wine with a teaspoon of flour and add that too. Bring to the boil, cover, and transfer to the oven, mark 3–4, 325°– 350°F; after half an hour remove the cover. Fry the mushrooms lightly in 2 ounces of butter, and set aside. After another half-hour of cooking, turn the *paupiettes* over and add the chestnuts and the mushrooms. Cook for another half-hour—the important thing is never to let the liquid boil hard: turn the heat down if necessary.

When the *paupiettes* are ready, cut off the threads, and arrange with the chestnuts, mushrooms and vegetables on a hot serving dish. Boil down the juice until it has a good concentrated flavour. Thicken it, if you like, with beurre manié (1 tablespoon flour mashed into 1 tablespoon butter, and added to the sauce in small bits: after 5 minutes of gentle cooking, it should become smooth and thick). Pour some of the sauce over the *paupiettes*, and serve the rest in a sauceboat.

Buttered pasta or boiled potatoes go well with this dish.

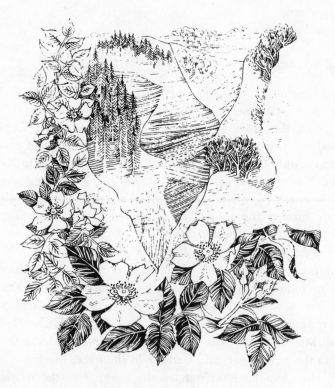

Filet de boeuf en croûte
(Fillet steak in pastry)

There are two ways of cooking steak *en croûte*—or steak *en chemise*. By one method, the uncooked fillet is enclosed in pastry and baked for 45 minutes. By another, the fillet is partially cooked before being wrapped in the pastry. I prefer this second method, as it gives the meat a brown crust, which adds to the flavour.

SERVES SIX
2 pound piece of beef tenderloin (centre part)
salt, pepper
4 ounces (8 tablespoons) butter
1 small onion, minced
8 ounces mushrooms, sliced
4 ounces chicken liver pâté,
  or canned pâté de foie
12 ounces puff pastry
beaten egg

Trim the meat of the fatty bits and pieces that many butchers do not bother to remove. Season the meat, spread it with a little of the butter, and place it on a rack in a roasting pan. Cook for 20 minutes at mark 7, 450°F. Remove and leave to cool.

Meanwhile cook onion in 1 ounce of butter until soft. Add mushrooms and cook quickly until slightly browned but not soft. Season, and leave to cool.

To assemble the dish, roll out the pastry into a rectangle large enough to envelop the fillet. Spread the pastry with the remaining butter, and put some of the mushroom mixture across the centre; lay the meat on top, and spread it with the pâté, then the remaining mushrooms. Wrap the pastry round the fillet, pressing the edges firmly together. Brush with beaten egg. Bake at mark 8, 450°F, for 30 minutes (medium rare). Serve with a red wine sauce, like the one on page 45.

Bef Stroganov

Originally the Stroganovs were a family of tough and enterprising Russian merchants. After the conquest of Kazan in 1552, the Tsar gave them huge grants of land in the Urals, which they colonized and exploited ruthlessly. Salt mines, iron and copper works, as well as the profits from trading and land, brought them riches and power until they became one of the great families of Imperial Russia. This recipe, from the end of the nineteenth century, was invented by the family's French chef and named in their honour.

It's a fine combination of French method and Russian ingredients. It also has the advantage of being quick and simple to prepare. Some versions of the dish, which has become so popular in Europe and America in the last few years, include tomato, and flour to thicken the sauce. I have even seen a suggestion that minced meat should be used. Such things are an insult.

SERVES SIX

1½ pounds well-trimmed beef tenderloin
salt, freshly ground black pepper
4 ounces (8 tablespoons) butter
4 tablespoons oil
1 pound onions, sliced
1 pound mushrooms, sliced
2½ teaspoons mustard powder
2 teaspoons sugar
2½ cups sour cream
parsley, minced

Cut the meat into ¼-inch-thick slices, then cut each slice into strips about 2½ inches long and ¼ inch wide. Season and set aside while the vegetables are cooked. Melt half the butter with the oil in a large frying pan, and cook the onions gently until they begin to soften without browning. Now raise the heat and add the mushrooms. By the time they are cooked without being too soft, the juices should have evaporated almost entirely, leaving the mixture moistened but not wet to the point of swilling. Keep mixture warm over a low heat. Mix the mustard and half the sugar to a paste with a very little hot water, and keep it by the stove. Now quickly fry the beef strips in another pan in the remaining butter (in two batches if necessary). They should brown in a few seconds, and not be allowed to overcook. Add them to the mushroom mixture, and stir in the mustard paste, then the sour cream. Correct the seasoning, and bring to just below boiling point. Turn into a dish and sprinkle with parsley.

The Russians serve *kartoplia solimkoi* with *bef Stroganov*, in other words matchstick potatoes made in exactly the same way as chips—the only difference is that the potatoes are cut into thin pieces about 2 inches long and ⅛ of an inch wide and thick. Their crispness enhances the piquant creaminess of the beef in its mushroom and sour cream sauce.

The recipe on page 215 shows how the method of *bef Stroganov* can be adapted to pork.

Fillet of beef with morels, or girolles

Canned mushrooms can be used for this recipe, or dried ones. You will need 4 ounces *drained weight*. If using fresh mushrooms, allow 6 to 8 ounces, as they will lose a good deal of liquid in the cooking.

SERVES FOUR
1 pound onions, sliced
milk
flour
deep fat for frying
4 tenderloin steaks
2 tablespoons freshly ground black pepper
6 ounces (12 tablespoons) butter
2 tablespoons fines herbes (tarragon, parsley, marjoram, chives, basil,
*   chervil, as available)*
⅓ cup dry sherry
4–8 ounces morels, girolles, or other mushrooms (see above)
1 heaping teaspoon cornstarch
⅓ cup beef stock
salt, pepper

Dip the onions in milk and drain them. Put them into a paper bag with a couple of tablespoons of flour and shake them about, then deep-fry them. Keep warm in the oven on crumpled kitchen paper spread over a baking sheet.

Rub the steaks with the pepper, and sauté them in half the butter about 3 minutes a side (time will depend on whether you like them rare, or medium rare). Remove and keep warm. Add remaining butter, herbs and sherry to the steak pan. Cook the mushrooms in it for a few moments only if they are canned, rather longer if they are dried or fresh. Mix the starch with the beef stock and add that to thicken the sauce slightly. Season.

Arrange the steaks on a serving dish, pour the mushroom sauce over them, and put the onion rings round the edge of the dish.

Mushroom croutons for roast meat

I have the feeling that, apart from roast beef and Yorkshire pudding, crispness is a quality underrated by English cooks when preparing meat dishes. And yet if one thinks of foreign dishes that have become popular here, it becomes obvious that the small crisp items usually served with them are an important part of their success. For instance, *boeuf à la bourguignonne,* with its triangles of fried bread, and *bef Stroganov,* with its straw potatoes —even our travesties of *tournedos Rossini* allow the steak to repose on its crouton of fried bread. The more unusual Italian liver and mushroom sauce, *salsa di fegatini,* served on toast with veal, is another good example. And so are these mushroom croutons, which can be served, too, with roast veal, and roast chicken or turkey. They can also be eaten on their own as a supper dish, or cut up into fingers to go with drinks.

SERVES SIX
1½ *pounds field or cultivated mushrooms*
2 *ounces (4 tablespoons) butter*
1 *large onion, minced*
⅓ *cup dry white wine*
salt, pepper
3 *tablespoons minced parsley*
¼ *teaspoon thyme*
nutmeg
1 *teaspoon flour*
6 *large slices fried bread*
1½ *ounces (about 2 tablespoons) grated Parmesan*

Slice the mushrooms. Set aside a teaspoonful of the butter and cook the onion in the rest. As it begins to soften, add the wine and mushrooms. When they are cooked, season with salt and pepper. Drain off any liquor, and reserve. Reduce the mushrooms to a slightly knobbly purée in a chopper or blender, or put through the coarse plate of a vegetable mill. Return to the pan with the mushroom liquor and add the parsley and thyme and some grated nutmeg to taste. Cook down until the purée loses its sloppiness. Mash the teaspoon of flour with the reserved teaspoon of butter, and stir it by bits into the purée to give a good consistency. Adjust the seasoning, spread mixture on the pieces of fried bread, sprinkle with Parmesan, and put under a fairly hot grill to colour appetizingly.

Cut the croutons, if you like, into smaller pieces and serve round the carved roast meat. No other vegetables are required, but provide a green salad to eat afterwards.

Rognons aux champignons
(Veal or ox kidney with mushrooms)

Veal kidneys are best for this delicious recipe, but they are not easy to come by, so ox (beef) kidney must be used instead. Allow extra time, a good hour and a half in a low oven when using ox kidney.

SERVES FOUR OR FIVE

1 *pound kidney*
2 *ounces (4 tablespoons) butter*
8 *ounces mushrooms, sliced*
salt, pepper
¼ *cup brandy*
⅔ *cup beef stock*
⅔ *cup dry white or red wine*
2 *tablespoons butter mashed with 2 tablespoons flour,*
   or ½ cup heavy cream

Cut the kidney into nice pieces and brown it lightly in the butter. Stir in the mushrooms and season. After they have been cooking for about 3 minutes, pour on the brandy and set it alight; turn the kidney and mushrooms about in the flames. Pour in the stock and wine, bubble up for a moment or two, then transfer to a casserole and complete the cooking in a warm oven, mark 3, 325°F.

When the kidneys are tender, you can strain off the sauce and thicken it in one of two ways. With red wine, beurre manié is best—add the mashed butter and flour to the sauce in little bits, stirring it all the time over a moderate heat. When it is thick, add the kidneys to reheat. If you have used white wine in the recipe, strain off the sauce, and reduce it until the flavour is very concentrated. Bring the cream to a boil, and add it to the sauce. Serve with croutons.

Tripe and mushrooms with sauce poulette

A mild and excellent dish of tripe, suitable for a dinner party (though it's a wise precaution to make sure in advance that your guests enjoy tripe).

SERVES SIX
2½ pounds tripe

COURT-BOUILLON:
2 medium carrots, sliced
2 medium onions, sliced
2 cloves
6 peppercorns
bouquet garni

SAUCE:
sauce poulette (*p. 35*), *made with chicken or veal stock*
¾ pound button mushrooms
2 ounces (4 tablespoons) butter
6 slices mild bacon
salt, pepper

Simmer tripe in the *court-bouillon* ingredients with just enough water to cover. Consult your butcher as to the time it will take to cook—some tripe has been so well blanched that it is ready in

30 minutes, but good old-fashioned tripe will require 2 or 3 hours. Cut tripe into strips when cooked.

Meanwhile make the *sauce poulette,* adding the trimmings from the mushrooms. Fry the mushroom caps in the butter. Pour boiling water over the bacon and leave for 5 or 10 minutes: drain, and cut into strips.

Mix tripe, mushrooms, bacon and sauce together. Cook for 5 minutes without boiling, season, then pour into a very hot serving dish.

Biscottes, toast or croutons of fried bread go well with tripe cooked in this way.

Veal tartare with mushroom salad, in the Piedmont style

We ate this excellent dish in the Belvedere Restaurant at La Morra in Piedmont, not far from the training school for truffle hounds. The view is endless. To France one way, over the Alps. Into Italy the other, with wave on wave of highly cultivated hills, not an inch of waste ground. Food in Piedmont is lovely, rather French in style by comparison with what we think of as Italian food, but with its own decided character.

VEAL:

12 ounces lean trimmed veal from the leg
lemon juice
salt, freshly ground black pepper
olive oil (or heavy cream)
8 slices of lemon, trimmed of most peel

SALAD:

¾–1 pound mushrooms, sliced
8 tablespoons olive oil
2 tablespoons wine vinegar
salt, pepper, sugar
parsley and chives, minced

Forty-five minutes before the meal, chop the meat in a chopper or put the veal twice through a meat grinder or mincing machine. Season with lemon juice, salt and pepper, and use just enough oil (or if you prefer it, some cream) to bind it smoothly. Form into eight nice round knobs, not quite as large in diameter as the lemon slices, and stand meat on top of slices. Chill for 20 to 30 minutes.

For the salad, pour boiling water over the mushrooms and leave for a minute, then drain. Mix oil, vinegar, salt, pepper and sugar, and stir in mushrooms while still warm. Set aside to cool, then drain and dress with herbs on a serving dish, leaving enough space for the veal and lemon.

Veal or lamb chops with mushrooms à la crème

As I have indicated earlier on in the various recipes for *mushrooms à la crème* (including morels and girolles), they make the most delicious sauce for small pieces of meat—veal and lamb chops, veal escalopes, sweetbreads, chicken breasts. The two elements can be prepared quite separately, meeting only on the serving dish. Or the meat can be cooked first, with the *mushrooms à la crème* prepared in the same pan after the meat has been removed. This second method has the advantage of incorporating the veal or lamb juices in the sauce, so binding the two parts of the dish in a proper unity. It's very much the French style, and is one of the reasons why their recipes produce better and tastier results than ours of a similar kind. For complete success, attention must be paid to the frying of the meat: if the butter catches, it will spoil the flavours. To avoid this, take the small trouble of clarifying the butter first, then the little salty particles which burn so easily and cause the trouble are left behind in the sieve.

SERVES SIX
salt, pepper
6 veal or lamb chops,
   or 1½ pounds blanched sweetbreads (or see above)
4 ounces (8 tablespoons) butter
¾ pound mushrooms (morels, girolles, etc.)
½ cup dry white vermouth, or a sweet fortified wine
¾ cup heavy cream

Season the meat and set aside for a while. Bring butter to the boil in a small pan, and pour it through a muslin-lined sieve into a pot. Put about two-thirds into a large pan, and fry the meat until nicely browned and cooked. Put the rest into a small pan and cook the mushrooms. When the meat is ready, transfer it to a serving dish and keep it warm. Deglaze the meat pan with the wine, scraping in the brown bits. Boil down to a syrupy consistency, tip in the mushrooms and their juices (which should not be too copious), and finally add the cream. Allow to boil and thicken for a few moments, then pour over the meat and serve. Boiled new potatoes or mashed potatoes are good with meat cooked this way.

Veal sauté with rice and peas

It's surprising how well mushrooms and peas go together; and it doesn't seem to matter whether they accompany fish or veal, as in this recipe. If you prefer it, reduce the quantity of veal, and the accompanying ingredients accordingly, so that the meat acts as a sauce to the risotto rather than as the main element of the dish.

RISOTTO:

4 *tablespoons* (*2 ounces*) *butter*
1 *medium onion, chopped*
1 *cup Italian or long-grain rice*
about 2½ cups hot chicken or veal stock
¾ *cup cooked peas*
¼ *cup grated Parmesan*

VEAL:

2 *pounds boned shoulder of veal*
1 *large onion, chopped*
6 *tablespoons* (*3 ounces*) *butter*
½ *pound mushrooms, sliced*
⅔ *cup chicken or veal stock*
⅓ *cup white port*
⅓ *cup heavy cream*
salt, pepper, cayenne

First prepare the risotto in the usual way (see page 78), adding the peas and cheese last of all. Tip into an oiled ring mould and keep warm.

Meanwhile cut the veal into ½-inch pieces, or a little smaller. Brown them with the onion, in 2 ounces of the butter, over a moderate heat, stirring the whole thing about. In a separate pan cook the mushrooms in the remaining butter. Pour the stock into the veal pan, and cook until the meat is tender and the juices reduced to a rich glaze. Add mushrooms, port, cream and seasonings, and reheat. Unmould the rice and pour the sauce into its centre. Very good.

Blanquette de veau (de poulet, d'agneau) (Blanquette of veal, or chicken or lamb)

Blanquette, a diminutive of *blanc,* could be translated as "little white stew." It is a popular French dish, and like some other popular white dishes—our own white sauce, for instance—it's a trap for the lazy or inexperienced cook.

The main problem is the veal. Stewing veal in butchers' shops is often poor stuff, blown up and flabby. It cooks to a slithy gristle, which is difficult to swallow. Unless you are certain of your butcher, buy a farmyard chicken instead. Lamb, again, for this kind of treatment needs to be of first-class quality. In many stews, the process of browning the meat thoroughly, with onions and carrots, counteracts the less amiable texture of cheap cuts, because it reinforces their robustness of flavour. In a *blanquette*, the meat should only be sealed in the fat to an opaque white, or the palest fawn. The same applies to the mushrooms and onions. In fact you are applying to cheap cuts the delicate method and ingredients usually kept for the finest pieces of white meat.

But please do not be put off. *Blanquette* can be a fine dish, costing less than fine dishes usually do.

SERVES FIVE OR SIX

2½–3 pounds shoulder of veal or lamb, cut into cubes, or 3½-pound
  chicken, cut in pieces
4 ounces (8 tablespoons) butter
5 cups veal or chicken stock
2 carrots, diced
1 leek, white part only
1 onion, stuck with 3 cloves
4-inch piece celery
bouquet garni
salt, pepper
18–24 pickling onions, peeled
6 ounces button mushrooms
lemon juice
2½ tablespoons flour
1 egg yolk
⅓ cup double cream
parsley, minced

Seal the meat over a moderate temperature in half the butter: it should not colour. Pour in the stock and add carrots, leek, onion, celery, bouquet and seasoning if needed. Bring to the boil and simmer until the meat is cooked—at least an hour.

Meanwhile prepare the garnish of onions and mushrooms. Melt half an ounce of butter in a pan and place the onions in it—use a large pan so that they form a single layer. Shake them about over the heat so that they glaze slightly, add 4 or 5 tablespoons of stock from the meat, and leave to cook. Cook the mushrooms in another half-ounce of butter with a little lemon juice—cover them so that they do not brown.

When the meat is cooked, remove it with a perforated spoon to a serving dish and keep it warm. Strain the stock. Cook the remaining butter and flour for a few minutes, and add the stock, which will have reduced in quantity, to make a sauce. Allow this to cook down fairly vigorously, and when it has a good flavour, add the mushrooms and onions and simmer for 5 minutes. Beat the egg yolk and cream together, add a little sauce, then slowly add mixture to sauce and stir it all together over a low to moderate heat, so that it does not boil and curdle the egg. Correct the seasoning with salt, pepper and lemon juice. Pour over the meat, sprinkle with parsley, and serve. Boiled potatoes, carefully and not insipidly cooked, are the vegetable to go with this dish.

Foie de veau et champignons à l'italienne
(Calf's liver and mushrooms in the Italian style)

Carême has the reputation of being a great chef whose complicated recipes are superseded by the necessary simplifications of modernity. One sees why this assumption is made, but lurking here and there in his magnificent books are the kind of quick and easy recipes we prefer today. This is one of them.

SERVES FOUR TO SIX

salt, pepper
12–18 slices calf's liver
4 ounces (8 tablespoons) butter
2 tablespoons minced parsley
2 tablespoons chopped chives
1 tablespoon minced tarragon
4–6 ounces mushrooms, chopped

2 tablespoons flour
1¼ cups dry white wine
1 tablespoon meat drippings from beef or chicken (optional)

Season the liver. Clarify 3 ounces of the butter by bringing it to a boil in a small pan, then pouring it through a muslin-lined sieve into a frying pan. Fry liver rapidly in the clarified butter. *Do not overcook*—2 or 3 minutes a side should be enough; liver is best when slightly pink in the middle. Remove to a serving dish and keep warm. Stir the herbs and mushrooms into the pan juices, then add the flour. Mix everything well over a gentle heat for a couple of minutes, and stir in the wine to make a sauce. Just before serving add the meat flavouring if used, and the remaining ounce of butter off the heat. Correct the seasoning, pour over the liver, and serve.

Rognons de veau (d'agneau) sautés, sauce à la crème
(Fried veal or lamb's kidneys in cream sauce)

This and the following two recipes come from one of my favourite cookery books, *Gastronomie Pratique,* by Ali Bab (which was the pen name of Henri Babinski). Even the salt is sometimes measured in grams; nothing it left to chance. The only unpractical thing about the book is its immense size. It's like cooking from a family Bible. I have translated his quantities as nearly as I can, but this need not stop you from making alterations of your own if your tastes are different.

3 tablespoons chopped onion
3½ ounces (7 tablespoons) butter
½ cup veal stock
1 pound veal or lamb's kidneys, sliced
scant ½ teaspoon salt
scant ½ teaspoon paprika
4 ounces mushrooms, sliced
½ cup heavy cream
vinegar
1 teaspoon minced parsley
3 tablespoons grated horseradish

Melt the onion in a generous ½ ounce of butter, without allowing it to brown. Pour in the veal stock and leave to finish cooking. Season the sliced kidneys with salt and paprika, and cook them for 5 minutes in the remaining butter, stirring them about all the time. Drain them and keep them warm. In the kidney juices, cook the mushrooms, and drain off their juices into the onion pan. Add the cream, a dash of vinegar or a little more to taste, and the parsley and horseradish. Heat them to just below boiling point, add the kidneys and mushrooms. Taste and adjust seasoning. Serve in the centre of a ring of boiled and buttered rice. "These creamed kidneys are excellent: all the ingredients of the sauce blend perfectly together without any one of them dominating the flavour."

Rognons de veau (d'agneau) panés, aux cèpes, sauce Colbert
(Veal or lamb's kidneys with ceps and sauce Colbert)

Ali Bab gives two versions of this recipe, one made with fresh ceps, the other with dried ceps (use the excellent Italian dried *porcini* if you can, or the Polish ones).

SERVES FOUR
8 ounces (16 tablespoons) butter
4 fine large ceps

4 *cloves garlic, cut in slivers*
1 *pound veal or lamb's kidneys*
flour
1 *beaten egg*
breadcrumbs
salt, pepper
3 *teaspoons minced parsley*
2–4 *tablespoons meat drippings or jelly*
lemon juice
nutmeg
Madeira

Clarify 3½ ounces of the butter by bringing it to a boil; pour it through a muslin-lined sieve into a bowl, and cool to tepid. Spike the cep caps (reserve the stalks) with the slivers of garlic and turn them in the clarified butter. Now leave them for the time being.

Trim and cut the kidneys into half-inch slices. Turn them in some flour, shaking off any excess, dip them in egg, and press them into the breadcrumbs so that they are nicely coated.

Now cook the kidneys in 1 ounce of butter for 3 to 4 minutes, seasoning them as they cook. Grill or broil the cep caps for 5 minutes on each side, basting them with the clarified butter. When they are done, remove the garlic slivers. Sprinkle ceps with salt, pepper, and 1 teaspoon of parsley.

Chop the cep stalks and cook them in 1 ounce of butter. Place them in a serving dish and arrange the kidneys and cep caps on top. Keep warm. To make the sauce Colbert, mix the remaining butter with the rest of the parsley. Heat the meat flavouring, add the parsley butter bit by bit, and season wih lemon juice, salt, pepper, nutmeg, and a dash of Madeira. Do not allow this sauce to boil. Pour over the kidneys and ceps and serve at once.

Brains baked with mushrooms and cheese

Use field mushrooms, if you have the chance, or any fine-flavoured woodland mushrooms.

1½ pounds brains
light stock
½ pound mushrooms, sliced
3 ounces (6 tablespoons) butter
salt, pepper, lemon juice
⅓–½ cup grated Gruyère cheese
¼ cup chopped parsley
1½ cups heavy cream

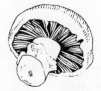

Soak brains in salted water to cover for at least an hour, then remove the fine membrane. Rinse brains and put into a pan, cover with stock, bring to the boil, and simmer for 10 to 15 minutes, until just done. Drain and slice thickly.

Meanwhile cook the mushrooms in one-third of the butter. Season with salt, pepper and a few drops of lemon juice. Grease an ovenproof dish with another ounce of butter and put the mushrooms in a layer on the bottom. On top put the slices of brain, and sprinkle them with the grated cheese. Mix parsley with the cream, season, and pour it over the dish. Dot with remaining butter and add some extra pepper. Place in a hot oven for 10 minutes or so, mark 7, 425°F, until everything is well heated through and the sauce has reduced slightly. Finish off, if you like, by browning under the grill: this is better than overcooking the brains by keeping the dish in the oven until it browns.

Ris de veau (d'agneau) à la poulette (Calf's or lamb's sweetbreads poulette)

SERVES SIX
2 pounds sweetbreads
4 tablespoons salt

chicken stock
2 *tablespoons lemon juice*
sauce poulette (*page 35*)

Cover sweetbreads with water, add the salt, and leave for at least an hour. Drain and rinse them, and put into a pan with enough stock to cover them and the lemon juice. Bring slowly to the boil, and simmer until they have lost their pink, raw look and become opaque. The time will depend on whether you are cooking small lamb's sweetbreads, or the large calf's.

Drain off the cooking liquor and use to make the *sauce poulette.*

Meanwhile run the sweetbreads under the cold tap, and when you can handle them comfortably, remove the bits of gristle and a certain amount of the white membrane (but not too much or they will disintegrate). Divide the sweetbreads into even pieces if they are small: slice them if they are large. Reheat them in the *sauce poulette* and serve with toast or croutons, or with buttered rice.

. . . with chicken

SERVES SIX

The recipe is exactly the same as for the sweetbreads in preceding recipe, or for the tripe on page 200. Choose a boiling fowl, and cook it in the usual way. Cut the meat into nice pieces and reheat in the sauce: 6 slices of bacon, blanched and chopped, make a good addition, as in the tripe recipe. Serve with buttered rice.

Ris de veau (d'agneau) à la crème (Creamed sweetbreads)

Choose veal sweetbreads if possible, as they are larger and easy to prepare. If they are not available, you will have to use lamb's sweetbreads. A good dish for an evening meal, as it is rich without being too copious. If you can find morels or girolles, they will make an even better dish than the cultivated mushrooms.

SERVES FOUR

1½ *pounds sweetbreads*
2 *ounces (4 tablespoons) butter*
8 *ounces mushrooms, sliced*
⅓ *cup port or other fortified wine*
1 *cup light cream*
salt, pepper, cayenne
8 *slices bread, fried in butter*

Soak and blanch the sweetbreads in the usual way (see preceding recipe). Slice them. Melt the butter and brown the sweetbreads and mushrooms lightly—take a little time to do this, as butter burns easily if the heat is too great. Remove to a dish and keep hot. Deglaze the pan with the port, stirring it up as it bubbles so that all the nice little bits from the frying are included. Add the cream, and boil for a minute or two longer until the sauce thickens. Put the sweetbreads and mushrooms back, season, and divide among the slices of bread.

Pork tenderloin or veal escalopes à la crème

An adaptation of the preceding sweetbread recipe to pork and veal. Chicken breasts could be cooked in the same way.

SERVES FOUR

1 *pound pork tenderloin, or 4 veal escalopes*
salt, pepper
beaten egg
breadcrumbs
2 *ounces (4 tablespoons) butter*
8 *ounces mushrooms, sliced*
¼ *cup Madeira, Marsala, or port*
⅔ *cup heavy cream*
lemon juice

Slice the pork thinly on the diagonal, to make small escalopes. Beat them out and season them. With veal escalopes, you need only beat them out and season them, as the butcher has done the slicing. Dip the meat in egg, and then in breadcrumbs. Bring butter to the boil in a small pan, and pour it through a muslin-lined sieve into a frying pan. Fry meat in the butter. Do not have the heat too high. After 2 minutes a side the escalopes can be transferred to a serving dish. Keep them warm while you make the sauce.

Add the mushrooms to the cooking juices, and fry them lightly. Season and stir in the wine. Boil hard for 3 or 4 minutes to reduce to a concentrated essence, then stir in the cream. Correct the seasoning with salt, pepper and lemon juice. Serve separately in a sauceboat. Buttered rice goes well with meat cooked this way.

Longe de porc à la vendômoise
(Loin of pork in the Vendômois style)

I love this dish both for itself and for its circumstances—because it's often the centrepiece of the midday picnic at grape harvest in the Loir valley. There's this beautiful roll of pork, 5 or 6 pounds of it, looking golden brown and white on the outside, surrounded with pale jelly. The vineyard owner's wife cuts it into slices, which reveal its pink inside, starred with black central pieces. Ideally these black pieces are truffle, or truffle peelings. More likely they are *trompettes-des-morts*, horns of plenty, which the family has gathered in the woods that border the vines. They do look like truffles when used in this way, but they lack the exquisite flavour.

One might be excused for thinking that with all the fuss, truffles are probably over-rated. When used simply and strikingly they are not, even if they are tinned. What I cannot stand are the tiny black flecks in canned pâtés and so on, which might as well be small beetles for all the flavour they contribute. Do at least try a tin once for this recipe. It will be an unforgettable dish.

SERVES TEN

4–5-pound loin of pork, boned, skinned

BRINE:

2 quarts water
1½ cups sea salt
1½ cups dark brown sugar
1 ounce saltpetre
½ bay leaf
1 sprig thyme
6 crushed juniper berries
6 crushed peppercorns

PLUS:

2–3 cloves garlic
4 ounces mushrooms or horns of plenty,
   or 1 tiny tin truffles, or truffle peelings
⅔ cup dry white wine
2 cups water

Be sure to bring the bones and skin home with you, as well as the pork. Bring the brine ingredients to the boil. Leave to cool, then strain into a scrupulously clean plastic bucket or crock. Weight the meat down with a foil-covered, clean stone, and cover. Leave for at least 24 hours, preferably 3 days. (When the pork is removed don't throw the brine away: use it for other pieces of pork —even roasting pork benefits from 8 hours of curing, and a leg can be left in for up to 10 days, but it should then be boiled.) Keep the pork bones and skin in the refrigerator.

When you want to cook the pork, rinse it quickly under the tap. Insert slivers of garlic into the meat and lay the sliced mushrooms, or truffle pieces, down the middle. Roll the meat up and tie it firmly, fat side out. Put it into a deep dish that just holds it nicely, tucking the bones and skin round the sides. Roast uncovered in a moderate oven, mark 4, 350°F for 30 minutes. Then add the wine and water and the juices from the tin of truffles, if used. Cover the pot with a double layer of foil and cook for a further 2 to 2½ hours, turning the heat down to mark 3, 325°F, when the liquid starts to boil.

Remove skin and bone from the dish of pork, but otherwise leave it undisturbed to cool. Next day remove the fat and put it into a little dish (this is for spreading on thick pieces of wholemeal bread to eat with the pork). Remove the jelly and chop it. Cut the pork into slices and put it on a dish, surrounded with its jelly. A bowl of green salad is the only other requirement—apart from the bread and wonderfully flavoured lard.

Pork tenderloin with girolles

An Austrian recipe of the Stroganov type, which is particularly delicious on account of the girolles. Cultivated or field mushrooms can be used instead, but the lovely flavour will not be quite the same. Although caraway seeds sound an odd flavouring for mushrooms, they work very well.

SERVES FOUR TO SIX
1 large pork tenderloin fillet
1 medium onion, sliced
1 clove garlic, minced
3 ounces (6 tablespoons) butter
¾ pound girolles
salt, pepper
scant ¼ teaspoon caraway seeds
scant ¼ teaspoon chopped fresh marjoram
2 thick slices back bacon, blanched
⅔ cup sour cream
3 tablespoons minced parsley

Slice and cut the meat into matchstick strips. Cook onion and garlic slowly in half the butter. When they begin to soften, add the mushrooms and raise the heat so that their juices run and evaporate, leaving a modest amount in the pan by the time they are cooked, as a basis for the sauce. Season.

Meanwhile season the meat with salt, pepper, caraway and marjoram. Cut the bacon into strips. In the remaining butter, fry the bacon until the fat begins to run, then raise the heat and add the pork. Stir it about all the time, so that it browns quickly without overcooking. Pour the mushroom mixture into the meat pan, add the cream, correct the seasoning, and bring back to the boil. Turn the whole thing into a serving dish, and sprinkle with parsley. Serve with bread, or new potatoes, or crisply fried matchstick potatoes.

As with *bef Stroganov*, the point is not to overcook the meat or the mushrooms. The method resembles Chinese cooking.

Scalloped ham with mushrooms and cheese

Good grocers who sell ham on the bone often dispose of the bits and pieces at a most advantageous price. They do very well for making a mousse or a scalloped dish like this one, as would leftovers from a baked ham. Always buy a little more than the recipe says, to allow for cutting away gristly skin.

SERVES FOUR

1½ cups béchamel sauce (see appendix)
nutmeg
2 ounces (4 tablespoons) butter
3 shallots, minced, or 6 tablespoons minced onion
6 ounces mushrooms, quartered
12 ounces cooked diced ham
3 tablespoons grated Gruyère or Cheddar
½ cup breadcrumbs
extra butter

Flavour the béchamel sauce with nutmeg. Melt the 2 ounces of butter and cook the shallots or onion gently until golden and soft. Add the mushrooms, and when cooked, stir into the béchamel with the diced ham. Divide among four deep scallop shells or small fireproof pots. Mix the cheese and breadcrumbs and scatter evenly over the ham mixture, dot with butter, and put in a very hot oven, mark 8, 450°F, or under the grill until brown and bubbling.

The dish can be prepared entirely in advance, with only the reheating in the oven or under the grill to be done at the last moment.

Scalloped chicken or turkey with mushrooms and cheese

SERVES FOUR

Follow the recipe above, substituting 12 ounces of cooked, diced poultry for the ham: or use a mixture of 8 ounces poultry and 4 ounces ham.

Jambon du Morvan à la crème gratiné (Gratin of Morvan ham, with a cream sauce)

There are many versions of this famous Burgundian dish. This one comes from Monsieur François Minot, the chef-patron of the Côte d'Or Hotel at Saulieu, in the Morvan, where one eats some of the best food in France. And therefore in the world. This dish is simple to make: mushrooms are the special addition to the recipe, along with the flavouring of tomatoes. The Morvan is particularly famous for its ham; it is not possible to buy exactly the same thing, but any first-class cooked ham can be used instead.

12 *slices cooked ham*
6 *ounces mushrooms, sliced*
1 *ounce (2 tablespoons) butter*
1 *cup Chablis or other dry white wine*
1 *large onion, minced*
3 *shallots, minced*
2 *large tomatoes, peeled and chopped (about 8 ounces)*
1¼ *cups heavy cream*
lemon juice
salt, pepper
1½ *tablespoons grated Parmesan cheese*

Arrange ham on a large, shallow ovenproof dish. Cook mushrooms in butter and scatter over the ham. Now make the sauce: cook wine, onion and shallots together until about a tablespoon of liquid remains and the vegetables are reduced to a soft purée. Add the tomatoes and simmer for 10 to 15 minutes. Sieve, pressing the pulp through, or put through food mill. Bring cream to the boil, and stir in vegetable purée gradually until the sauce is thick and slightly grainy but smooth. Season with lemon juice, salt and pepper, and pour over the ham and mushrooms. Sprinkle with the cheese. Put into a hot oven, mark 8, 450°F, for about 10 minutes. If the top isn't brown enough, put under the grill for a few moments.

Boiled and buttered rice goes well with this dish.

Crépinettes

These small cakes of well-flavoured, minced meat are first cousins to our English faggots. They also have a family resemblance to Pojarsky cutlets, but their external wrapping is provided by caul fat, and not by egg and breadcrumbs. The caul is that irregularly patterned veil of fat which encloses the pig's internal organs. When stretched out, it looks beautiful, but in the butcher's shop it hangs up in a contracted fatty strip. Don't expect to find it at the supermarket; for this and other interesting parts, you should go to a small butcher. Once you find a source of caul fat, make the most of it. I find it's useful to keep a plastic bag of caul fat in the freezing compartment of the refrigerator: it is much better than bacon for wrapping round pâtés, and with very lean meats such as venison and veal, wrap the chops or pieces in caul fat before grilling or roasting—in other words, it is a quick substitute for larding because it bastes the meat continually as it cooks. It catches the heat and provides an attractive brown surface to the meat.

Crépinettes are usually made of all-pork sausage meat (rusk and other fillers are not allowed in France). You can mince up your own from shoulder of pork, or buy some high-meat-content sausages and discard the skins. But this is only the basis. Almonds, truffles, chopped mushrooms (ceps are particularly good), chopped

ham, chicken, turkey, game, can all be mixed with the pork. If the meat is on the lean side, add very thick cream or melted butter to the mixture—not much, and certainly not enough to make it sloppy. Finer mixtures are often flavoured with a spoonful or two of brandy.

And do not forget the seasonings—the garlic, the herbs, seeds and spices. Always fry a spoonful of the mixture before you envelop the crépinettes in their pieces of caul fat, so that you can check and adjust the flavourings.

Simple crépinettes, made from a basic mixture like the one below, are often served in a bed of mashed potatoes (plenty of butter and milk). But other purées can be served instead, according to the meat: apple, chestnut, celeriac and potato, or a highly seasoned tomato stew.

SERVES FOUR
1 *pound pork sausage*
1 *medium onion, chopped*
1 *clove garlic, minced*
4 *ounces mushrooms, chopped*
butter
3 *tablespoons minced parsley*
small bunch of chives, chopped
salt, freshly ground black pepper
a piece of caul fat

Put sausage in a bowl. Cook onion, garlic and mushrooms in a few tablespoons of butter until they begin to soften, then raise the heat as the mushroom juices begin to flow—there should not be a lot of liquid at the end. Mix with the sausage, and stir in the herbs and seasoning. Fry a small piece of the mixture to test the flavours. Divide into eight pieces.

Soften the caul fat in a bowl of tepid water, stretch it out, and cut eight squares about 4 inches each side. Place a piece across your left hand, put a knob of sausage mixture in the centre, and fold the caul fat round it to make a completely enclosed parcel. As you do this, flatten the knob slightly until it is about ¾ inch thick and a nice oval shape. Repeat with the remaining sausage. Fry in a few tablespoons of butter for about 12 minutes, turning them so they brown evenly. Or grill or broil them. Or bake them—give them 20 minutes at mark 5–6, 375°–400°F. Whichever method you choose, the aim is to have the caul fat nicely browned.

Pork, egg, and mushroom pies

One of the best pie recipes, so long as a high-meat-content sausage is used. The mushroom, spice, and onion flavourings blend deliciously with the pork, and the pastry benefits from the rich juices. My own idea is that pies and tarts are best eaten warm.

If a picnic is planned, I make up these pies the day before and store them in the fridge—then they are ready to go into the oven an hour before we leave. If they are wrapped in foil they will keep their heat for a surprisingly long time.

SERVES FOUR

1 pound shortcrust pastry
1 pound sausages
4 tablespoons port or Madeira
4 tablespoons minced parsley
1 medium onion, chopped
2 ounces (4 tablespoons) butter
6 ounces mushrooms, chopped
¼ teaspoon each mace, cloves, black pepper, nutmeg, all ground
salt
4 hard-boiled eggs
beaten egg

Divide the pastry into four. Roll out the first piece, and trim it to a rectangle about 4½ by 7 inches. Cut an arrow-head shape out of each corner, pointing inwards, and keep the trimmings. This will make it easier for you to bend up the sides of the pastry to make a box shape when the filling has been put into it. Repeat this with the three other pieces, guarding all the trimmings carefully, as they will be needed for making lids for the pies.

Let the pastry rest while the filling is put together. Remove the sausage meat from the skins and put it into a bowl. Add the wine and parsley. Cook the onion gently in the butter, and when it begins to soften, add the mushrooms and raise the heat slightly so that you end up with a moist rather than a wet mixture. When they are cooked, stir in the spices and salt.

To assemble the pies, divide the sausage mixture into eight pieces, and place one in the centre of each piece of pastry, leaving the outer rim free. Divide the mushroom mixture among the four pies and spread it over the sausage. Cut the eggs in half and place them, cut side down, on top of the mushrooms. Cover them in their turn with the remaining pieces of sausage mixture, pressing the whole thing gently into a box shape. Bring up the pastry rims, pressing the corner edges to join firmly. Cut away excess pastry. Roll out all the trimmings and cut four oblong lids. Brush the outside of the pastry boxes with egg and place the lids on top, again pressing the edges together to seal. Slash two or three openings in the centre of each lid, and decorate with pastry leaves or diamonds. Brush the tops over, and bake at mark 6, 400°F, for about 30 to 40 minutes, until golden brown.

If the pies are being eaten fairly hot, as a main course, creamed cucumber goes with them well (pieces of cucumber blanched in boiling water for 10 minutes, then drained and finished in butter, with a final addition of cream and chives).

Leg of lamb with gratin of ceps and potatoes

A magnificent dish, so long as you use a fine-flavoured leg of lamb. The gratin is put into the oven about half an hour after the lamb, so that they are both cooked and ready at the same time.

SERVES EIGHT
4–5-pound leg of lamb
4 cloves garlic, cut in slivers
oil
3 ounces (6 tablespoons) butter

PLUS:
ingredients for gratin of ceps and potatoes (page 119)

Make cuts in the lamb and slide garlic slivers into them. Brush over with oil, and place in a roasting pan. Give it 15 minutes at mark 6, 400°F, then daub it over with the butter, add several tablespoons of water to the pan, and reduce the heat to mark 4, 350°F. Cook for another 1¼ or 1½ hours until the meat is tender and well cooked. Baste it from time to time with the juices. Protect with buttered paper if it becomes too brown.

Meanwhile make up the gratin in a large oval dish, so that it comes rather shallower than usual. Bake for an hour with the lamb, on a shelf above it, protecting it with paper or a piece of foil.

Slice up the lamb and arrange it on top of the gratin, with a spoonful or two of the cooking juices. Serve immediately.

Lamb or veal chops chasseur

Lamb or veal chops are delicious when served with *sauce chasseur*, which you will find on page 48.

Allow two lamb cutlets per person, or one thick veal chop. Flour them lightly, or coat them with egg and breadcrumbs, then fry them in a mixture of butter and oil, half and half. Depending on the size of the pan and the number of the chops, you may have to do them in batches.

Arrange them on a hot serving dish, pour a little of the sauce over them, and serve the rest separately.

Lamb cutlets with purée soubise and mushrooms

Both the French and the English like lamb with onion sauce; the flavour is even better if some mushrooms are added to the dish. As a change from the usual soubise sauce of onions and béchamel, I recommend purée soubise, because the rice gives it more body.

SERVES FOUR

MEAT:
8 best end of neck lamb cutlets
salt, pepper
2 ounces (4 tablespoons) butter

MUSHROOMS:
1 ounce (2 tablespoons) butter
1 pound mushrooms, sliced
⅓ cup medium-dry sherry or stock
nutmeg, salt, pepper
⅓ cup heavy cream
purée soubise (page 305)

Trim and season the cutlets. Leave them for an hour or two to absorb the seasoning. Then fry them in the butter, about 8

minutes if you like them pink inside, 12 or more if you like them
well done. Do not cook them so fast that the butter burns. Remove them from the pan and keep them warm. Add the ounce
of butter to the pan and then the mushrooms. When they are
nicely browned, stir in the sherry or stock and deglaze the pan
well. Skim off any fat that rises. Add the cream and taste for
seasoning.

Reheat the purée soubise and put it into the centre of a round
serving dish. Arrange the cutlets on top and the mushrooms with
their cream sauce round the edge. Serve very hot.

Grilled meat en brochette

One has to be careful about meat kebabs, meat cooked *en bro-
chette*. It's often cooked to an aromatic leather. Chew, chew, chew.
Which is why I avoid such dishes in restaurants and make them
at home instead. The general idea is a godsend, because it gives
perfectly ordinary ingredients an allure, an air of the Arabian
nights, which would be entirely lacking if they were served in
the usual way. The skewers can be prepared hours in advance of
cooking. Brush them with oil and they will keep beautifully moist
as the flavours begin to work together. The final cooking takes
about 10 minutes (use an electric spit if you can).

All kinds of mixtures can be made, once the basic idea is grasped
—that is that lean meat is improved in flavour and tenderness by
sandwiching it between herbs, vegetables, and pork belly or fat
bacon. Although special herb blends can be bought which add a
little Middle Eastern authenticity, there is nothing wrong with
the herbs in the garden—bay leaves and sage, cut in quarters, can
be strung on the skewers; tarragon, parsley, and chervil can be
finely chopped and added to the initial marinade or the final pan
sauce, or both.

Brochettes should be put under a hot grill, and turned when
they begin to brown at the edges. The time depends on the meat
you are cooking, and whether you like it pink in the middle. It
is better to undercook rather than overcook, particularly when
dealing with chicken or calf's liver and lamb, which are the best

kinds of meat for this dish. Serve on a bed of buttered rice or green beans. Piquant sauces can be served as well, e.g., tomato, but the best and simplest thing is to make a little concentrated sauce from the pan juices as in the recipe below.

SERVES SIX

6 *slices calf's liver*
  or *¾ pound chicken livers*
  or *1 pound lamb fillets*
  or *6 lamb's kidneys and 3 slices calf's liver*
  or *kidney, liver, and prepared sweetbreads*
12 *thin slices bacon*
6 *bay leaves or 12 sage leaves*
18 *medium mushrooms, halved*
6 *tomatoes, quartered and seeded*
12 *small onions, blanched for 10 minutes*
salt, pepper
oil

SAUCE:
⅔ *cup veal or chicken stock*
⅓ *cup Madeira or port or sherry or dry white vermouth*
walnut-sized knob of butter

Cut meat into even-sized pieces—the number should be divisible by six. Cut bacon into the same number of pieces, discarding any rind. Cut bay leaves and sage leaves into half-inch pieces.

Now lay out your ingredients to be skewered in six lines on a chopping board or table, and see that they are properly alternating. Place on six skewers, making sure that there is always a piece of bacon against a piece of meat.

Season the skewers of food, brush generously with oil, and leave them in a cool place until 15 minutes before the meal. Place them under a hot grill for 7 to 10 minutes, turning them as the edges begin to catch. They should be a little crisp outside and slightly underdone in the centre. Lay them on a bed of buttered rice or French beans and keep warm. Pour the stock and wine into the pan juices, boil everything up, stirring well, until the flavour is strong and appetizing. Remove from the heat, stir in the butter, and pour over the skewers. Serve immediately.

Alexis Soyer's mushroom and kidney sandwich

Alexis Soyer was one of the French chefs who came to London and made his reputation in the middle of the last century. For a time he was chef at the Reform Club, but he had a strong social conscience and was occupied with culinary good works of a practical kind. He helped organize soup kitchens for the Irish peasants in the potato famine, and for the silk workers in Spitalfields. His greatest work, though, was to reorganize the hospital catering for Florence Nightingale in the Crimean War. He wrote a book about his experiences there, his *Culinary Campaign,* from which this recipe comes.

SERVES SIX
12 really large mushrooms
butter, melted
salt, pepper
6 lamb's kidneys, sliced
6 croutons or pieces of buttered toast

Brush the mushrooms over with a little melted butter, season them well, and grill or broil them. Quickly cook the kidneys in a few tablespoons of butter—they should not be overcooked. Set six of the mushrooms, *underside up,* on the six hot croutons or pieces of toast. Divide the kidneys among them, and place the remaining mushrooms on top, *underside down,* to form a "sandwich." Serve immediately.

Escargots à la poulette

On wet nights in the countryside in France, village byways and gardens are not deserted as they would be in England. Pinpoints and beams of torchlight flash high and low. Dark lumpy shapes move mysteriously about. The snail-hunters are out in force, with sacks draped over their heads and shoulders to keep out the worst of the rain. They have sticks and wire baskets. Their usual prey is the dark-speckled garden snail, *Helix aspersa,** but what they would like to find is the *gros bourgogne,* the Roman or vineyard snail, 2 inches across with a beautiful pale brown and white shell. Both kinds are found in this country too. Often when I put the milk bottles out on a wet night, I see a good number of garden snails moving majestically up the doorsteps and over the porch, or humping along the gravel.

Snails should be kept in a bucket with a pierced lid (but weight it down or they will escape). Give them lettuce or cabbage or dandelion leaves to eat. Some people add thyme to improve their flavour. Others only give them flour. After 10 days they can be eaten. And for this recipe allow at least a dozen per person.

Put on your rubber gloves, and swish the snails about in a bowl

* *I understand that* Helix aspersa *were introduced to America in the nineteenth century and are to be found in California, especially the southern part, Virginia, Arizona, Louisiana, and South Carolina, but very few people hunt them, although they are perfectly edible.*

of water with a handful of salt. When they've exuded a good deal of foamy slime, change the water and repeat until it is clear (4 changes). Simmer them in a *court-bouillon* for 40 minutes (see tripe recipe, page 200, above). Remove them from their shells with a needle, which has been stuck eye-end into a kernel of corn. Set the snail meat aside and throw away the shells.

Make the *sauce poulette*, page 35, with extra mushrooms and bacon if you like. Reheat the snails in some butter for a few minutes, then add to the sauce. Serve in individual pots with toast or fried bread.

N O T E : With canned snails, you need only reheat them in butter before adding to the sauce. Drain them well first, when you remove them from the tin.

Potée d'escargots solognote
(Snails in the Sologne style)

We have a small cave-house in a cliff-village in the north of the department of Loir-et-Cher—half of it leans up against the cliff face, and looks quite normal; the rest—the secret half—burrows into the rock, making use of a worked-out quarry tunnel. That department is firmly divided in two by la Loire, the great river of French history, which in summer at least has a modest sleepy look. Blue water winding erratically between banks of pale gold sand held together by willow trees. Sometimes we cross it, rather daringly because it is a real boundary to the mind, and go into the Sologne. This is a strange, flat world of endless woodland and forest, opening on occasion to reveal a small settlement or a drained mere which now provides sumptuous beds for asparagus. As in most country of this kind, architecture is neither abundant nor striking. The old cottages have a transitory look. They make one see how in the Middle Ages, men sitting inside might be killed by a dagger thrust through the daub walls. And yet one becomes trapped by the Sologne. First perhaps by Alain Fournier and his *Grand Meaulne* (*The Lost Domain*), or by the thought of the delights of Sancerre, which lies through and out the other side. Or by the woodland mushrooms, the girolles and ceps, by the snail dishes and game served in the local restaurants.

If you collect your own snails, prepare them as in the preceding recipe and simmer them in a *court-bouillon* (page 200). Otherwise buy 3 tins of snails (for four people) from the delicatessen—if you are lucky, you may be able to choose between French brands and the English Mendip snails, canned by Paul Leyton of the Miner's Arms at Priddy in Somerset, where he also has snails on the menu.

The recipe comes from La Croix Blanche, at Chaumont-sur-Tharonne, not many miles from the birthplace of Alain Fournier.

SERVES FOUR

6 *dozen snails, or 3 tins snails*
2 *ounces (4 tablespoons) butter*
12 *ounces cultivated mushrooms, sliced*
8 *ounces girolles, chopped*
¼ *cup water*
¾ *cup ground almonds*
salt, pinch paprika
parsley, minced

SNAIL BUTTER:

4 *ounces (8 tablespoons) butter*⎫
8 *tablespoons minced parsley* ⎪
12 *cloves garlic, pounded with* ⎬ *mash together*
8 *tablespoons oil*   ⎭

Prepare the snails in the usual way (see pages 227–8) and set them to drain. Just before the meal, melt the butter in a flameproof pot, and fry the mushrooms until lightly coloured. Add the water, cover, and leave until the mushrooms are cooked. Now add the almonds, the snails, and the snail butter. Stir together and season with salt and paprika. After reheating for 2 minutes—be careful not to cook hard or long, as this will toughen the snails—serve in the cooking pot, sprinkled with parsley. Provide plenty of bread, and white wine.

Poulet aux morilles (two recipes)
(Chicken with morels)

We first ate this best of all dishes at the Cheval Rouge in Montoire on a hot night in early May. And naturally we praised the dish to the proprietor's wife when she did her usual round of the tables. "Oh, yes, it's the season for morels," she replied. Whenever we comment on some particularly good dish there, it always turns out to be the season. Their menu is geared to the seasons and not to the rotation of a deep-freeze. "This goat's cheese is superb," or "We did enjoy the biquet, the young kid," and the response contains a faint note of irritation at our comment on the obvious: "But it's the season, Madame." How easily we forget that things are at their best in their proper season, when they're at their most abundant—and cheapest. But it must be acknowledged that some seasons are better than others, need more celebration. Certainly the season of morels is a great festival of the year for anyone who likes food (and who can find them).

There are many variations of this recipe, and you can alter it to suit yourself. The three main ingredients are a good chicken, morels and a great deal of cream—some form of alcohol is desirable, too. Guinea-fowl or a young turkey could be used equally well for the following recipes, but substitute port for the white wine of the first recipe.

I

SERVES SIX
3 pounds chicken pieces
seasoned flour
2 ounces (4 tablespoons) butter
2 tablespoons oil
⅓ cup dry white wine
½–2 pounds morels, cleaned, quartered
4 cups heavy cream
1 large egg yolk

salt, freshly ground black pepper
lemon juice (optional)

Turn the chicken in seasoned flour and colour lightly in the butter and oil. Pour in wine and cook briskly until it has almost evaporated, turning the chicken pieces about in the juices. Add morels and cream and leave to cook uncovered until the chicken is done. Remove it, and as many morels as possible, to a hot serving dish. Boil down the sauce by about half. Thicken the sauce further by beating up the egg yolk with a little of the sauce, then cooking it all together, just below boiling point, for about 5 minutes. Correct the seasoning (a little lemon juice may be added to bring the flavour of English cream nearer to the French, which has a slightly sharpish tang). Pour over the chicken and serve. Boiled and buttered rice goes well with this dish, or plenty of really good bread.

Obviously economies can be made—e.g., by substituting chicken stock for half the cream. But I think morels are an occasion for extravagance and rejoicing. Economize with the other courses.

II

SERVES SIX
3-pound dressed whole chicken
1 medium onion, chopped
salt, pepper
butter
1–2 pounds morels, cleaned, quartered
4 tablespoons oil
2–3 cups double cream
⅓ cup brandy or Calvados (or whisky)
2 large egg yolks

Put the chicken into a roasting pan. Mash up the onion with seasoning and a lump of butter and put it into the cavity. Roast the chicken in the usual way. Meanwhile cook the morels in several tablespoons of butter and the oil, adding the cream after about 5 minutes. Leave to cook down gently but steadily for about

20 minutes. When chicken is cooked, cut it into pieces, put them into a pan over a moderate heat, pour the heated alcohol over them, and set it alight. Turn the pieces of chicken in the flames. Add the chicken pan juices, loosened over the heat with a little water if necessary, to the morel sauce. Beat the egg yolks with a little sauce, then return mixture to the sauce, cooking without boiling for about 5 minutes. Correct the seasoning.

Put the chicken on a serving dish, and pour the sauce over it. Always serve this kind of cream sauce very hot, with very hot plates.

Poulet, pintadeau, ou dindonneau aux girolles
(Chicken, guinea-fowl, or turkey with girolles)

The method for this recipe is rather different from chicken with morels, because girolles must not be cooked too long. They are therefore cooked separately for only 10 minutes, but over a brisk heat so that their juices evaporate.

SERVES FOUR
3-pound fowl, whole or in pieces
3 ounces (6 tablespoons) butter
4 shallots, minced
⅓ cup brandy
⅓ cup port
salt, pepper
4 cups cream (or half cream, half stock)
1 pound girolles

Brown the poultry in 2 ounces of the butter. Add the shallots. Flame with the brandy, moving the pieces about in the flames. Then pour in the port and stir it around so that all the bits and pieces which have stuck to the pan are amalgamated in the sauce. Add seasoning and the cream, or cream and stock, and cook covered for about half an hour, or until the bird is tender. Remove to a warm serving dish, and boil down the sauce until it is nice and thick.

Meanwhile cook the girolles in the remaining butter, raising the heat as the juices run so that they evaporate. After about 10 minutes, add the mushrooms to the reduced sauce and simmer together for a few minutes, stirring all the time. Correct the seasoning, pour over the bird, and serve at once.

Poultry and game birds stewed with ceps

This general method of stewing meat with ceps can be adapted to poultry (chicken, turkey, guinea fowl) or to game birds, and you can vary the herbs of the bouquet garni accordingly. The flavour is far superior in concentration and fineness to any of the stews which rely on cultivated mushrooms. Dried ceps can be used, but fresh ones are best. In northern Italy, such dishes are scattered with slices of white truffle as a final grace note.

SERVES SIX TO EIGHT
poultry or game bird(s), cut in serving pieces
seasoned flour
½ cup olive oil
2 ounces (4 tablespoons) butter
¼ cup brandy or other spirits
1 medium onion, chopped
2 cloves garlic, minced
1 large carrot, chopped
bouquet garni
up to 2½ cups stock
1 pound ceps, caps sliced, stalks chopped
salt, pepper
parsley, chopped
triangles of fried bread, or buttered rice

Turn poultry pieces in seasoned flour and brown them in half the oil and all the butter. Flame with warmed brandy, moving the pieces about. Add onion, garlic, and carrots, and stir them about in the pan juices for 10 minutes. Keep the heat on the low side. Put in the bouquet, and pour about half the stock into the pan— tough birds should just be covered, and more tender ones should be only half-covered. Meanwhile fry the ceps in the remaining oil for 5 minutes at a brisk heat. Add to the poultry. Cover and complete the cooking. Pour in more stock if the sauce begins to dry up, but there should not be too much of it—one is aiming at concentration of flavours. Transfer the pieces of cooked poultry or game to a serving dish and keep warm. Season the sauce to taste, skim off any fat, and pour sauce over and round the meat. Sprinkle with parsley. Arrange triangles of bread, or the rice, round the edge of the dish and serve immediately.

Poulet à la dauphinoise
(Chicken in the Dauphiné style)

Walnut orchards are one of the beauties of the Dordogne and Corrèze, and of many other parts of southern France such as the Dauphiné. The rough grey-walled enclosures of green grass, the smooth silver-grey of the trunks, and the yellowing green of the leaves in autumn have a soothing quietness as one drives along the country lanes. Mostly the walnuts will be sold to French and foreign commercial bakers, like Fullers (the Dauphiné includes Grenoble, Montelimar and Gap, which are all famous for their confectionery), and to housewives, but some will be turned into a black liqueur, *crème de noix*, or crushed for walnut oil. Once this was much used by painters, but I imagine that the price caused them to turn to cheaper substitutes long ago. Nowadays walnut oil is a luxury for the knowledgeable cook. Put it at the top of your list of things to bring home from France; it's expensive there, but in England the price seems to jump beyond contemplation. I found this recipe in a French periodical; its combination of walnuts, walnut oil and ceps is unusual and good.

SERVES SIX

½ pound shelled walnuts (36 walnuts in their shells)
4-pound roasting chicken, cut in pieces
3 ounces (6 tablespoons) butter
6 tablespoons walnut oil
4 ounces smoked bacon, cut in strips
1 onion, minced
5 shallots, minced
1 clove garlic, minced
1 pound small ceps, sliced
bouquet garni
salt, pepper
¼ cup brandy or marc
½ cup port
1 egg
4 tablespoons cream

When preparing this dish, it is wise to cope with the walnuts well in advance. Choose a peaceful moment, when you can listen to the radio or talk to a friend. Pour boiling water over the shelled nuts, leave them for a few moments, then drain them and remove the fine skins. The fresher the walnuts, the easier this job is— this is really an autumn dish when ceps are in the woods, and the first walnuts arrive from France. I won't deny that this is a fiddly job, but it's worth the trouble because the skins can spoil dishes of this kind with their bitter flavour. Set aside half a dozen of the nicest pieces for final decoration, and put the rest in a bowl beside the other ingredients.

Brown the chicken, in a large frying pan, in half the butter and all the walnut oil. Remove to a dish and keep warm. Put the bacon into the pan, and when it colours, remove to the dish of chicken. Finally cook the onion, shallots and garlic in the butter and oil. And when they are ready, return the chicken and bacon to the pan. Be careful never to burn the fat, or the flavour of the juices will be spoilt.

Meanwhile cook the ceps in the rest of the butter, and put them into the frying pan with the chicken. Add the walnuts and bouquet. Flame with half the brandy or marc, then pour in the port. Cover and simmer for about an hour, or less if the chicken is cooked sooner.

Meanwhile beat up the egg with the cream and remaining brandy. When the chicken is cooked, arrange it on a serving dish with the ceps, bacon, and walnuts. Strain the cooking juices into a pan, and thicken with the egg mixture. Cook a moment or two without boiling and pour over the chicken. Decorate with the reserved nuts.

Poularde à la crème aux cèpes du Revard (Chicken with a cream and ceps sauce)

This recipe is from the Hotel-Restaurant International Rivollier at Aix-les-Bains; the ceps used here come from Mont Revard, which overlooks the Lac du Bourget. They have a specially good flavour, but the dish can be made with ceps from a good deal further north. Or you could use cultivated mushrooms, preferably the rather large ones—but do not expect quite such a fine result.

SERVES FOUR
3-pound whole chicken
7 ounces (14 tablespoons) butter
1¼ cups dry white wine
2 cups chicken stock
2 pounds ceps, sliced
salt, pepper
2 cups creamy milk
¾ cup cream
2½ tablespoons flour

Melt 2 ounces of the butter. Colour the chicken slightly in a deep fireproof cooking pot, adding the melted butter gradually so that it doesn't stick. Leave the bird on its side, add the wine and stock, and leave to cook for 40 minutes or so (lid on the pan). Turn the chicken twice during this time, and when it's cooked, remove it, cut it into pieces, and keep warm on a serving dish. Cook the ceps in 2½ ounces butter meanwhile. Season.

To make the sauce, reduce the chicken cooking liquid very rapidly to several tablespoons. Pour in the milk and the cream. Mash the remaining butter with the flour, and use to thicken the sauce, adding it bit by bit and keeping the heat moderate so that the sauce barely boils. Strain on to the ceps and reheat the whole thing together, adjusting the seasoning if necessary. Pour over the chicken and serve very hot.

Poulet Célestine

This recipe for chicken with mushrooms, cooked in a tomato sauce, was invented, according to Lucien Tendrot in *La Table au Pays de Brillat-Savarin*, by Monsieur Roussdor, the head chef at the Café du Cercle at Lyons in the 1860s. He called his new dish after his wife, Célestine. A large farm chicken, cut in serving pieces, can quite well be used instead of the small half-chickens, which are most likely these days to be tasteless commercial birds.

SERVES SIX

3 *ounces (6 tablespoons) butter*
3 *small chickens, split in half*
½ *pound button mushrooms*
2 *large peeled tomatoes (about 10 ounces), diced*
¾–1 *cup dry white wine*
4 *tablespoons meat drippings or jelly*
¼ *cup brandy*
salt, pepper, cayenne
parsley and chives, minced
1 *small clove garlic, minced*
triangles of bread fried in butter

Clarify the butter: bring it to a boil in a small pan, then pour it through a muslin-lined sieve into a frying pan. Brown the chickens in the butter. Add mushrooms and tomatoes. Cook for 10 minutes. Now add wine, meat flavouring, and brandy. Season and continue to cook gently until the chicken is done. Remove to a large serving dish. Skim fat from the sauce if necessary, add herbs and garlic, and boil down hard until the flavour and consistency are concentrated to an agreeable richness. Pour over the chicken, and serve surrounded with the triangles of bread.

Poulet sauté chasseur (Huntsman's fried chicken)

One of the best versions of pan-fried chicken, which can be adapted to rabbit or pigeon, or to small items like lamb and veal chops. Choose a farmyard roaster, four to five pounds dressed weight, and ask the butcher to cut it into 10 pieces.

SERVES FIVE TO SIX
1 *chicken, cut in pieces*
seasoned flour
cooking oil
4 *shallots, minced*
8 *ounces mushrooms, quartered*
¼ *cup brandy (optional)*
2 *cups chicken stock*
3 *tablespoons tomato paste*
⅔ *cup dry white wine*
bouquet garni
2 *tablespoons butter*
2 *tablespoons flour*
salt, pepper
parsley, tarragon and chervil, minced

Turn chicken pieces in seasoned flour. Brown them lightly in oil in a large frying pan. Add shallots and mushrooms. When they begin to colour, pour brandy, if used, into the pan and turn the chicken about in the flames. Mix stock and tomato concentrate, and pour into the pan with the wine. Tuck in the bouquet garni.

Cover and leave to simmer until cooked—up to an hour, depending on the chicken. Meanwhile mash together butter and flour.

Place cooked chicken in a serving pot. Add butter and flour paste to the sauce in small bits, stirring all the time. Keep below boiling point—the sauce will thicken in about 5 minutes. Correct seasoning. Pour sauce over chicken. Sprinkle with chopped herbs and serve.

Triangles of fried bread can be used to garnish the dish. Vegetables are not necessary, but potatoes, green beans or crisply cooked celery would be appropriate.

Poularde en demi-deuil
(Chicken in half-mourning)

A French recipe, which can also be used for a small turkey. The black shapes of the truffle slices show through the semi-transparent skin of the bird, hence the name of the dish. Fresh truffles give a wonderful flavour, but even with one tinned truffle this is food for a special occasion. Take great care choosing the bird.

SERVES SIX
5-pound whole roasting chicken
1 fresh or tinned truffle
11 cups chicken stock
sauce suprême (*page 34*), *made with stock from the chicken pot*
rice boiled in stock from the chicken pot

The day before you intend to eat the chicken, cut the truffle into slices, and slip them underneath the breast skin of the bird, as decoratively as you can manage. Leave in a cool place—not the fridge—until required: this gives the bird time to absorb flavour from the truffle.

Put the stock into a large cooking pot, bring it to the boil, a rolling boil, and plunge in the chicken. Lower the heat when the stock returns to the boil, and keep it simmering until the bird is cooked—about 50 to 60 minutes. After half an hour, strain out enough stock to make the rice and sauce. Set the rice to cook, and make the *sauce suprême*. Place the bird on a hot serving dish when it is cooked, pour some of the sauce over it, and serve the rest in a sauceboat. Put the rice into another dish.

Poularde Derby

A recipe of great luxury, invented by Escoffier for the pleasure of Edward VII. A *poularde* is a fattened pullet, and "Derby" means that the dish includes both truffles and foie gras. Escoffier's own description of the dish, in his *Guide to Modern Cookery*, is bleak to the point of nonchalance: "Stuff a pullet with pilaff rice and pot-roast it. Dish, and surround it with collops of foie gras tossed in butter (and placed on small, fried croutons), and alternate these with large, whole truffles, cooked in champagne."

SERVES SIX
½ *pound (about ½ cup) long-grain rice*
7 *truffles, cleaned*
salt, pepper
1 *fine roasting chicken*
2 *ounces (4 tablespoons) butter*
¾ *cup hot water*
¾ *cup champagne*
4 *ounces foie gras*
6 *slices bread, fried in butter*

Boil rice in plenty of salted water, rinse it, and drain it well. Chop the liver of the chicken and one truffle, and mix into the rice with salt and pepper to season. Stuff the chicken with this mixture. Melt the butter in a deep flameproof pot, and brown the chicken all over. Add seasoning and hot water. Cover, then leave for 1½ hours, until the chicken is cooked: turn it over occasionally, and add more water if necessary. Meanwhile put remaining truffles into a pan with the champagne and some salt and pepper, and simmer for 10 minutes. When the chicken is cooked, put the stuffing in the centre of a serving dish. Cut the bird into six pieces.

Spread the foie gras on the croutons of bread, and arrange them alternating with the chicken around the rice: the truffles can go on top. Boil up the truffle juice with the chicken juice. Pour over the dish, and serve.

Chicken and mushroom cutlets

These delicious cutlets, based on the Russian *kotlety pozharskie*, can conveniently be prepared one or two days in advance. Store them in the refrigerator, and fry them just before the meal.

SERVES FOUR TO SIX
2–3 ounces cultivated mushrooms, or ceps, or morels, finely chopped
9 ounces (18 tablespoons) butter
1½ pounds boned raw chicken (or half chicken and half veal)
2 cups breadcrumbs
⅓ cup light cream
3 tablespoons chopped parsley
salt, pepper
1 egg, beaten

Cook mushrooms in 1 ounce of the butter and leave to cool. Mince chicken. Soak about two-thirds of the breadcrumbs in the cream. Add to the chicken and mince again, or put through the meat grinder, with the veal if used. Cream 4 ounces of the butter to soften it, and mix in the meat, the mushrooms and the parsley. Season to taste.

With wet fingers—keep a bowl of water handy—form the mixture into oval cakes about ½ inch thick. There should be enough for about 16 to 18. Turn them in beaten egg and then in the remaining breadcrumbs. They can now be put into the refrigerator.

Clarify the remaining butter by first bringing it to a boil in a small pan, then straining through a muslin-lined sieve. Put half the clarified butter into a large frying pan, and cook the cutlets gently on both sides until they are crisp and golden brown on the outside, and soft but cooked through inside—this will take

15 to 20 minutes. Place on a serving dish, and pour the remaining clarified butter over them.

Chicken croquettes with mushrooms (or truffle)

Croquettes are simple enough to make—the difficulty comes with the seasoning and cooking, because they should be mild yet full of flavour, crisp outside and creamy in the centre. Remember that as all the ingredients are cooked beforehand, a minimum of time is needed for the final deep frying—about three minutes, just long enough to brown the egg and breadcrumb coating.

SERVES FOUR
3 ounces (6 tablespoons) butter
2½ ounces minced cooked ham
5 tablespoons flour
2 cups boiling milk
7 ounces cooked chicken, minced
3 ounces mushrooms, chopped,
  or 1 small tin truffle peelings, or 1 truffle
salt, pepper
2 egg yolks
2 tablespoons heavy cream
1 egg, beaten
breadcrumbs or crushed biscottes
fat for deep frying

Melt 2 ounces of butter and heat the ham in it. Stir in the flour, cook for 2 minutes, then, off the heat, amalgamate with the boiling milk. Cook until a very thick sauce is formed. Add the chicken, and remove from the heat. Cook the mushrooms in an ounce of butter, and season them well; stir into the chicken mixture. (Alternatively chop the truffle and add with its juice to the sauce; no additional butter will be needed.) While still hot, beat in the egg yolks and cream. Correct seasoning. Spread out in a shallow dish and leave to cool in the refrigerator until firm. Form into 8 croquettes, dip in beaten egg, roll in breadcrumbs or *biscottes* and deep-fry for about 3 minutes until golden brown all over. Serve immediately.

The croquettes can be prepared well in advance, and stored in the refrigerator. This leaves only the frying to do at the last moment.

Salsa di fegatini
(Chicken liver sauce for veal)

One of the family sent me this recipe from La Lanterna restaurant in Perugia. I thought it most original—until I came across an almost identical sauce the following week, in the *Forme of Cury*, that roll of mediaeval recipes compiled about 1390 by the cooks of Richard II. *Sawce noyre* was served with capon in those days: at La Lanterna it's spread on hot, thin slices of veal (lightly fried escalopes or roast veal), and served with pieces of toast in between also spread with the sauce. You can order it too as a first course on its own, when it's eaten with toast like a pâté.

1 *ounce dried* porcini *or ceps,*
   or 2 *ounces mushrooms, chopped*
1 *pound chicken livers, chopped*
1 *slice raw Parma ham or unsmoked ham, chopped*
1 *small onion, chopped*
1 *clove garlic, minced*
2 *tablespoons minced sage*
sprig rosemary
1 *slice lemon, chopped*
olive oil
2 *cups dry white wine*
juice of ½ lemon
salt, pepper

Pour hot water over the dried mushrooms, and leave to soak for 15 minutes or according to the instructions; drain and chop. Cook the first eight ingredients in a little olive oil, until the livers are half-cooked. Mince finely, or use a food mill. Add wine and a little lemon juice. Simmer for half an hour, uncovered. Correct seasoning and add the rest of the lemon juice if necessary. The liquid evaporates to leave a strongly flavoured, spreadable paste rather than a sauce. It can be stored for up to 10 days in a screw-top jar in the refrigerator: it can also be made in half-quantities quite successfully.

Chicken liver and mushroom pâté

Another good combination of chicken liver and mushrooms, this time in a firm, smooth-textured pâté. It can be eaten with thin toast, or spread on steak baked *en croûte*.

½ pound chicken livers
4 ounces (8 tablespoons) butter
1 medium onion, chopped
1 clove garlic, minced
2 ounces mushrooms, chopped
1 tablespoon Madeira (optional)
salt, pepper, nutmeg
clarified butter (optional)

Trim gristly white part from the livers. Cook them in 3 ounces of butter for about 2 minutes a side. They should still be pink in the centre. Remove them from the pan, and put onion and garlic in to cook gently until they begin to soften. Add mushrooms and cook for a further 4 or 5 minutes. Put with the chicken livers. Melt the remaining butter in the pan, stir in the Madeira if used, and scrape in all the delicious brown bits and pieces left over from the cooking of livers and onion and mushrooms. Add to the rest of the ingredients, and either liquidize in a blender or put through a food mill; this depends on the texture you prefer. Season to taste. Put into a pot, smooth down the surface, and cover with clarified butter if you intend to keep the pâté for a little while. Once the butter has solidified, put a sheet of foil over the pot, and store in the refrigerator until required.

N O T E : Like most pâtés, this one tastes best after a couple of days.

Filetti di tacchino bolognese
(Turkey breasts with ham, cheese and white truffles)

Turkey breasts are easy to buy nowadays, and can be sliced into fillets with a sharp knife. Allow about a pound for four people. Unless you can afford canned white truffles, you will have to substitute cultivated mushrooms. This delicious Italian method of cooking turkey, which I have taken from Elizabeth David's *Italian Food* (Macdonald, 1954; Knopf, 1958), can be adapted to veal escalopes, and slices of pork tenderloin, if slight adjustments are made to the cooking time.

SERVES FOUR
1 pound turkey fillets
thinly sliced cooked ham (see recipe)
salt, pepper
flour
butter
white truffles, or 6 ounces mushrooms, sliced
grated Parmesan cheese
turkey or chicken stock

Flatten the fillets, then cut an equal number of pieces of ham to the same size. Season and flour the turkey. Melt a generous 2 ounces of butter in a pan and cook the fillets gently for 5 minutes a side (don't let the butter burn). *Do not cook the truffles,* but if you are using mushrooms, cook for 5 minutes in the remaining butter until lightly browned.

Place pieces of ham on top of the turkey. Cover with thin slices of truffle or a layer of mushrooms, then a layer of cheese. Pour about a tablespoon of stock over each fillet. Cover the pan and cook gently for another 5 minutes or so. "Some of the cheese spreads, amalgamates with the butter and the stock in the pan, and forms a sauce. Serve quickly, for if the dish is kept waiting the sauce will dry up and the cheese will become hard."

Filetti di tacchino al Marsala
(Turkey breasts with Marsala)

Like the preceding recipe, this is another Italian way of cooking delicate cuts of meat. As well as being suitable for veal and pork, it can be adapted to sweetbreads, which should first be soaked, blanched and trimmed (see page 211).

SERVES FOUR
1 pound turkey fillets (or blanched sweetbreads)
salt, pepper
flour
butter
⅔ cup Marsala, or ⅓ cup each Marsala and stock
8 ounces mushrooms, sliced (or thinly sliced white truffle)

Flatten, season and flour the fillets (NB: if using sweetbreads, do not flatten but divide into convenient pieces, or cut into slices). Cook gently until lightly browned in 3 ounces of butter—about 5 minutes a side. Pour on the Marsala, or Marsala and stock, and bubble for a few moments before removing meat to a warm serving dish. Boil pan liquids down to a slightly syrupy sauce, stirring all the time. Beat in an ounce of butter and pour over the meat.

Meanwhile cook the mushrooms in 2 ounces of butter, unless you are using white truffles, which need no cooking but can be heated for a moment in some butter. Place mushrooms around the fillets.

Confit d'oie à la basquaise
(Goose with ceps in the Basque style)

Tins of *confit d'oie* are one of the best things to bring home from a holiday in France. You may also find them in good delicatessens. It's a preserve of salted goose, cooked and stored in its own fat, and a speciality of south-west France, the foie gras area. I suppose it began as a way of using up the sad carcasses once their real commercial point, their livers, had gone off to the market. The goose farmer's perquisite. All this being so, *confit d'oie* is still not cheap. Combined with ceps, it makes a splendid dish to be eaten in small quantities. I've tried to make *confit d'oie* from an English goose, but it was not successful. The overfattened foie gras geese are the only ones to use. I understand that American geese work very well.

SERVES THREE
1¼-*pound tin* (*600 grams*) confit d'oie
2 *pounds ceps*
6 *tablespoons oil*
4 *tablespoons minced parsley*
1 *clove garlic, minced*
salt

Open the tin and reheat the goose gently in its own fat. Slice the cep caps and chop the stalks. Put the oil into a frying pan, plus a few tablespoons of goose fat from the *confit d'oie*. Cook the ceps in this, and when they are just done mix in the parsley and garlic and stir the whole thing together. Season with salt.

Drain and cut up the hot goose. Place it on a serving dish, surrounded by the ceps. Eat with plenty of good bread, or a few boiled potatoes. The left-over goose fat should be preserved carefully: it's excellent for frying potatoes, or a dish of ceps and potatoes as on page 120.

Pâté de canard, truffé
(Truffled duck pâté)

Although the generality of mushrooms does not appear in pâtés, truffles do. Whenever the mixture is particularly fine or rich, there you will find the small black nuggets which indicate their presence. Fresh truffles in reasonable quantity are obviously the ideal when you are making a special game or duck pâté, because canning removes the subleties of their pervasive and exquisite flavour. On the other hand, if you are in France, it's worth bringing home a small can or two, because they can still contribute something good even in their reduced state (canned truffles can be bought in England, but the prices are far too high).

SERVES EIGHT TO TEN
1 *large duck with its liver*
2 *pounds lean pork*
½ *pound hard fatback or fat pork belly*
⅓ *cup brandy or Madeira*
salt, pepper
quatre-épices, *or a mixture of nutmeg, mace, cinnamon, and allspice*
1 *large egg*
2 *ounces truffles*
4 *ounces extra duck or chicken livers*

Bone the duck (or ask the poulterer to do it for you), but leave the legs intact with their bones. Reserve the liver. Cut away as much of the rest of the duck meat as you can, without damaging the skin: select a nice piece of breast and cut it into long strips, then mince the rest of the duck meat with the lean and fat pork. Mix in the brandy or Madeira and seasonings, bind with the egg, cover and leave for an hour or two.

Lay the skin of the duck, inside upwards, on a board. Put half the forcemeat in the middle. Remove gristly bits from the livers, including the one from the duck, and place them in the middle. Distribute the sliced truffle among them. Cover with the remaining forcemeat, and pat into shape so that the livers are quite enclosed.

Wrap the skin round the pâté, and sew it into shape with button thread. Find a terrine into which the duck can be fitted without any room to spare. Bake uncovered, at mark 4, 350°F, for 1½ hours.

Cool under a light weight. Store in the refrigerator for at least 24 hours before serving; keep the pâté covered with foil once it comes out of the oven.

This recipe can be used for game pâtés, too, without the skin being wrapped around, of course. Hare, pigeon, pheasant, partridge, for instance. For these lean creatures, increase the proportion of fat pork in the recipe above. Allow ¾–1 pound boned game to about 2 pounds total weight of pork.

English game pie

As in many other European game dishes, mushrooms are an essential flavouring in this old recipe, which has been slightly adapted to fit in with our methods of cooking to-day. Field mushrooms are the best, but they do not always coincide with game in the poulterer's shop, so you will most likely have to make do with cultivated ones instead. Choose pheasant or grouse which are not in their first youth, or partridge; or woodpigeons, which always need prolonged cooking. If you are short on game, buy some chuck steak to make up the quantity. Cut it into cubes and brown it in a little oil, before simmering it with the birds.

2–4 game birds, according to size
bouquet garni
stock or water
chuck steak (optional: see above)
1 large onion, chopped
8 ounces mushrooms
2 ounces (4 tablespoons) butter
2½ tablespoons flour
6–8 slices bacon (optional)
3–4 hard-boiled eggs
salt, pepper
parsley, minced
puff or short pastry
beaten egg

Put birds and bouquet into a large pan; cover with stock or water, bring to the boil, and simmer, covered, until the meat begins to part from the bone and can be separated into nice large pieces. Arrange them in a pie dish (put the steak underneath, if used). Brown onion and mushrooms lightly in the butter, stir in flour, and add enough of the game stock to make a rich sauce. Leave to simmer. If you wish to use bacon, divide the bacon pieces in two and make them into little rolls: these should be lightly grilled or broiled, then arranged round the meat. The eggs should be

shelled, then quartered or sliced, and added to the pie dish. Season well with salt, pepper, and parsley. Pour in the onion and mushrooms and as much sauce as is required almost to fill the dish. Cover with puff pastry in the usual way, or use short pastry if you prefer it; brush with beaten egg and bake for about 30 minutes at mark 8, 450°F, until the pastry is well risen and golden, and the contents of the pie bubbling hot.

Rabbit or chicken pie

SERVES SIX TO EIGHT
For pies of tender meat like rabbit or chicken, a slightly different method from the one above should be used. Assemble the ingredients, which, apart from the meat, will be the same and continue as follows:

Cut the rabbit or chicken in serving pieces, and turn it in the flour. Place in a pie dish. Fry onion and mushrooms until lightly coloured, then add them with their juices. Tuck the grilled bacon, which is much to be desired with less well-flavoured meat like rabbit and chicken, and the quartered hard-boiled eggs into the gaps. Season with salt, pepper, and parsley—also with thyme, which is a great improver of rabbit in particular. Pour in half a pint of stock. Cover with pastry in the usual way and brush with beaten egg.

Cook for 20 minutes at mark 8, 450° F, until the pastry has risen nicely and begun to turn golden brown. Lay a piece of brown paper, wax paper (greaseproof) or foil on top of the crust so that it doesn't colour too much, and lower the heat to mark 3, 325°F. In an hour the meat should be cooked—test it with a larding needle or skewer by way of the central hole in the pastry lid. Give it a little longer if need be.

Cailles farcies au porto et à la truffé
(Quails with a truffle and port stuffing)

This French recipe can easily be adapted to other game birds, such as pheasant: the cooking time would need to be increased, but that is all.

STUFFING:

½ *pound chicken livers*
8-ounce piece hard back pork fat
½ *pound mushrooms*
1 *small onion, halved*
½ *cup parsley*
4 *tablespoons butter*
1 *glass port*
salt, pepper, nutmeg
1 *nice truffle, preferably fresh*

QUAILS:

8 *quails*
8 *thin slices pork fat*
4 *tablespoons butter*
4 *tablespoons port*

First make the stuffing: trim the gristly bits from the chicken livers, and cut the pork fat from the skin (hard back fat is the part cut from chops or loin of pork, the layer of fat attached to the skin) and weigh it—you will need 5 to 6 ounces. Put the livers, fat, mushrooms, onion and parsley through the food mill. Cook them in the butter over a high heat for 2 minutes, stirring all the time. Put into a bowl, and add the port and seasonings. Cut the truffle into 8 pieces.

Divide half the stuffing among the quails, and push a piece of truffle into the centre of each one. Tie the slices of pork fat like jackets over the breasts of the quails. Brown them all over in the butter, add the port, and simmer for 10 to 15 minutes. Meanwhile divide the remaining stuffing between 8 small ramekins or soufflé dishes. Put the quails on top (remove the string) and place the ramekins in a hot oven for a further 10 minutes, mark 7, 425° F. Serve, if you like, with the *sauce Périgueux* (or *sauce périgourdine*) on page 44.

Côtes de chevreuil Saint-Hubert
(Venison cutlets in the style of Saint Hubert)

Saint Hubert is the patron saint of huntsmen, but in view of his story I always feel he was an inappropriate choice. As a young man, this noble Gascon of the eighth century spent much of his time hunting, to the exclusion of many other more worthwhile activities. He was out one Good Friday when the deer he was chasing confronted him, and he saw a shining crucifix between its horns. This vision converted him to the religious life; first he became a hermit, living in the woods (he is also the saint of foresters and woodcutters), and eventually Bishop of Liège in what is now Belgium. His feast day is November 3, right in the middle of the hunting season. In culinary terms, "Saint-Hubert" means a garnish of mushrooms, preferably woodland mushrooms such as ceps, sometimes with a truffle, when used in connection with game: the accompanying sauce is invariably a *poivrade*, pepper sauce.

12 *venison chops*
1 *pound high-meat-content sausage*
½ *pound ceps or field mushrooms, finely chopped*
4 *juniper berries, crushed*
4 *ounces (8 tablespoons) butter*
caul fat
4 *tablespoons oil*
salt, pepper

POIVRADE:
1¼ *cups red wine*
2 *medium onions, chopped*
6 *tablespoons brandy*
6 *tablespoons olive oil*
salt, black pepper
1 *carrot, diced*
6 *tablespoons corn oil*
5 *tablespoons flour*
4 *cups beef stock*
2 *tablespoons tomato paste*
bouquet garni
venison bones (optional)
⅔ *cup red wine vinegar*
8 *peppercorns, crushed*

From the *poivrade* ingredients, mix together half the red wine, half the chopped onion, the brandy and the olive oil, and season them well. This is a marinade, and the chops should be soaked in it for several hours; overnight, if you like.

While they are soaking, it is a good idea to make the sauce, which will then be ready for reheating just before the meal. Brown remaining onion and the carrot in the corn oil, stir in the flour, then the beef stock and tomato concentrate, with the bouquet garni. If you have been able to get some extra venison bones, put these in too. Simmer for 2 hours, covered. Strain, and skim off the fat. Put the vinegar into a small pan, and add the marinade from which the chops have been removed (let chops drain well), together with the peppercorns. Reduce by about half. Add to the brown sauce, simmer for another 30 to 45 minutes, pour in the remaining wine, and reheat before serving.

Now for the chops. Mix the sausage meat (discard the sausage skins) with the chopped mushrooms and the juniper berries. Using about a third of the butter, bring it to a boil in a small pan, then pour it through a muslin-lined sieve into a frying pan. Brown the chops on one side only in this butter. The moment they are cool enough to handle, spread the browned side with the sausage and mushroom stuffing, to make a thick layer. Wrap each chop in a piece of caul fat, place them in an ovenproof dish, fairly close together, and bake them for 20 minutes at mark 5–6, 375°–400° F. Baste them with the remaining butter. Serve with mashed potatoes, and the sauce.

N O T E : Any sauce remaining is useful with roast venison, or venison crépinettes—add some stoned canned black cherries, and a little red-currant jelly. It's also good with beef. The recipe above is easily adapted to veal.

THE MAIN
MUSHROOMS
OF JAPANESE
AND CHINESE
COOKING

A mushroom: stuck
To it a leaf
From a tree somewhere.

Anyone who has ever picked over a basket of wild mushrooms will understand the quiet delight of this seventeenth-century haiku by the great Japanese master Basho.

The mushroom with its leaf, Basho's mushroom, is the matsutake (*Tricholoma matsutake*), the great delicacy of Japanese mushrooms, on a par with our finest cep, *Boletus edulis*. "The arrival in early October"—this is Joan and Peter Martin in *Japanese Cooking* (Penguin, 1970)—"of the matsutake mushrooms, flatly nestling in their beds of fern, is one of the first signs that autumn is truly here." The high prices paid for this prized mushroom from the red pine forests (*matsu* means pine; *take*, mushroom) are not regretted, because it is "superb, with an aroma and flavour quite unlike any other mushroom." If you are lucky you may find canned matsutake. Or you might try substituting one of our *Tricholoma* species, the wood blewit. Certainly they work well in the Japanese recipes for undried mushrooms, with their unusually fresh flavour, a kind of light earthiness. Equally good, perhaps even better, are the edible ceps. And cultivated mushrooms can be used, though their flavour is a little on the weak side.

The great mushroom, though, of Chinese and Japanese cooking, with a role equivalent to our own cultivated mushroom's, is the shiitake. This is the most common dried mushroom on sale in oriental shops (and in many delicatessens). If you ask for dried Chinese or Japanese mushrooms, this is what you will be given. It's a tree fungus growing on the trunk of the shiia and other hardwood trees—hence the name. Which means that its cultivation is quite different from our own indoor mushroom-producing industry, being a sideline of forestry. The point is that the "bed" on which the shiitake will grow must be a log of wood, not the elaborately prepared mattress of compost which is compacted into huge oblong trays for the comfort of our European cultivated mushroom. In other words, it's an outdoor industry with all the problems of weather and situation.

This type of mushroom-growing may not seem so odd to us in the future. We may one day find the corners of our state forests bristling with yard-long pieces of wood neatly stacked in inclining rows. The list of mushrooms which it might be possible to cultivate successfully consists mainly of woodland species, some of them like the oyster mushroom growing on, rather than under, trees. There is also talk of growing shiitake in Europe. It's a matter of convincing forestry commissions that further varieties of mushroom are worth their trouble and attention. I hope these moves are successful. We are far too tied, particularly in England, to the one mushroom, which is by no means the finest in flavour.

A primitive form of cultivation of shiitake has been practised first in China, then in Japan, for well over a thousand years. It was a question of helping the natural processes along, of simulating natural conditions, and then of hoping for the best. As in Europe, the reproduction and growth of mushrooms was not properly understood until the nineteenth century, and the latter part of the century at that. At last, in the twenties, scientists discovered how to prepare the spawn, and mushroom growing could be expanded to a profitable industry.

While Philip Miller was describing in his *Gardener's Dictionary* of 1741 the methods by which gardeners around London were managing to produce mushrooms, Japanese growers were beginning to look systematically for trees on which the shiitake had started to grow. They would cut off the branch, and place it alongside new logs, hoping that the spawn would spread naturally to them.

It sounds simple enough, and the method is basically the same to-day. I suspect it was more successful than Hannah Glasse's rough and ready method of boiling up mushrooms and throwing them and their water on to manure-covered hotbeds, which is described in her *Art of Cookery* (6th edition, 1758). But it involves more heavy labour in the dragging about of the logs. It needs skill and knowledge, too, as the right wood must be chosen for the logs, and the logs must be cut at the right time.

The scientists have refined but not altered the old method. No one goes looking for a tree on which the shiitake is already growing nowadays. Spore emulsions are prepared in the laboratory, then they are injected into or brushed over the bruised and moistened logs. The logs are then propped up at a low angle from the ground, in a good situation. This cannot be created artificially, in the way that our mushroom grower can prepare huts or caves to receive the mushroom trays. A place must be found at the edge of a wood, where there is the right amount of wind. And it must be above the fogs of the valley. The ground must be moist, but well drained, never soggy. Then one needs the right mixture of dampness and warmth in the weather.

Several months later, the logs are moved to a "raising yard." This time they are propped up more steeply, in serried ranks like an army's row upon row of defensive stakes. There they stay until the shiitake are ready for picking. The whole process takes longer than our three-month cycle. On the other hand, the bed logs last for several years, whereas our mushroom compost has to be renewed after each batch of mushrooms.

The shiitake grower has another advantage, because his mushroom is tough, and stands up well to handling and delays (though it is best eaten within a couple of days of being picked). It can be dried quickly, too, either in specially heated sheds or, as far as the small grower is concerned, in the sun. In other words, the grower has a double product—the fresh shiitake, which must go reasonably fast to the markets of Japan, and the dried shiitake, which make such a successful export. He can also send them to factories where they will be canned or pickled in vinegar, along with wild mushrooms.

As I have said, both Japanese and Chinese cooks make great use of the shiitake, but the Chinese have a speciality of their own which can be bought in some oriental shops. This is a crunchy, gelatinous-textured relation of the "Jew's ear" (*Auricularia auricula*), another tree fungus. The Chinese call it wood ear, or cloud ear, or silver ear. Our Jew's ear is edible but not highly regarded among mushrooms, and according to Hsiang Ju Lin and Tsuifeng Lin in *Chinese Gastronomy* (Nelson, 1969), the popularity of the wood ear in China has a certain element of perversity. They group it with other texture foods such as shark's fin, bird's nest and *bêche-de-mer,* observing that they are "absurdities" unless prepared with the right sauces and stocks. On their own they are "as appetizing as a piece of paper." An element in their high reputation is the chance they give the cook to show off his taste and skill: "Perhaps in their ultimate artificiality, they are the most sophisticated of food." Try the recipes using them in this section, and see how you find them.

Another mushroom which is popular in southern China, southeast Asia and Madagascar is the padi-straw mushroom (*Volvariella volvacea*). It is grown out of doors, on rice straw as the name suggests, and is marketed fresh or dried. I have never seen it on sale in England, but judging by a note and recipe in Gloria Bley Miller's *The Thousand Recipe Chinese Cookbook* (Athereum, 1966; Paul Hamlyn, 1966), it is available in America. There are two edible species of *Volvariella* in northern Europe, but they are both rare. One interesting thing: the oldest mushroom picture in existence, from a market in north Africa in Roman times, is of a *Volvariella*, though a different species from the padi-straw mushroom. This, like most of the scientific information in the section, comes from *Mushrooms and Truffles,* by R. Singer (Interscience Publishers, New York, 1961), a book for anyone who is interested in the present and future cultivation of mushrooms.

I hope your illusions will not be spoilt, or your sense of what is fitting in the realms of *chinoiserie,* when I add that the cultivation of *Agaricus bisporus,* our own familiar supermarket mushroom, is big business in the East as well—particularly in Korea and Taiwan. So you need not feel regretfully unauthentic if you use them when making Chinese and Japanese dishes. Indeed some recipes stipulate "fresh" mushrooms or even "champignons." The word "fresh" might include a number of mushrooms, wild as well as cultivated, but "champignons" is unmistakably our cultivated western mushroom.

How to prepare shiitake
(Lentinus edodes)

Unlike Italian, Polish or Yugoslav dried ceps, which are sliced and unidentifiable without their packaging, shiitake are dried whole. They vary in size from half an inch across to about two inches. The gills underneath are a mass of creamy fawn pleating. The caps are brown on top, sometimes slashed to show a paler brown like an Elizabethan sleeve, sometimes as wrinkled and grooved as a tortoise's shell. This strange appearance sets them apart from the other mushrooms we eat, as does their firm, slightly chewy texture, and their strong distinctive taste.

On account of the prolonged and laborious method of cultivation, shiitake are more expensive even on their home ground than our fresh commercial mushrooms are to us. You will notice that most recipes in Japanese and Chinese cookery books count them out individually—4 shiitake, 6 shiitake—rather than by weight. Neither is there the range of purely mushroom dishes that we have in the West (though as you will see from the following matsutake recipes that they grill, broil and fry fresh mushrooms just as we would do). The reason for this is not just the price, but the pronounced flavour of the shiitake itself. Only the dried Italian *porcini* (ceps) give as much flavour among our mushrooms, though quite a different one. Shiitake are used as a seasoning, an important one like the slices of fresh ginger. They are also esteemed as a luxury (and therefore to be enjoyed sparingly) on account of their texture, and the way in which they still retain their flavour after having given so much to the dish in which they have been used.

Shiitake do not need prolonged soaking. Twenty to thirty minutes are enough if you cover them with cold water. With warm or moderately hot water, they will be soft after about fifteen minutes. They do not swell up enormously, but soften to pliability. The tough stalks should be cut off and discarded after soaking. Sometimes the caps are left whole so that the beauty of the mushroom adds to the final appearance of the dish; sometimes they are halved or quartered. Do not be in a hurry to throw away the soaking water, as it is occasionally needed in the recipe.

The Chinese names for this mushroom vary from dialect to dialect. The name given to them by a Cantonese shopkeeper in Soho may not match the one you find written in a book of Peking cookery. Different systems of romanization do nothing to clear the situation. In this book I propose to stick to the Japanese name, shiitake. The Japanese are the big growers; they export more than three million pounds a year to countries all over the world, including China, so I think this is fair. In an oriental store, you are likely to find only two kinds of dried mushroom from the East, shiitake and the rarer, more expensive wood ears. A glance through the plastic bag will show you which is which; and on a catalogue, whatever the names may say, the shiitake will be the cheaper of the two.

The recipes in this section can give only a brief indication of the way Japanese and Chinese cooks use mushrooms. They are not, I think, difficult to follow; the ingredients are almost all available from oriental stores, or from good grocers who carry a selection of oriental foods. If not, they can be obtained by mail order. I have tried quite deliberately, and with only one exception, to choose dishes that may be incorporated harmoniously into an otherwise western meal (though they should be accompanied by boiled or steamed rice, rather than by potatoes and two vegetables). This may offend the purist, but on reflection I cannot see why it should. For the real thing, one must seek out a restaurant which aims to provide Chinese or Japanese food for Chinese and Japanese clients. Authenticity in such matters is out of the question—unless one has lived for long periods in the countries concerned—and striving for it is likely to be wearing and ridiculous. The best thing is to take what one likes, and make it one's own. French cooks took all they could from Italy in the sixteenth and seventeenth centuries, and by grafting it on to their own style developed the finest cooking in the world. Who goes to Paris and complains about the pasta?

This means that it is even more difficult than usual to predict the number of servings. What looks like a tiny amount of food will go quite a long way because it has a strong flavour. In a Chinese household, if extra guests arrive, you do not make more of what you are already preparing; you add two or three extra dishes, because everyone eats a little of everything, and a lot of rice so as to make the most of the flavours (nearly all the recipes following can be backed up with rice or noodles). As a matter of fact I always think that the predictions in Western cookery books —including this one—are rather silly. Who has a family with average capacity? It depends on what people like, and how much they like it. It also depends on how much you are prepared to fill up with bread, rice, potatoes and so on. Or on whether you are serving the dish as part of a two, three, four, five, or six course meal. Most people can look at the main ingredients of a recipe, take in the general method, and know instantly how far it is going to go in their family. Recently I told an American acquaintance that I bought one pound of chuck steak for a family stew for four people (and we do not have the right kind of figures for bread and potato eating). She was horrified at my meanness. Yet most of my English friends consider we eat rather a lot. And French friends regard our table as lavish.

So please treat my predictions, particularly in this section, with a critical caution.

Japanese recipes

Hamaguri ushiojitate
(Clear clam soup)

The *kombu* listed in the ingredients is a processed Japanese seaweed which comes in dark greenish black sheets. It's used as a flavouring for soups and stock, as we might use a bouquet garni.

12 *sprigs watercress, or young spinach leaves*
1 *teaspoon salt*
3-*inch square* kombu
24 *clams or cockles*
6 *slices lime or lemon peel*
6 *large fresh mushrooms*
1 *tablespoon soya sauce*
monosodium glutamate (*optional*)
sake (*optional*)

Blanch the watercress or spinach in a little water with half the salt for 1 minute. Drain, and set aside. Scrub the clams or cockles, then put them into a large pan with 2½ pints (U.S., 4 cups) of water. Add the *kombu*. Bring to a boil, then remove the *kombu*. Leave for 2 minutes or until the clams or cockles open. Strain off the stock into a clean pan, discard all the shells but six, arrange the clams or cockles in them, and place in six bowls with the reserved watercress or spinach, and lime or lemon peel.

Now bring the strained liquor to the boil with the mushrooms, soya sauce and remaining salt, and add a seasoning of monosodium glutamate, if you like, but not very much. A dash of sake is also a good idea, if you can get it. Boil for a few moments. Put a mushroom into each bowl, then carefully pour in the soup down the side so that the arrangement is disturbed as little as possible.

Dried mushrooms stuffed with shrimps

I always like the mixture of shellfish and mushrooms, almost any mushrooms. It's the combination of sweet piquancy and earthiness. For this recipe pick out the largest of your dried mushrooms, the deepest ones with the most regular shape.

20 *dried mushrooms*
1 *cup dashi (see page 268) or chicken stock*
4 *tablespoons soya sauce*
4 *tablespoons mirin (see page 268) or dry sherry with some sugar*
½ *pound shelled shrimp or prawns*
½ *egg white*
1 *teaspoon salt*
monosodium glutamate
1 *teaspoon cornstarch*

Cover the mushrooms with cold water and soak until soft. This takes upwards of 15 minutes. Discard the stems, cutting them away carefully. Bring the next three ingredients to the boil in a pan, and gently cook the mushrooms in this liquid for about 10 minutes. Most of the liquid will have disappeared. Drain the mushrooms and spread them out on a rack to cool. Pound or blend the shrimps to a paste, and add the remaining ingredients, using just a little monosodium glutamate. More egg white can be added —it is difficult to judge the exact quantity of half an egg white.

Put a spoonful of this mixture on the gill side of each mushroom cap, so that it's nicely stuffed. Steam until the shrimp mixture is set. Eat hot or warm.

Chawan-mushi
(Steamed egg custard with chicken and fish)

An excellent supper dish. The unusual—to our way of thinking— collection of nicely seasoned bits and pieces is distributed among individual pots, then the egg and stock mixture is poured over the top. The ideal pots to use are china or glass egg coddlers, with well-fitting lids, but any small pots will do so long as they are covered with foil.

SERVES FOUR

CUSTARD:
4 *eggs*
1 *cup dashi (see page 268) or chicken stock*

1 teaspoon salt
1 teaspoon mirin (see page 268) or dry sherry with some sugar
½ teaspoon soya sauce
¼ teaspoon monosodium glutamate

CHICKEN:
4 ounces chicken breast, thinly sliced
1 teaspoon mirin, or dry sherry with some sugar
1 teaspoon soya sauce

SEAFOOD:
4 large prawns or shrimp in their shells
4 ounces good white fish
½ teaspoon sake
salt

VEGETABLES:
4 dried mushrooms, soaked
4 French beans

Mix custard ingredients, and strain. Mix chicken ingredients and leave for at least 5 minutes. Shell the prawns and split them in half with a sharp knife: cut the fish into julienne strips and sprinkle with sake and a little salt. Quarter the mushrooms, and discard their stems: blanch the beans in boiling salted water until barely cooked; drain and slice diagonally. Divide chicken, seafood and vegetables among four pots (see above), pour the custard over them, cover them, and steam in a large pan of water for 20 minutes—a self-basting roaster works well. Or cook them in a moderate oven in a bain-marie until just set, without being brown on top—30 minutes. Serve immediately.

Norimaki-zushi
(Vinegared rice and seaweed rolls)

One of the basic ingredients of Japanese cooking is seaweed, which has the triple function of providing flavouring, wrapping, and colour contrast. If at first thought this seems odd, think of the British cooked seaweed, the cooked laver which is familiar enough to people on the Bristol Channel, in Scotland and Ireland. It used to be a favourite dish in the not uncivilised Bath of Gainsborough and Beau Nash, and one may still buy it by mail order from Cardiff's main store, James Howell. But it has never been as much part of our lives as it has of the Japanese. One is always coming on seaweed and its colours, and its sinuousness, in Japanese writing. When I wrap the green-black sheets of seaweed round the rolls of *norimaki-zushi*, I am still unblasé and novice enough to be reminded of seaweed in *Genji* or the *Pillow Book* or of a twelve-hundred-year-old poem in *The Collection of Ten Thousand Leaves* about the girl leaning on her lover as the seaweed rests on the open sea. As yellow egg, white rice, brown mushrooms and black seaweed combine, I remember the poet D. J. Enright writing in *The World of Dew* that any Japanese maidservant can arrange diced vegetables on a plate with wonderful effect, since she comes of a people at once the most and least aesthetic in the world, with the most unusual gift for colour matching. Perhaps he might have said flavour matching or flavour combining. And I think, too, that Japanese cooking is a way of walking into Japanese culture.

In this dish (which makes a beautiful hors d'oeuvre), sheets of prepared seaweed or *nori* are rolled round *zushi* (vinegared rice) and a varying collection of delicious bits and pieces. The roll is then cut down into slices (like a jam roll), so that when they are arranged on a dish, or in a lacquer box, the effect can be as colourful as the clusters of a *mille-feuille* paperweight.

Dashi, made from seaweed and dried bonito, is the basic Japanese soup stock, their *court-bouillon*. A packet of instant dashi powder, to be mixed with water, is perfectly satisfactory for this recipe: chicken stock or plain water can be used instead. Dried gourd strips will have to come from an oriental supplier, but you may find sheets of *asakusa-nori* at some health food shops. Mirin, the sweet Japanese rice wine, has a flavour entirely of its own;

the only substitute is dry sherry with extra sugar. Japanese food may seem rather sweet, and there is no reason why you should not reduce the amount of sugar given below.

VINEGARED RICE:
1½ cups rice
2 cups water
½ teaspoon salt
3 tablespoons wine vinegar
1½ tablespoons sugar
pinch monosodium glutamate

EGGS:
2 eggs
1 scant tablespoon sugar
1 generous tablespoon mirin, or dry sherry with some sugar
¼ teaspoon salt
vegetable oil

MUSHROOM AND GOURD:
3 large mushrooms, dried
1 ounce gourd strips
5 tablespoons soya sauce
2 tablespoons sugar
2 tablespoons mirin, or dry sherry with some sugar
⅔ cup dashi or stock

SPINACH:
6 ounces leaf spinach
salt

FISH:
3–4 ounces fillet white fish
2 tablespoons sugar
½ teaspoon salt
red food colouring

4 sheets asakusa-nori

To prepare the rice, put it into the boiling, salted water. Cook uncovered for 10 minutes, cover, and then leave for 10 minutes.

The rice should be firm and the water absorbed; pour off any excess water. Mix in vinegar, sugar, and monosodium glutamate, and spread out to cool on a dish. The Japanese fan the rice until it is cold, which gives it a glossy appearance.

Beat the eggs, sugar, mirin or sherry, and salt together. Brush a large hot frying pan with vegetable oil and cook the egg mixture in a thin layer. Roll up, remove and slice down into strips.

Soak the mushrooms and gourd in water until soft, 30 minutes. Drain well, and slice the mushrooms, discarding the stalks. Cook in the soya sauce, sugar, mirin or sherry, and dashi or stock, which will be largely absorbed. Drain.

Wash spinach. Put into a pan, cover and cook in its own liquid. Do not overcook. Drain well, and season.

Pour boiling water over the fish. Leave for 5 minutes. Drain and mash, adding sugar and salt and a drop or two of colouring to turn the mixture pink. Dry to a fluffy mass in a pan over a low heat.

To make up the *norimaki-zushi*, crisp the sheets of *asakusa-nori* under the grill; or pass them to and fro over a gas flame. Lay the first one down on a bamboo table mat, and place a second one slightly overlapping it. Spread them with half the rice, leaving a

½-inch margin all round. On this base lay the various bits and pieces in lines across the rice to make a striped effect—again, use about half of each filling.

Roll up very carefully, using the mat to help you, and pushing the filling back into the roll as it squeezes out. Repeat with the other sheets of *asakusa-nori,* and the remaining rice and fillings. Chill for 3 hours, or longer if you like, then cut down into about 8 slices.

Any rice left over can be formed into small oval cakes, and pressed on to pieces of smoked salmon or other cured fish, cut into oblong pieces about 1 by 2 inches, or on to shelled prawns. Place the fish in the palm of your left hand, and gently press the rice on to it: then reverse on to a plate. These little cakes are called *nigiri-zushi.*

Tempura

In other words fritters, because the European fritter is thought to have been the origin of this popular Japanese food. When the Jesuit missionaries arrived with Saint Francis Xavier in sixteenth-century Japan, they ate the dish on Ember Days, fast days occurring at four periods of the year—the *quattuor tempora*—when ordinations could take place. The first Tokugawa ruler, Ieyasu, died about sixty years later from a surfeit of *tai tempura,* fritters of sea bream or *tai,* the most prized of Japanese fish. Some at least of the missionaries' works had made devoted converts.

If you have an electric deep frier, you will find tempura easy to organize on the *fondue bourguignonne* principle—which is to say that all the separate ingredients that go to make up a tempura are prepared beforehand, and the cooking is done last of all at table with no loss of sociability for the cook. This is the ideal, because these rather delicate fritters should be eaten immediately, straight from the pan, each person dipping his piece into a small bowl of sauce the moment it's ready.

In Japan, chopsticks are used for both cooking and eating tempura. But unless you are very skilful with them, you will find it easier, when cooking, to make use of a perforated spoon in the normal way. Fondue forks are the obvious solution, if you have them.

Prepare the three elements of the dish—sauce, seafood and vegetables, batter—in the following order:

SERVES FOUR

SAUCE:
4 tablespoons sake ⎫
2 tablespoons mirin ⎰ or 6 tablespoons mirin, or dry sherry with some sugar
4 tablespoons sugar
⅔ cup dashi or stock

Simmer together for two minutes. Pour into a bowl, or individual bowls, and leave to cool.

SEAFOOD AND VEGETABLES:
16 mushrooms, or shiitake
24 large prawns or shrimp in their shells
24 mussels, scrubbed and scraped
2 aubergines (eggplants)
4 spring onions

Cut stalks of fresh mushrooms level with the caps, or soak the shiitake until soft, drain them, and discard stems. Shell the prawns. Open the mussels in a large pan, covered, over a very high heat: remove them from their shells (keep the cooking liquor for another dish). Cut the aubergines into 8 or 12 pieces each, according to their size. Trim roots and damaged outer skin from the spring onions. Arrange elegantly on a dish. (Other ingredients can be added—e.g., cubes of firm white fish fillets, pieces of young carrot, red and green pepper and so on.)

BATTER:
The master of a tempura restaurant in Tokyo, the famous Ten-ichi restaurant, has written a small book on the special foods of the capital. In it he gives this recipe for the correct, very light batter. He observes that the old way of reading the characters of the word *tempura* gives you "flour" and "silk-gauze." "The whole word could mean to wear light stuff of flour, as a woman wears

silk-gauze that desire may be stimulated in the beholder by glimpses of the beauty underneath." This gives you a good idea of what the fritters should look like when they are ready to eat.

Break an egg into a measuring container, and whisk it smooth. Add four times its bulk of water, then five times its bulk of flour. In other words, if your egg occupies one liquid ounce, you should end up with ten liquid ounces of batter. Whisk well.

TO COOK:

Heat a pan of deep oil to between 350° and 360°F. Dip the individual pieces of food into the batter, shake off the surplus, and deep-fry for a few minutes until the coating is crisp and a rather whitish brown. With the spring onions, you will find it easier to use your fingers for dipping them into the batter rather than a perforated spoon. If you are not handing out the cooked fritters straight from the pan, arrange them on an elegantly folded napkin on a serving plate and keep them warm in the oven. Obviously the cooking has to be done in batches, so that there is no risk of the oil losing heat.

NOTE: Half the quantity can be used to make the first course of an otherwise Western dinner.

Sukiyaki

Sukiyaki is a *nabemono,* or one-pot dish—*nabe* meaning pot. This means that it is usually cooked at table, so that people can help themselves to the food when it is cooked to exactly the right degree. The basis of sukiyaki is prime fillet steak (Japan is famous for its beef, particularly in the Kansai region of Kyoto, Osaka and Kobe). Ideally the meat should be netted with fine threads of yellow fat. If it is well chilled, it can easily be cut into paper-thin slices. In Kyoto, fresh matsutake mushrooms would be used, as they grow abundantly around the city—but we must make do with the dried shiitake, unless we can find some fresh ceps. Bean curd can be bought fresh, canned or in packets of powder for making up. There are three kinds: *tofu,* which is white; *yakidofu,* which has been grilled; and *aburage,* which has been deep-fried. The first two are suitable for sukiyaki.

SERVES FOUR

4 ounces shirataki or vermicelli
1½-inch cube beef suet
1 pound trimmed fillet steak, in paper-thin slices
3 onions, sliced thickly
1 stalk celery, sliced diagonally
8 ounces Chinese (or Savoy) cabbage, sliced
4 ounces spinach leaves
8 dried mushrooms, soaked 10 minutes in hot water, stems removed,
   or 8 fresh ceps
4 ounces bamboo shoots, sliced
¼ pound tofu, or yakidofu, cut into 1-inch cubes

SAUCE:

½ cup dashi or stock
½ cup soya sauce
6 tablespoons sugar
2 tablespoons mirin or dry sherry with some sugar

PLUS:

4 eggs
4 bowls hot boiled rice

Boil Japanese noodles (shirataki) or vermicelli in salted water for 5 minutes. Drain and cool. Arrange with the rest of the first list of ingredients on a large platter or tray. Mix sauce ingredients together. Break each egg into a small bowl and beat. Put the rice into 4 bowls. Each person is given a bowl of egg and a bowl of rice.

TO COOK:

Heat frying pan over a table cooker (or use an electric frying pan), and rub it with the cube of suet. Quickly put in some of the beef: when it is lightly browned, turn it over (chopsticks are the best implements). As people eat the first slices of beef, which they dip first into egg and then into the rice bowl, cook the rest.

Then pour some of the sauce into the pan and stir it up with the meat juices. Add a selection of the other ingredients, keeping everything at a steady boil—not too fast, or the juices will evaporate. The cabbage will add a certain amount of moisture, so will the onion and celery; the rest of the sauce should be added gradually. The first time you make this dish, it is a good idea to have some extra sauce to hand, in case the liquid boils too fast and disappears.

Overcooking is the worst fault of sukiyaki—vegetables should have some bite and a fresh flavour to them. If beef overcooks, it becomes tough.

Any cooking liquor left can be poured into the egg bowls and drunk as soup.

Sautéed mushrooms and cucumber

Mushrooms and cucumber are two crisp smooth textures which combine well together—see the French recipe on page 122. By contrast the delicious item in this recipe is the crunch of toasted sesame seeds.

SERVES TWO TO FOUR
1 cucumber
salt
6 large fresh mushrooms (field or cultivated)
4 tablespoons sesame seeds
4 tablespoons oil
4 teaspoons sugar
6 tablespoons soya sauce

Wash the cucumber and cut it into slices. Sprinkle with salt, and leave in a colander for at least 30 minutes to drain. Cut the mushrooms into ¼-inch-thick slices. Toast the sesame seeds in a dry frying pan, stirring them about gently, until they hop and crackle in the heat; then crush them in a mortar or nut grinder or electric coffee mill. Drain and dry the cucumber. Heat the oil in a pan and put in the cucumbers and mushrooms. Cook briskly until the cucumbers are beginning to soften. Add sugar and soya sauce and stir everything about for another minute. Put on to a serving dish and sprinkle with the sesame seeds.

Mushrooms grilled with mirin

Large fresh ceps, or good-sized field mushrooms can be substituted for matsutake in this recipe from Joan and Peter Martin's *Japanese Cooking* (Penguin, 1970). Remember that matsutake, the pine mushrooms which are such a delicacy in the autumn, can be as large as 10 inches across—the equivalent to 6 of them in this recipe would be 18 nice-sized ones of another variety. But there is no need to worry—making adjustments to a simple recipe like this one is easy: if there seems too little of the marinade, increase the quantities in proportion. Matsutake are also grilled plainly, then served as they are, with soya sauce, lemon juice and monosodium glutamate on the table for each person to season his mushrooms to his own liking.

SERVES TWO TO FOUR
6 *matsutake, or 18 ceps or field mushrooms*
2 *ounces mirin, or dry sherry plus some sugar*
3 *tablespoons light soya sauce* (usukuchi)

Wash and slice the mushrooms into thick pieces. Mix the wine and soya sauce and pour over the mushroom pieces. Leave to marinade for an hour. Drain well, then grill or broil for 2 or 3 minutes on each side, brushing with the marinade from time to time. When cooked, serve immediately.

Dobin mushi
(Mushrooms steamed in an earthenware teapot)

This dish is prepared in special teapots: the lids are large enough to serve as bowls to drink the soup from. Dr Aga Kagawa, the author of *Japanese Cook Book*, from which this recipe comes, suggests that you plug the spouts with fresh pine needles, or with other sweet-smelling leaves, just before serving the *dobin mushi*. Use small marmites with lids as a substitute, or soup bowls with a foil lid.

SERVES SIX
3 *matsutake, or 6 shiitake, soaked*
4 *tablespoons sake*
1 *teaspoon salt*
8 *ounces chicken breast*
18 *sprigs watercress*
24 *gingko nuts or chestnuts, shelled*
2½ *cups dashi, or broth, boiling hot*
2 *teaspoons soya sauce*
2 *tablespoons Seville orange juice or lemon juice*

Discard mushroom stems, and slice caps. Pour the sake and half the salt over them. Leave while you assemble the other ingredients. Slice the chicken breast into small pieces and strain over them the juices from the soaked mushrooms. Divide the mushrooms, chicken, watercress, and nuts among the six teapots or bowls. Add the boiling dashi or broth, the soya sauce and the remaining salt, and place the teapots or bowls in a steamer (improvise with a self-basting roaster) with enough boiling water to come halfway up the pots. Steam for 20 minutes. Add the orange or lemon juice just before serving. People remove the lids from their pots and pour in the soup: with the aid of chopsticks, they remove the nice bits and pieces remaining in the pot, and dip them in the soup before eating them. Then they drink the soup which remains.

Matsutake gohan
(Rice with matsutake mushrooms)

Another recipe from Joan and Peter Martin's *Japanese Cooking* (Penguin, 1970), which can be used for cultivated mushrooms or field mushrooms.

SERVES SIX TO EIGHT

3 cups rice
5 cups water
1 piece kombu *seaweed (optional but desirable)*
6 tablespoons light soya sauce
4 tablespoons sake
6 ounces matsutake, or button mushrooms, sliced
½ teaspoon salt

Wash and drain the rice an hour before cooking it. Put with water, *kombu* if available, soya sauce and sake into a large pan and bring to the boil. Extract *kombu* as soon as the water begins to bubble. Add mushrooms and salt, cover, and simmer for 15 minutes or a little longer until the water has been absorbed. Raise the heat for 30 seconds, then remove pan from the stove and allow it to rest 10 minutes before putting it into a serving dish.

Chinese recipes

Mushroom soup

The Chinese equivalent to *consommé aux champignons* is a delicate soup with the light flavours of chicken, ginger and onion supporting the mushrooms. If you care to make the two soups on consecutive days, you will understand in the clearest way possible the difference in flavour, texture and function between the oriental mushroom and our own commercial *Agaricus bisporus.* The compactness and concentrated taste of *Lentinus edodes* means that the quantity is specified by number rather than weight—four dried mushrooms, or six, at the most twelve (except in the unusual mushroom dish on pages 285–6—unusual, that is to say, from a Chinese point of view, being much closer to a Western recipe like, for instance, the mushrooms and anchovies on page 128).

Although chicken stock in China is made from a boiling fowl or from a carcass, just as it is in Europe, there is a difference, an important one, in the aromatics. We use carrots, parsnips, onions, a bouquet garni of thyme, parsley and bay; they use spring onion and a slice or two of fresh root ginger, with perhaps some rice wine or soya sauce. Also they emphasize the meat flavour by including a piece of pork spareribs (an idea to be borrowed, particularly if you are relying on a carcass). If you want to serve the boiling fowl in the European style, this poses a problem: the best way to solve it is to use the Western aromatics, but in smaller quantities so that the flavour—for instance of carrot, or bay—is not too assertive.

12 *dried mushrooms*
1 *large spring onion*
1 *slice fresh ginger root, peeled*
4½ *cups chicken stock*
2 *tablespoons soya sauce*
sugar
.*salt*

Put mushrooms in a bowl. Cover them with not quite boiling water and leave for 30 minutes. Reserving liquid, remove mushrooms and cut them in half, discarding the stems. Put with onion, ginger, stock, and mushroom-soaking liquid into a pan. Add the soya sauce, about ½ teaspoon of sugar, and salt if needed to taste. Cover tightly (jam the lid on with foil, if it doesn't fit well) and simmer for an hour. Before serving, remove the onion and ginger, and correct the seasoning.

This soup would be served with rice and bowls of meat and vegetables, to be drunk during the meal. But there is no reason why you should not enjoy it at the beginning of the meal like any other soup, and follow it with the kind of things you normally eat.

Tung kua t'ang
(Winter melon soup)

This is a lovely soup, beautiful to look at, varied and clear to the taste. It has the further merit of being simple to make. Do not worry too much about finding the correct Chinese ingredients, apart from the mushrooms, which are essential. Substitutes for other items work successfully. In fact the success of the soup depends on using a good chicken stock: in other words, make it when you have been cooking a boiling fowl (or have been able to buy giblets).

SERVES FOUR
3 *cups chicken stock*
1 *pound winter melon or cucumber, peeled*

4 dried mushrooms, at least 1 inch across, soaked
1½ ounces canned Yunnan ham or Smithfield ham, or lachschinken, *or*
  Danish smoked bacon, cut into 1-inch squares

Put the stock into a pan. Cut the melon or cucumber into ¼-inch-thick pieces, about 1 inch across, and add to the stock. Drain the mushrooms, discard the hard stalks, quarter mushrooms, and add to stock. Bring to the boil and cook gently for 15 minutes, pressing the mushroom pieces once or twice to extract the maximum amount of juice into the soup. Place the ham or *lachschinken* or bacon into the soup bowls, and pour the contents of the pan over it.

Chinese steamed fish

The snag about Eastern cooking from an English point of view is the difficulty of getting fish—and vegetables—in good fresh condition. Japanese sashimi, the raw fish hors d'oeuvre, which can be exquisite in flavour and texture, is perfectly disgusting when made with stale squid or bream. This recipe is delicate and subtle in flavour when the bass or John Dory or chicken halibut or turbot has come fairly rapidly from the sea. With poor fish it tastes insipid. If you are in doubt and cannot rely on your fishmonger's understanding of the word "fresh," choose sole. Because of its peculiar chemistry, the flavour develops two days after it has been caught: with other fish, such as plaice, it begins to deteriorate from the moment of death.

SERVES FOUR
1½-pound whole white fish
1 level teaspoon salt
1 tablespoon soya sauce
1 tablespoon Chinese rice wine, or dry sherry
1 tablespoon grated fresh ginger root
3 spring onions or 2 small leeks, cut in 2-inch lengths
2 tablespoons corn oil
5 dried mushrooms, soaked, quartered, stems removed
½ teaspoon sugar
4 slices very fat bacon, or pork back fat

Rinse and dry the fish. If it is a round fish, such as bass, make diagonal cuts on both sides of the backbone. If it is a flat fish, skin it. Rub in the salt and place it on an oval dish which will fit easily into the steamer (improvisation with a self-basting roaster may be needed: stand the dish on two heatproof pots—there should be enough space between the dish and the roaster for the steam to circulate freely). Mix all remaining ingredients, except the bacon or pork fat, and pour them over the fish. Lay the bacon or pork fat on top of it. Cover tightly and steam for 10 to 20 minutes, according to the thickness of the fish. Serve with all the juices and bits and pieces but remove the bacon if it looks unsightly.

Red-cooked pork leg or shoulder

"Red-cooked" because of the beautiful reddish brown tone given to the meat by the soya sauce. This kind of slow-cooked dish surprises many Westerners, who think that all Chinese food comes from a frying pan. If you are preparing a meal of several dishes, this is a sensible one to include, as it can be prepared a day or two in advance. Just before the meal it can be reheated. Or it can be served cold, cut in slices, with the jellied cooking liquid. "The sensation of jelly melting against the hot rice in your mouth must be unique to Chinese eating," says Kenneth Lo in *Chinese Food,* "like the warm, many-scented earthiness which rises in waves from the land when the snow first starts melting in the spring. The nascent flavour of the jelly seems to be enhanced by being freshly released."

SERVES EIGHT AS A MAIN COURSE
4–5-pound leg or shoulder of pork
½ cup soya sauce
4 sections star anise
2 tablespoons superfine sugar
¼ cup Chinese rice wine, or dry sherry
2 tablespoons chopped mild onion
2 cups cold water
8 dried Chinese mushrooms, 1–1½ inches diameter, soaked and left whole

In red-cooking, the meat must be blanched first (with red-cooked fish, it is usually fried, but that's a different story), so cover it generously with cold water, set it over a high heat and boil briskly for 5 minutes. Put meat in a colander and rinse it under the cold tap. Discard the blanching water. Now score the part of the meat which is *not* covered by skin with four cuts, and place it, scored side down, in a clean pan. Add soya sauce, anise, sugar, wine, onions and cold water. Bring to simmering point and cover, turning it over every half-hour or so. After 2½ hours, or sooner if the meat seems nearly ready, add the soaked mushroom caps (discard the stems), and complete the cooking—until meat can be pierced with chopsticks. Remove the meat to a deep dish, and keep warm if it's to be eaten straightaway. Place the mushrooms decoratively on top. Measure the cooking liquid; there should be about 10 ounces—if there's more, boil it down; if there's less, add some hot water. Pour round the meat.

Chinese-style, the meat would be pulled off the bone by the diners during the meal. More practical, for our way of eating, is to slice the meat from the bone, always including the skin, and lay it on a dish with the mushrooms and sauce.

Stir-fried chicken with mushrooms

One of the easiest dishes to include in a western meal. As you can substitute fresh for Chinese dried mushrooms, the only ingredient likely to cause a little difficulty is the ginger.

SERVES FOUR AS A MAIN DISH

1 *pound boned chicken breast*
4 *teaspoons cornstarch*
1 *egg white*
4 *tablespoons Chinese rice wine, or dry sherry*
salt
8 *tablespoons oil*
2 *slices fresh ginger root, peeled*
4 *heaping tablespoons finely chopped onion*
12 *large Chinese mushrooms, soaked, quartered, stems removed,*
   or *½ pound fresh mushrooms, sliced*
2 *tablespoons soya sauce*
⅓ cup chicken stock

Chill the chicken, then slice it as thinly as possible and cut each slice into strips about ½ inch wide and 1 inch long. Mix them with half the starch in a bowl until they are coated; add egg white, wine, and a teaspoon of salt, and mix well. Heat half the oil in a frying pan, and stir-fry the ginger and onion for a few seconds, until they begin to have a whitish appearance, then put in the chicken. Stir it about for a minute, until chicken is opaque and just cooked. Remove to a dish and keep warm. Pour remaining oil into the pan and fry the mushrooms for a minute and a half, scraping the pan well. Put chicken back in pan, and add soya sauce. Quickly mix remaining starch with chicken stock, tip into the pan (keep stirring), and cook for a moment or two until the meat and mushrooms are glazed with a clear brown sauce. Correct seasoning if necessary.

This simple stir-fried chicken with mushrooms recipe, from *The Thousand Recipe Chinese Cookbook,* by Gloria Bley Miller (Atheneum, 1966; Paul Hamlyn, 1966), can be varied by substituting one

of the mixtures below for the mushrooms mentioned in the master
list of ingredients:

I.

¼ *pound fresh mushrooms, sliced*
6 *shiitake, soaked, stemmed, quartered*

II.

½ *pound fresh mushrooms, sliced*
½ *pound Chinese leaf (celery cabbage), sliced*

III.

¼ *pound fresh mushrooms, sliced*
2 *stalks of celery, sliced*
4 *ounces shelled walnuts, roughly chopped*

IV.

¼ *pound fresh mushrooms, sliced*
¼ *pound bamboo shoots, sliced*

V.

6 *shiitake, soaked, stemmed, quartered*
¼ *pound bamboo shoots, sliced*
¼ *pound shelled walnuts, roughly chopped*

VI.

1 *cucumber, peeled, sliced*
¼ *pound fresh mushrooms, sliced*
6 *water chestnuts, sliced*
4 *stalks celery, sliced*

Chicken stuffed with dried mushrooms and chestnuts

Chestnuts are a great favourite with the Chinese, as they are with
us. This is a most sympathetic dish to our Western idea of things.
The point of hanging the chicken up in a blast of cold air is to
dry out its skin, which will then become particularly crisp and
succulent as it roasts: this is the method used to make the skin
of Peking duck such a pleasure to eat. In Peking, though, the dry
cold air is supplied by the Gobi desert and not by an electric fan.

4–5-pound *whole roasting chicken*
14 *shiitake mushrooms*
20 *chestnuts*
½ *cup chopped onion*
4 *tablespoons soya sauce*
salt
pepper
2 *tablespoons sherry*
peanut or corn oil

Hang the chicken up by a piece of string in front of an electric fan, or the cool air from an electric fan heater. Leave it for 2 hours.

Meanwhile soak, then slice, the mushrooms, discarding stems. Peel and chop the chestnuts. Mix mushrooms and chestnuts with onion, two-thirds of the soya sauce, ½ teaspoon of salt and a dash of pepper. Stuff the dried chicken with the mixture and truss securely.

Mix sherry with remaining soya sauce and rub it over the bird. Then brush it over with oil. Put on to a rack over a roasting pan with a good inch of water in it, and put into a mark 5, 375°F, oven for 20 minutes. Reduce the heat to mark 3, 325°F, for another 40 minutes or until the bird is cooked. Baste from time to time, and add more water to the pan if necessary. Serve in the Western style; or cut up and arrange on a warm dish in the Chinese manner.

Steamed chicken with padi-straw (grass) mushrooms

I include this recipe (from Gloria Bley Miller's *Thousand Recipe Chinese Cookbook*) in case you have the good fortune to come across some dried padi-straw mushrooms or some of the rare, edible *Volvariella* species which grow in Europe.

SERVES SIX
10 *dried padi-straw mushrooms, soaked 15 minutes*
4 *pitted Chinese red dates, or prunes, soaked 25 minutes*
1 *piece dried tangerine peel, soaked 30 minutes*

4 *ounces bamboo shoots, sliced thinly*
2–3 *slices fresh ginger root, peeled, chopped*
2 *tablespoons cornstarch*
½ *teaspoon salt*
½ *teaspoon sugar*
2 *teaspoons soya sauce*
1 *roasting chicken, including giblets*

Cut mushrooms, dates, or prunes and peel into julienne strips. Put with bamboo slices and ginger into a bowl.

Mix next four ingredients to a smooth paste and stir into the mushroom bowl, turning everything over well.

With a cleaver, cut chicken into pieces 1½ by 2 inches, and put them on a heatproof dish which will fit inside your steamer with a little room to spare at the sides. Cut the giblets into ½-inch pieces and add them to the chicken.

Spoon the contents of the mushroom bowl evenly over the chicken. Steam until done—30 to 40 minutes.

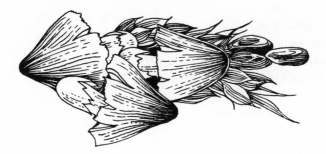

Fried rice

Now that there are so many Chinese cooked food shops in England, fried rice has become a popular snack or light meal. Basically it is yesterday's boiled rice, heated up and scrambled with egg. To this simple formula—which is not quite so simple to make up successfully as you might imagine—it is usual to add some interesting details. Here is Kenneth Lo's recipe from *Chinese Food* (Penguin, 1972), which I've chosen because it gives you the most successful result. Fried rice can be soggy and greasy. On the other hand, it can be delicious, particularly as a supper dish with a bowl of clear soup. Two things to remember: prepare all the ingredients and have them arranged logically, near the stove, and make sure that everyone is sitting down to the table by the time the rice is cooked (just as you would with a soufflé). As Kenneth Lo says, the ingredients for fried rice can be varied. You should aim to have onion and ham or bacon as well as the eggs, but chicken, pork, beef, cucumber, bamboo shoots, prawns and shrimps can be used. Your choice will depend on the contents of the refrigerator. It is a good way of using left-overs discreetly. Experiment by including field mushrooms or oyster mushrooms or rubber brush mushrooms, instead of the cultivated kind.

SERVES FOUR

4 eggs
1 teaspoon salt
4 ounces cooked pork, diced into pea-sized pieces
3 tablespoons soya sauce
½ teaspoon sugar
½ cup vegetable oil
2 medium onions, chopped
⅓ cup cooked green peas
⅓ cup button mushrooms, quartered
2 ounces cooked ham, diced
3 cups boiled long-grain rice

Beat eggs with half the salt for 10 seconds. Marinade the pork with soya sauce and sugar. In a very large frying pan, heat about a third of the oil and stir-fry the onions for one minute, without frizzling them. Put in peas and mushrooms, and fry for half a minute, stirring all the time. Push everything to one side of the pan. Add half the remaining oil, and when it is hot, scramble the eggs in it. As eggs begin to set, push them to the opposite side of the pan, and remove the whole thing from the heat. *In another pan*, heat the remaining oil and stir-fry the marinaded pork and the ham for 3 minutes. Add the cooked rice and mix everything well together for 1 minute more. Be sure to keep everything moving. Now tip this mixture into the centre of the large frying pan. Put it back over a very high heat and stir everything vigorously together for 1 minute only. Turn on to a warmed dish and serve immediately.

Stir-fried Chinese cabbage with mushrooms and bamboo shoots

I notice that Chinese cabbage, celery cabbage or Chinese leaf (*pe-ts'ai* and *pai-ts'ai* to the Chinese themselves) is creeping quietly but steadily into good greengroceries all over. It is by far the best of the Brassicas, and simple to grow. Indeed, whenever I see gardens full of the usual rank-smelling cabbage, I wonder why we still bother with such things when this pleasurable relation is in all the seed catalogues.

Stir-fried, as in this recipe, Chinese cabbage keeps its fresh taste and crunch, but benefits from the heavier crispness of bamboo shoots and the chewiness of mushrooms. A fine vegetable dish, on its own, or with a Western meal.

SERVES FOUR
1 pound Chinese cabbage (or Savoy, if you must)
4 ounces canned bamboo shoots
6 dried mushrooms, soaked
oil
about 1 teaspoon salt
about ¼ teaspoon sugar

Slice cabbage so that it falls into strips about ¼-inch wide, across the leaves. Rinse and slice the bamboo shoots. Reserve a few tablespoons of the mushroom soaking water, then quarter the mushrooms, discarding the stems. Heat the frying pan, and pour in just enough oil to cover the base thinly. Stir-fry the cabbage for 1 minute, keeping it moving and turning the whole time, so that all the strips are coated thinly with oil. Add bamboo shoots, mushrooms, salt, sugar, and reserved mushroom soaking liquor. Bring to a sharp boil, cover, and cook for 5 minutes, or until the cabbage is cooked but still crisp. Correct seasoning. Serve immediately.

Aubergines (eggplant) à la chinoise (Aubergines in the Chinese style)

Chinoiserie is one of the joys of European civilisation, and I see no reason to apologise when it breaks out in cooking. Authenticity is not its aim (I should like to take a visitor from Peking into the eighteenth-century rococo Chinese room at Claydon House in Buckinghamshire and watch his face), but pleasure. Or perhaps delight is the word, delight in the exotic, that "bright world of the imagination, where we take our true holidays," as Edward H. Schafer says in *The Golden Peaches of Samarkand*.

SERVES FOUR

1 pound aubergines (eggplant), peeled, diced, salted
cooking oil
1 ounce dried mushrooms, soaked, stemmed, quartered
6 ounces lean smoked Danish bacon, cut in squares
6 ounces cooked chicken, diced
4 ounces chopped walnuts
⅓ cup soya sauce
6 tablespoons Madeira
2 tablespoons sugar
pinch of monosodium glutamate (optional)

Fry the well-drained aubergines in oil, and when they are half-cooked, add the mushrooms, bacon, and chicken. Mix remaining ingredients in a bowl. When the aubergines are cooked and the other ingredients well heated, pour in the contents of the bowl. Stir the whole thing together, and serve when really hot.

Sautéed mushrooms

The combination of mushrooms with oyster sauce is a good one, and a favourite of the Chinese, particularly of the Chinese in Kwangtung, on the southern coast. You might like to take the advice of the Lins—"Do not talk when eating mushrooms, or you spoil the flavour. Chew a mushroom as little as possible, only press out its hidden juices between tongue and teeth." This remark points out very clearly the difference in texture between shiitake and most European mushrooms.

Oyster sauce is made from oysters and soya sauce, and can be bought at oriental stores. Or you can make your own, which is quite simple to do. Open half a dozen oysters, chop them roughly and put them into a small pan with their juices. Cover them closely and simmer for about 15 minutes. Strain the liquor into a bowl, pressing it out of the chopped oyster, which can then be discarded. Season with 1 to 2 tablespoons of soya sauce. Store in a screw-top jar, and keep in the refrigerator.

SERVES THREE TO EIGHT
30 *large dried mushrooms*
3 *tablespoons oil*
¾ *teaspoon sugar*
generous ¼ *teaspoon salt*
1½ *teaspoons soya sauce*
3 *tablespoons sesame seed oil*
8 *tablespoons oyster sauce*
1 *cup beef or chicken stock*
3 *teaspoons cornstarch*
extra sugar

Soak mushrooms in enough hot water to cover them, for 30 minutes. Drain them, reserving the liquid, and discard the stems. Fry the caps briefly in the oil, then add sugar, salt and soya sauce. Mix well, then pour in the mushroom-soaking liquor, sesame seed oil and just under half the oyster sauce. Simmer until the liquid has almost disappeared, leaving just a spoonful or two. Arrange the mushrooms in a pile on a serving dish, caps upwards.

Quickly stir together the remaining ingredients—the rest of the oyster sauce, the stock, cornflour or starch and a good pinch of sugar. Pour it into the mushroom-cooking pan, and stir everything well together so that it thickens evenly. Taste and correct the seasoning—a little more sugar may be needed, for instance. Pour over the mushrooms.

This dish may be served as part of a Chinese meal—or it can be eaten Western style with grilled steak or veal escalopes, or as a vegetable dish on its own or with rice.

Mushrooms from *The Dragon Book*

It seems odd, in these days of television and universal movement, that my first idea of foreign countries should have been exclusively poetical. Geography lessons I found useless. They emptied the world with a boredom of sketch maps, isobars, crops and rainfall. It was a desert—until I encountered the poets. Italy came alive with Browning and the "wind-grieved Apennine." Then China, with Arthur Waley. His translation of *The Everlasting Wrong*, Li Po's lament for Yang Kuei Fei, the Pearl Concubine (who was ultimately sacrificed by her Emperor lover to political necessity), was perfectly attuned to my state of emotional starvation at a girls' boarding school. China was full of hibiscus and solitary pines, jagged mountains and dancing girls with long sleeves and moth eyebrows. Just as well that someone gave me *The Dragon Book*, an anthology by E. D. Edwards which includes poetry but also Chinese sayings and proverbs, and funny stories—and recipes. Crabs fed with sesame seeds and salads of yellow chrysanthemum petals seemed exotic, but they made my mouth water and gave me a more rounded idea of the Chinese character than Li Po—or rather Arthur Waley —had done. (I don't think that Browning's Italians ever *ate* anything: they rode—on horses or in gondolas, they collected statues, they sang, but none of them ever twirled spaghetti on a fork.) Years later, when I had my own kitchen, this was one of the first Chinese recipes I used from that anthology:

SERVES TWO TO FOUR
2 ounces (4 tablespoons) butter
1 large clove garlic
½ pound fresh mushrooms, whole
1 slice fresh ginger, peeled, slightly crushed
1¼ cups stock
2 lumps sugar
2 tablespoons soya sauce

salt
1 *tablespoon cornstarch*

Melt half the butter and cook the garlic in it gently until it begins to soften, then crush it with a wooden spoon or a fork. Add the mushrooms and cook for 5 minutes. Pour in the stock, and add the slice of ginger. Simmer slowly until the mushrooms are cooked—about 5 more minutes or a little longer. Pour off the stock into a small saucepan, remove the ginger, and put the mushrooms into a dish. To the stock, add the remaining butter, the sugar, soya sauce, and salt to taste. Boil for a minute, then tip some of the liquid on to the starch. Mix it well, return to the pan, and stir over a low heat until the sauce thickens to a rich brown. Coat the mushrooms with the sauce, either more or less of it according to taste, and according to whether the dish is to be part of a Chinese meal, or to be eaten on its own or as a vegetable with steak or chicken.

Wood ears
(Auricularia polytricha)

The crumpled blackish muddle of dried wood ears resembles the charred remains of a log before it finally disintegrates to ash. How can such an unpromising substance come to be worth eating? And yet after 20 or 30 minutes in a bowl of hot water, the pieces swell into cloud-like shapes—perhaps this accounts for the name cloud ears—of a light gelatinous firmness. One sees why this and related funguses are known throughout the world by the name of ears—there's the Latin "ear" name, *Auricularia,* our own "Jew's ears," the French *oreille de Judas,* and the less shameful, more poetic names given them by the Chinese, wood ears, cloud ears.

As one turns them over in the water to loosen the clusters, the delicate shaping and colours vary considerably. Some are blackish brown and tightly wrinkled together, like ruching in a fabric. Others, small perfect shells, are a reddish brown fading to mauve in the shallow curve. All of them have a hint of transparency that indicates the clean crunchy texture. Buried amongst them you may find traces of their original home, fragments of wood, a seed or two, and a few dried leaves which still retain a little of their green. Such souvenirs must be discarded of course, and the water will need changing several times before the gritty sand is separated from the intricate curves.

Try chewing a small piece. It is almost entirely texture, with the faintest air of mushroom flavour that one seems to smell rather than taste. And this light clean texture is the reason for its popularity with the Chinese. In *Chinese Gastronomy*, the Lins group it with other texture foods such as bird's nest, and the heavier, more resilient *bêche-de-mer* (the sea slug or sea cucumber). They give a recipe combining the wood ear and the sea slug. It comes from Yuan Mei, the great gourmet of eighteenth-century China. He deplored the opulent vulgarity and showiness of court banquets under the Ching dynasty, which was not Chinese at all but Manchu. "What matters," he said, "is the unique taste of each food" (this was two hundred years before Curnonsky took a stand against the decadence of haute cuisine in France, asserting that everything should taste *of itself*). It is a wonderfully black dish, as black as Italian *cacciucco*, the fish stew of Leghorn, and not difficult to make. You will find it on page 298.

Here, though, as a simpler beginning, are two recipes from *The Joy of Chinese Cooking*, by Doreen Yen Hung Feng (Faber, 1952), followed by an unusual recipe for wood ears and pickled cabbage steamed with pork, and *Yuan Mei's bêche-de-mer gourmet*.

Pig's liver with wood ears

A most savoury mixture. The pig's liver is much improved by the combined method of frying and scalding.

SERVES FOUR

1 *pound pig's liver, cut in ¼-inch-thick slices*
¾ *ounce wood ears, soaked*
½ *cup oil*
3 *spring onions, cut in 2-inch lengths*
salt
2 *teaspoons sugar*
4 *tablespoons soya sauce*
2 *tablespoons dry sherry*
3 *teaspoons cornstarch, mixed with 4 tablespoons water*

Cut liver into pieces about 2 inches by 1 inch. Separate the wood ears as much as possible. Heat a couple of tablespoons of the oil in a large frying pan, add onions, and stir-fry for 15 seconds. Next put in the wood ears, sprinkle with a little salt, and give them 10 seconds, stirring all the time. Remove from the pan, to a dish.

Add the rest of the oil to the frying pan, and heat it well. Put in the liver and cook for 30 seconds, turning it over so that the slices are sealed by the heat. Remove them to a bowl and pour enough boiling water over them to cover. Stir gently, leave for 10 seconds, then pour out into a sieve held over the sink, so that the meat is well drained.

Put the remaining ingredients into the bowl, then return the liver to it and mix everything well together. Reheat the frying pan and cook the liver mixture for 15 seconds. Put in the wood ears to reheat for a few seconds—keep stirring all the time. Transfer to a warm serving dish. Eat immediately.

Braised satin chicken

"Golden needles" are dried lily flowers. They come in yellow strips and need to be soaked before cooking. Get them if you can, because their flavour is unlike anything else, so that there is no substitute.

SERVES FOUR
4 dried shiitake, soaked
⅓ cup wood ears, soaked
12 golden needles, soaked
½ teaspoon sugar
¼ teaspoon salt
¼ teaspoon pepper
1 slice fresh ginger, peeled, chopped
2 tablespoons soya sauce
2 tablespoons dry sherry
½ roasting chicken, cut in several pieces
6 tablespoons oil
⅔ cup hot water

THICKENING:
1 tablespoon cornstarch
a little water
¼ teaspoon sugar
dash soya sauce

Slice the shiitake, discarding their stems. Separate the clusters of wood ears. Cut the golden needles in two. Put the next six ingredients into a bowl, mix them well, and rub into the chicken. Leave for 10 minutes or so, then drain chicken. Heat the oil in a frying pan and brown the chicken all over. Add the mushrooms and golden needles and the hot water. Simmer, covered, until the chicken is cooked, turning it over from time to time—about 30 to 40 minutes.

Place the mushrooms and golden needles on the serving dish. Slice the chicken and place it on top. Mix the thickening ingredients and stir into the pan juices. After simmering a few moments, pour sauce over the chicken and serve.

Pickled cabbage steamed with pork

Chinese pickled cabbage comes in brine-filled jars. If you cannot buy it, use sauerkraut instead. Tangerine skin comes in 2-inch squares, more or less, and will need a brief soaking like the mushrooms. Kenneth Lo remarks that you can prepare your own by drying tangerine peelings in a mark ½, 250°F, oven, for half an hour —but you will need to use double the quantity for the same effect.

SERVES FOUR

1¼ cups pickled cabbage or sauerkraut
⅓ cup wood ears, soaked
2 large shiitake, soaked, stems discarded
1 small piece tangerine peel, soaked
6 water chestnuts
½ pound minced pork
¼ teaspoon pepper
¼ teaspoon salt
1 tablespoon soya sauce
½ teaspoon sugar
1 teaspoon cornstarch
2 tablespoons corn or salad oil
⅓ cup cold water

The important thing is to taste the pickled cabbage or sauerkraut, after rinsing it. If it is too salty, leave it in a basin of cold water for up to 15 minutes, until the pungency of the brine has been reduced to an agreeable level. Drain it well, then chop it with the next five ingredients to make a moderately fine mash: it can be put through a mincing machine or grinder. Mix with remaining ingredi-

ents, taste a tiny amount with the tip of your tongue to check the
seasoning, and put into one or two serving dishes. Steam, covered,
for 30 minutes until the pork is cooked.

Yuan Mei's bêche-de-mer gourmet

Bêche-de-mer, sea slug or sea cucumber, has been boiled and dried
before it gets to the oriental provision merchants. It looks like a
dried banana, not in the least like an ex-inhabitant of the seas. You
will need to soak it well, until it is soft. By the end of the recipe,
its texture will be one of "tender resilience."

SERVES FOUR
½ *pound dried* bêche-de-mer, *soaked*
½ *ounce dried wood ears, soaked*
2½ *ounces shiitake, soaked*

STOCK:
3 *ounces dried prawns or shrimp*
2 *tablespoons sesame oil*
2¾ *teaspoons sugar*
6 *small pickling onions, peeled*
3 *slices fresh ginger, peeled*
3 *cups water*

3 cups chicken or beef consommé
2 tablespoons soya sauce

Clean the soaked *bêche-de-mer* and cut it into ½-inch chunks. Separate the wood ears. Discard the stems of the shiitake, but keep the water in which they have been soaked.

To make the stock, put the prawns into a large container with the sesame oil and 2 teaspoons of sugar. Cover with about a quart of boiling water. After 10 minutes, pour into a sieve over the sink. Put the prawns into a saucepan with the remaining stock ingredients, not forgetting the last ¾ teaspoonful of sugar. Simmer for 1 hour, then strain off the stock and discard the prawns.

Put the stock into a clean pan with the *bêche-de-mer*, the wood ears, and the shiitake and their reserved soaking water. Simmer for 2½ to 3 hours.

Silver tree fungi in crystal soup

A recipe for devotees of mushrooms, and of Chinese regional cookery, because it is the only one in this section which cannot easily be incorporated into a Western meal. Although it could be part of a particularly savoury buffet table, it should be served in the context of Szechuan food, which Hsiang Ju Lin and Tsuifeng Lin, in *Chinese Gastronomy,* describe as "a brilliant freak." Much use is made of hot peppers—chilis, in other words—and after the first shock of their flavour has passed, leaving a mellowness, comes "the *manifold flavour* characteristic of Szechuan, in which the sour, salty, sweet, fragrant, bitter and hot can all be tasted at once."

One sees why this sweet mushroom soup is served towards the end of a banquet. After four or five courses of such spiced and savoury food, its elegant clarity makes a perfect finish. "On the other hand, when the dishes are served together—as sometimes in a party meal at home—then such a dish can only be served in conjunction with at least four or five other savoury dishes, adjacent to a dish which is particularly spicey and rich." This is Kenneth Lo writing, and I suggest that if this recipe captures your fancy as it did mine, you turn to the complete Szechuan meal he describes in his *Chinese Food* (Penguin, 1972). After quick-braised beef, sweet and sour pork, marinaded venison and quick-fried hot diced chicken, it comes like a beautiful resolution or coda.

SERVES SIX TO TEN
1 *ounce dried wood ears, soaked*
1 *egg*
4 *cups water*
½ *pound amber-coloured sugar crystals, or ordinary lump sugar*

Clean the soaked mushrooms and break the clusters into pieces.

Beat egg thoroughly, then add 4 or 5 tablespoons of the water, and beat for a further 5 seconds. Heat sugar and remaining water in a clean pan. When the sugar has melted and the liquid is almost at the boiling point, stir in the beaten egg. When it rises to the top of the syrup in a thick layer, pour the whole thing into a muslin-lined sieve set over a heatproof bowl—the purpose of the egg is to clarify the syrup, making it crystal clear.

Drain the wood ears and add them to the syrup. Put the bowl into a steamer and give it 1½ hours. Serve warm or chilled.

Epilogue

But when all's said and written,

there is nothing better than field mushrooms

that you have gathered yourself,

on toast, for breakfast.

APPENDIX:
FIVE BASIC
RECIPES FOR
REFERENCE

Basic béchamel sauce

4 tablespoons butter
4 tablespoons flour
2¼ cups hot milk
medium carrot, quartered
medium onion, quartered
2 cloves
bouquet garni
salt, pepper

Melt butter, stir in flour and cook for 2 minutes without allowing
the mixture to colour. Pour in the hot milk gradually at first, then
in larger amounts, stirring the sauce all the time with a wooden
spoon or a hand whisk. Add remaining ingredients and cook down
steadily to a good consistency; allow at least 20 minutes, better
still an hour, for the sauce to thicken and mature in flavour. Strain
before serving.

Sauce à la crème

There are many recipes, but the simplest is to add a generous
amount of heavy cream to a thick béchamel—¼ pint for instance.
Reheat and stir in a knob of butter just before serving.

Basic velouté sauce

4 tablespoons butter
4 tablespoons flour
1¼ quarts chicken stock
12 white peppercorns
3–4 ounces mushroom stalks, peelings, etc.

Melt the butter, stir in flour and cook slowly for 2 or 3 minutes
without allowing the roux to brown. Stir in the heated stock to
make a smooth sauce. Add remaining ingredients and cook for
an hour. The sauce should coat the back of a spoon, without being

gluey. Aim to reduce the sauce to between a pint and a pint and a quarter. Strain, and store covered.

Basic fish stock

2 *pounds bones, heads and skin of fish (turbot and sole remains are the
    best, because they add a gelatinous smoothness to the stock)*
2 *medium onions, each stuck with 2 cloves*
1 *carrot, sliced*
bouquet garni
8 *peppercorns*
2 *quarts water*

Put all ingredients into a large pan. If the water does not cover the bones, add a little more. Simmer steadily for 30 minutes. Strain, and reduce to a concentrated flavour if required for a sauce. Add seasoning at this point, not before.

Purée soubise

This purée goes well with roast and grilled meats, and makes an excellent dish on its own when mixed with fried mushrooms, and served with little croutons of fried bread.

1½ *pounds onions, sliced*
4 *tablespoons butter*
¾ *cup long-grain rice*
3 *cups chicken or veal stock*
salt, white pepper, sugar
½ *cup heavy cream*

Blanch the onions in boiling, salted water for 4 minutes, then drain them well. Melt one-third of the butter in a pan, add onions, rice, stock and seasoning—a pinch of sugar should be enough. Simmer, uncovered, until the rice is well cooked, then sieve. Reheat when required with remaining butter and cream. The purée should be really thick.

Index

Mushroom(s) (*continued*)
  barley soup in the Middle-
    European manner, 58–9
  Bordeaux style, 99–100
  butter, 175
  cake with a cream sauce, 76–8
  caps, filled with chopped olives,
    98–9
  caviare, from Russia, 104–5
  and chicken
    steamed with padi-straw,
      286–7
    stir-fried, 284–5
    stuffed with chestnuts and,
      285–6
  cooked in vine leaves, 72–3
  with coriander, 109
  in cream (à la crème), 83–4
    veal (or lamb) chops with,
      202–3
  creamed cucumbers with, 122–3
  croquettes, 78
  croutons, for roast meat, 198–9
  and cucumber
    creamed, 122–3
    sautéed, 275–6
  Dauphiné style, 90–1
  Dragon Book, 292–3
  dried, 3, 31–2
    in Chinese recipes, 279–91
    stuffed with shrimps, 265–6
  and eggs, 127–34
    scrambled with, 127–8
  and fish
    baked in foil, 149–50
    paupiettes with, 156
  flan à la crème, 85–7
  forcemeat, 49
  fritters with tomato sauce, 71–2
  with fruit, 126–7
  Genoese style, baked, 101–2
  with grapes, 126
  Greek style, 106–7
  grilled, with mirin, 276–7
  ketchup, 33
  and kidney sandwich, 226

Mushroom(s) (*continued*)
  loaves, 91–2
  in Madeira sauce, 89–90
  marinaded, 109–11
  with mirin, 276–7
  mussel soup with, 60–1
  and olive stuffing, 49–50
  with oysters, 177–8
  paste, 106
  pie, 75–6
  powder, 32–3
  puffs, creamed, 88–9
  purée, 40–1
    Laguipiere's recipe, 42
  quiche (tart), basic recipe for,
    74–5
  with red fruit, 126–7
  and rice, 278
  sandwiches, 105–6
    and kidney, 226
  sautéed, 290–1
    and cucumber, 275–6
  with shellfish, 175–81
    and oysters, 177–8
  soubise, 125–6
  soufflé, 132–4
  and sour cream sauce from Rus-
    sia, 38–9
  steamed, 277–8
  stir-fried
    chicken with, 284–5
    Chinese cabbage and bamboo
      shoots, 289
  stuffed, Italian style, 100–1
  stuffed with mushrooms, 97–8
  tart (quiche), basic recipe for,
    74–5
  tomato sauce, fritters with, 71–2
  with tomato and orange sauce, 108
  in vine leaves, 72–3
Mushroom salad(s), 112–18; basic
    recipe, 112–13
  broad bean and, 115
  with lemon and herbs, 114
  lobster and, 113
  onions with sultanas and, 117–18

Vendômois style, loin of pork (longe de porc), 213–15
Vinaigrette, for kipper or matjes herring salad with mushrooms, 173
Venison (chevreuil) cutlets, 253–5
Vine leaves, mushrooms cooked in, 72–3
Vol-au-vent
à la normande, 160–1
ragoût de laitances aux morilles, 170–1
Volvariella volvacea, see Padi-straw mushroom

Walewska, Marie, 169
Waley, Arthur, 292
Walnut(s)
in aubergines à la chinoise, 290
in champignons farcis aux noix, 96
chicken à la dauphinoise, 234–6
and mushroom sauce, 47–8
White fricassey of mushrooms, 84
White truffles
bagna cauda, 143
with cheese, 141–2
with eggs, 142–3

White truffles (*continued*)
turkey breasts with ham, cheese, and, 245–6
White wine
eel stew (bouilleture d'anguilles), 186–8
sauce for chicken, 43
sauce for fish, 42–3
Whiting à la dieppoise, 167–8
Wine sauce
red, 45–6
eggs in, 130–1
white, for chicken, 43
white, for fish, 42–3
Winter melon soup, 280–1
Wood-blewit (*Tricholoma nudum*), 2, 14, 21 and *illus.*, 258; list of recipes using, 21
Wood ear (*Auricularia polytricha*), 15 and *illus.*, 260–1, 293–300; list of recipes using, 15
and pig's liver, 295–6

Yang Kuei Fei, 292
Yuan Mei, 294
her bêche-de-mer gourmet, 298–9